Project Sponsorship

An Essential Guide for Those Sponsoring Projects Within Their Organizations

DAVID WEST

WSP Management Solutions, UK

GOWER

Published by
Gower Publishing Limited
Wey Court East
Union Road
Farnham
Surrey, GU9 7PT
England

Gower Publishing Company
Suite 420
101 Cherry Street
Burlington
VT 05401-4405
USA

www.gowerpublishing.com

David West has asserted his moral right under the Copyright, Designs and Patents Act, 1988, to be identified as the author of this work.

British Library Cataloguing in Publication Data
West, David.
  Project sponsorship : an essential guide for those
  sponsoring projects within their organizations.
  1. Project management. 2. Sponsors.
  I. Title
  658.4'04-dc22

  ISBN: 978-0-566-08888-9 (pbk)
  ISBN: 978-1-4094-1079-9 (ebk)

Library of Congress Cataloging-in-Publication Data
West, David, 1959-
  Project sponsorship : an essential guide for those sponsoring projects within their
  organizations / by David West.
    p. cm.
  Includes index.
  ISBN 978-0-566-08888-9 (pbk) -- ISBN 978-1-4094-1079-9
  (ebook) 1. Project management. 2. Strategic planning. 3. Business planning. I. Title.
  HD69.P75W465 2010
  658.4'04--dc22

                                                                        2010024944

Mixed Sources
Product group from well-managed
forests and other controlled sources
www.fsc.org Cert no. SA-COC-1565
© 1996 Forest Stewardship Council

Printed and bound in Great Britain by
MPG Books Group, UK

WITHDRAWN

Project Sponsorship

CONTENTS

PART 3   UNDERSTANDING PROJECT MANAGEMENT

LIST OF FIGURES

LIST OF TABLES

PREFACE

I am deeply indebted to Stephen Bennett and Laura Honey, who have read and commented on each chapter of my book. Their comments, suggestions, questions and encouragement have been an inspiration.

I would also like to thank Gower publishing and in particular Jonathan Norman for their support and advice.

The understanding of projects that I have accumulated over my career is due to working with great companies and outstanding people too numerous to mention individually. You know who you are and I thank you.

Finally I would like to thank my long-suffering wife Claire who bears my projects with patience, support and love.

Review for
Project Sponsorship

Having previously had the pleasure of working with David on some very challenging projects, I was delighted to be asked to review his book. In my experience, very much more has been written and said about project management than project sponsorship, and David's text meets a real need. Effective project sponsorship is an essential discipline for all but the simplest projects, and can be the difference between a success and a high profile and expensive disaster. Sponsors must understand why a project should proceed and remain vigilant that this justification remains good as circumstances, and all too often costs change. And they must be able to translate the reasons for a project into a practical and well articulated remit for project management to deliver. In short, they must be both the guardians and translators of the interest of investors and funders. Through cogent analysis; reference to apposite examples; and a well structured explanation of practical techniques David has provided an excellent guide to the realities of effective project sponsorship. Reviewing this text has provided me with a valuable opportunity to reflect on best practice and how to apply it. I have no hesitation in recommending it to others.

Bill Reeve, Director of Rail Delivery for Transport Scotland

INTRODUCTION

There are several possible reasons for you to have picked up and begun reading this book.

- You are a Project Sponsor and you are aware that you need to reinforce your knowledge of project sponsorship in some areas.
- You are about to become a Project Sponsor and you need to learn the basics quickly.
- You wish to become a Project Sponsor and need to acquire knowledge of project sponsorship before putting yourself forward for the role.
- You need to improve the quality of project sponsorship within your organization.

Let me reassure you now that everything you need is in this book. The problem for me has been how to cope with the varying levels of knowledge already possessed by each reader. I do not want to bore you with material that you already know but neither do I want to leave out important guidance that you lack and need.

Consequently I have structured this book in three parts.

Part 1 is a general section which covers the value that Project Sponsors add and how to select Project Sponsors. It is therefore of interest both to Project Sponsors and the organization appointing sponsors.

Part 2 addresses specifically the Project Sponsor's role on a project. If you already have a good understanding of project management then Part 2 adds everything you need for good project sponsorship.

Part 3 deals with the interface between the Project Sponsor and the project manager. There are, of course good, mediocre and bad project managers. I cover here the common failings of less than good project managers, identifying what you should expect to see from the project manager, the questions to ask and how to tell a good answer from a bad one.

I hope that you do have the time and curiosity to continue with me through to the end. The standard of project sponsorship and project management can be greatly improved and needs to be. Good, well-informed project sponsorship is fundamental to this.

Project sponsors are of course both male and female. I will try and avoid using 'he' but 'he or she' can sometimes be awkward. If I do say 'he' from time to time, please forgive me, I do mean to address both genders at all times equally.

Happy reading!

PART 1

THE NATURE OF PROJECT SPONSORSHIP AND SPONSORS

CHAPTER 1

THE VALUE OF PROJECT SPONSORSHIP TO THE ORGANIZATION

In this chapter we will explore the value of project sponsorship to an organization by reviewing three elements:

1. The value of a project to the organization
2. The role of the Project Sponsor
3. The value of the Project Sponsor.

THE VALUE AND RISK OF PROJECTS

There are innumerable changes and aims that organizations seek to achieve through projects. For example, a company may wish to change its accounting systems. It may wish to do this in order to provide better management information or achieve efficiencies, or both. A car manufacturer may need to upgrade an old model or relocate manufacturing to a country with lower labour costs in order to increase sales and profits. NASA undertook the Apollo space programme to fulfil President John F. Kennedy's aim of landing a man on the moon. The very nature of projects is that they are almost all unique and different from the everyday business of the organization. A car manufacturer's business is making cars. Planning and building a new factory in a different country is a major undertaking, dramatically different to its everyday business. Manufacturing cars is a continuous production line process: building a new factory starts with, perhaps, a competitive need to reduce costs and an idea of how to go about it. The project concludes when the new factory is built and commissioned, staff hired and trained and the enterprise is turning out cars. If the cost of planning, designing and building the new factory has been in accordance with the budget set when the project was approved by the board, and if the costs of labour and materials in the new country are as budgeted, and if the cost of shipping is also as forecast then all looks set to deliver the value that the project was designed to achieve. That value stems from production costs which are lower than in the organization's existing facilities. However, the attentive reader will have noticed a number of 'ifs'. Projects are fraught with risk. Responsibility for managing this risk and delivering a project that adds value to the organization, or aborting the project if it will not, rests with the Project Sponsor.

If we look again at the example of an organization that wishes to change its accounting system, this might on the face of it seem a much less daunting prospect than relocating manufacturing facilities overseas. However, in 2002 W.S. Atkins, 'one of the world's leading providers of professional, technologically-based consultancy and support services'[1] suffered a dramatic nosedive in its fortunes. In its 2001 annual report it stated 'During the year the Group commenced a major initiative to put in place a global knowledge management system, the core systems for Finance and Human Resources for the UK Operations will also be replaced in 2002.' This involved investment in a 'Shared Service Facility' in Worcester which was to open in January 2002, but this project did not go entirely according to plan. Failures in the new Worcester facility resulted in late invoicing of £20m–25m of work and debt rocketed. The *Daily Telegraph* reported that W.S. Atkins 'stunned investors in October with a howitzer of a profits warning'.[2] The effect on the share price was catastrophic as shown below.

W.S. Atkins was then, and continues to be, a strong, reputable and growing company and it recovered from the setback, as Figure 1.1 shows, but for a few months it lost almost all of its value on the stock market. Some in the engineering industry who knew the underlying strength of the company made a killing on the shares, but there were casualties at board level and it can't have been an enjoyable experience for those there at the time. If a problem of this nature can befall 'one of the world's leading providers of professional, technologically-based consultancy and support services' it is a salutary lesson to all of us.

Coming more up to date, at the time of writing, Terminal 5 at London's Heathrow airport has recently been opened. It is an architectural and engineering masterpiece. However, in the first few days of its operation failures in the baggage handling system resulted in masses of cancelled and delayed flights, attracting widespread criticism in the press and real distress for many passengers. There is hardly a comedy sketch writer that is not sincerely grateful to British Airways (BA) and the British Ariports Authority (BAA) for this source of new material (except those actually travelling of course). The problem with Terminal 5 was not due to late delivery or cost overrun but with putting this magnificent new facility into operation. It was the interface between the project and the existing organization that failed, and this is the crux of project sponsorship.

1   W.S. Atkins plc annual report for the year ended 31 March 2001.
2   Soaring debt drives Atkins into red, Alistair Osborne, Associate City Editor, *Daily Telegraph*, 12 December 2002.

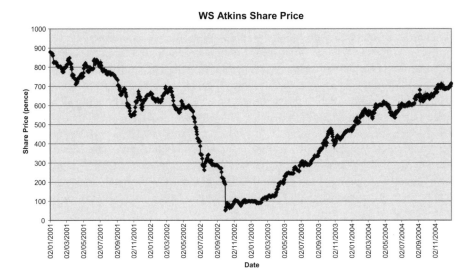

Figure 1.1   W.S. Atkins' share price

Given the obvious risks of such dramatic change to their operations, one might wonder why companies like Atkins and BA embarked on these changes. The simple fact is that they had to. The business environment is dynamic. Competitors are constantly improving and customers continually demand better value. If you don't change you probably will not survive and you certainly won't grow.

Technology is also an ever more important driver of change. Consider for example the impact that technological advance has had on the music industry. I am 48 years old. When I was a boy, music was sold on vinyl records. You played singles at 45 rpm and long playing records (LPs) at $33^1/_3$ rpm. My parents had a record cabinet full of 78s, which had been the standard media for musical recordings from 1898 until the late 1950s. Vinyl records made 78s and the gramophones used to play them obsolete. They also made the production line for 78s obsolete. The music industry was dominated by 78s for around 60 years: vinyl records dominated for not much more than 20 years. They competed for much of that time with magnetic tape in cassette and cartridge formats of various sizes. One advantage of magnetic tape over the vinyl record was that a record player was very sensitive to movement. Consequently only cassette or cartridge formats were suitable for in-car entertainment. Sony brought out their Walkman in 1979 and it was by the standards of the day a very small portable cassette player suitable for clipping on your belt and going jogging. Around 1982 compact discs emerged. By 1985 Dire Straits' *Brothers in Arms* became the first CD to sell a million copies and vinyl was in near-terminal decline. Walkman-style CD players replaced the cassette Walkman players. In 1999 MP3 players started to appear. My iPod goes everywhere with me. It has my entire CD collection on it as well as all my digital photographs, innumerable podcasts, videos etc. Just think about the research and development projects, new factories, new distribution channels and marketing projects that each of these step changes in technology have generated. The transition from film to digital photography is a similar example of technological change matching and stimulating customer demand and in the process completely changing the status quo of an industry.

The matching of a customer's needs and wants with appropriate, developing technology is a business opportunity which drives the necessity for change and consequently projects. As seen in the music industry, the pace of developing technology is accelerating and major strategic change is occurring with ever greater frequency.

The Project Sponsor is increasingly vital to an organization's very survival. The pace of technological change grows ever faster, and, as customers, the more we get, the more we want. The translation of new technology into new products requires projects and these projects make demands on the organization's finances which may have long payback periods. It is the Project Sponsor's primary role to manage the business case of the projects and ensure that the organization is 'doing the right things' as well as 'doing things right'.

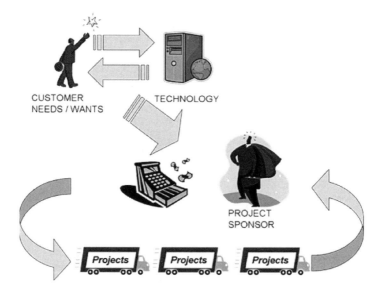

Figure 1.2   The project production line

So change projects are fundamentally vital to any organization's survival and growth. But there are huge risks involved in making these changes to your organization which, if you get them wrong, can threaten the organization's very existence. Whilst it is possible to manage change within your organization successfully it is not possible to manage the dynamic business environment whilst your organization stands still. You must change, but you must also successfully manage that change. An obvious point perhaps, so why does it go wrong so often? Project management is a well-established discipline with many thousands of qualified, experienced and competent practitioners. Nobody is perfect however, and sometimes projects fail because of project management failures. We will explore some of the important causes of these failures later and arm the Project Sponsor to avoid them. More often though, projects fail at the interface between the project and the organization, and this brings us to the role of the Project Sponsor.

THE ROLE OF THE PROJECT SPONSOR

> *Project sponsorship is an active senior management role, responsible for identifying the business need, problem or opportunity. The sponsor ensures the project remains a viable proposition and that benefits are realised, resolving any issues outside the control of the project manager.*[3]

The secret of a successful project is in the relationship between the Project Sponsor and the Project Manager. I liken the relationship to an hourglass in which the Project Sponsor and the Project Manager both fit in the neck of the hourglass. The Project Sponsor manages the top half of the hourglass, which contains all the relevant parts of the organization with a stake in or role to play in the project. The Project manager manages the bottom half of the hourglass which contains all the consultants, designers, contractors, manufacturers and so on, with a role in delivering the project. Figure 1.3 illustrates this relationship.

The roles of the Project Sponsor are essentially fourfold:

1. Identifying business need, problem or opportunity
2. Owning the business case
3. Hiring the project manager
4. Translation.

We will now address each of these in turn.

---

3   *Association for Project Manegement Body of Knowledge*, 5th edition, definitions; available at http://www.apm.org.uk/page.asp?categoryID=4.

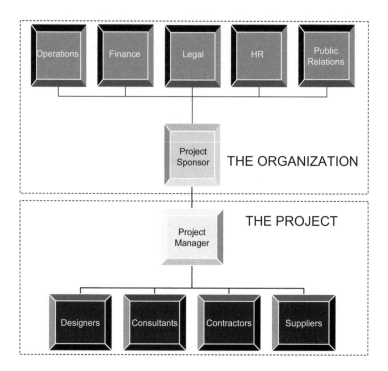

Figure 1.3   The hourglass

Identifying Business Need, Problem or Opportunity

As we have already said, organizations need to change in order to survive and grow. Before we can change we need to know why we must change and into what. To do this we must identify a business need, problem or opportunity, analyse it and come up with an outline of the requisite change.

The identification of a business need, problem or opportunity may initially come from any level within the organization. If it is a significant project it will require sufficient definition to put forward a board paper before further development is sanctioned. Even at this early stage this process needs a Project Sponsor; someone to take ownership, investigate the issue, write up and present the board paper.

If the issue has been identified by the CEO they may delegate it to someone to develop and present the paper. If a manager at a lower level in the organization is the catalyst, they are unlikely to be comfortable with presenting a board paper and may look to a more senior colleague to champion the idea. If the need emerges from an operating division or finance, for example, then there should be a senior manager within that division who can sponsor the project.

Owning the Business Case

We will cover the business case in much more detail in Chapter 6, but for now let us work with the simple assumption that the business case contains an estimate of the value of the benefits which the project will deliver together with an estimate of the costs to make the change (both evaluated in present day terms). If the value of the benefits exceeds the cost then there is a case for proceeding with the project.

We have seen that projects are unique, have a beginning and an end, and are usually very different in nature to the routine operations of the organization. Project management is a specialist discipline and consequently it is quite normal for organizations to hire in project managers when it has a requirement rather than carry them as a permanent overhead. If the project manager's employment depends on a project going ahead, it is inappropriate for them to be made responsible for the project's business case.

Projects generate momentum. A project may start as someone's good idea, and they will persuade others that it is a good idea too. People begin to invest time and energy in the project, and as they do so they become reluctant to stop, they don't want to see what they have been doing as a waste of time and money. It is also really difficult to kill off your own brainchild.

If you look again at the hourglass in Figure 1.3 you can see that project managers have a number of organizations and staff working for them. They may feel quite protective of them and the project. These are natural human emotions, but they may not best serve the interests of the organization.

The business case for the project will evolve throughout the lifetime of the project. In the beginning rough estimates of project benefits and costs are made. These are refined and improved as the project is developed and better information becomes available. With this refinement it may be that costs increase and assessed benefits decrease such that the project no longer has a business case. The organization needs to be able to cancel unviable projects, and for this reason the business case needs to be owned by someone in a position to be as dispassionate as possible in the best interests of the organization. This person is the Project Sponsor.

Hiring the Project Manager

The Project Sponsor has taken ownership of the business need, problem or opportunity and its business case: it is logical therefore that they take the lead role in establishing the team necessary to develop it. The first step will be to identify the project manager. Chapter 8 will cover team selection issues in much more detail; at this stage, let me emphasize three key points:

1. People always owe a debt of loyalty to the person who has hired them. Consequently the Project Sponsor must take the lead role in hiring the project manager and once appointed the project manager must take the lead role in hiring the rest of the project team. Any other arrangement undermines the relationships required.
2. This process is very different to buying a commodity. You're looking for experience, knowledge, skill, intelligence and energy. A good project manager will more than pay for themself over the life of the project.
3. The Project Sponsor–project manager relationship is critical. Do not hire someone you cannot get on with just because they appear to be the best. However, equally beware of choosing a project manager who is a clone of you. These are different roles requiring different skills.

Project Translation

The fourth key role of the Project Sponsor is translation, by which I mean enabling communication between the organization and the project team. In most cases the project manager and Project Sponsor will speak the same language. To this you need to add the common jargon of the project manager and the project team; a vocabulary that includes arcane phrases such as Gantt chart, programme, critical path, work breakdown structure (WBS) and float. Likewise the organization will have its own language related to the context of its business e.g. manufacturing, health, IT, government, education and so on.

Furthermore, each division of the organization will have its own language. Finance will use different language to legal, human resources or public relations departments for example.

The Project Sponsor is the intermediary between the organization and the project manager, and in the early stages, the project manager is likely to need some help understanding the organization, what it is trying to achieve and the input and requirements of each of the departments. Conversely, the project manager may need some help getting messages across to the organization.

Language is one of our key tools for passing information, ideas and feelings between people. One of the common problems with translation between different languages is the false friend: a word in one language which sounds very much like a word in another language yet has a very different meaning. For example in German, the word *gift* is translated into English as poison.

I was project manager for the design and construction of a pathology laboratory some years ago for the Royal Air Force. My team had completed the concept design and were interviewing contractors to carry out detailed design and construction. The Project Sponsor was an RAF Wing Commander: a pathologist by profession. We had a day of interviewing six shortlisted design and build contractor teams. The client team comprised our Project Sponsor, myself, my conceptual architect and my quantity surveyor (cost consultant). At the beginning of each interview I would outline the procurement process, and then ask the contractors to present their relevant experience and credentials to do the job. We would then ask questions. When it came to question time the Project Sponsor just had one question which he asked each team: 'Can you tell me what you think pathology is, please?' A simple enough question, particularly for contractors bidding to design and build a pathology laboratory, but it caused incredible consternation amongst the contractor teams. Until this point most of the talking had been done by the managing directors of the contractors, but at this question they would all turn to their architect for a response. The architects made a good effort at answering but it was clear that their understanding of pathology came from television dramas such as *Quincy* or *Silent Witness* in which the hero or heroine dashes from cutting up corpses to solving crimes and back again. It caused such difficulty for the contractor teams that, when we broke for lunch after the first three interviews, we started discussing it.

My quantity surveyor at this point asked me what pathology was (I have subsequently forgiven him) and I said that when I had bid for the project management role I had looked it up in the dictionary and it meant 'the study of disease'. At this point, much to my relief, the Project Sponsor said that was absolutely right and that most of his patients walk into his consulting room and walk out again afterwards. He considered, quite rightly, that was an important point if you are bidding to design a pathology laboratory.

So here was a situation in which the word 'pathology' meant one thing to the professional pathologist and something very different to the general public who had been deceived into thinking they knew what it meant by the television.

The Project Sponsor has a key role to play in making sure that the project team and the relevant departments of the client organization understand each other.

THE VALUE OF THE PROJECT SPONSOR

The value of the Project Sponsor is the product of the value of the project to the organization and the role of the Project Sponsor.

Change is fundamental to survival in business just as in the natural world. Organizations must evolve to suit the developing business environment or become extinct, replaced by a more adaptable competitor. In nature, evolution is a matter of gradual genetic mutation generating variations in species of which only the best adapted survive. In the business world, organizations have the choice to change themselves and pre-empt the emergence of a fitter competitor. Championing that choice and seeing it through to a successful conclusion is the role of the Project Sponsor.

Because change is out of the ordinary for the organization it carries with it unfamiliar risks. We have already looked at examples of spectacularly successful change projects and some spectacular failures.

The ingredients of a successful project are:

- Identifying the vision of what the changed organization needs to be.
- Identifying the right project to get it there. This usually involves testing different options in a feasibility study to identify which delivers the best value for money.
- Selecting a good team to manage the development of the project.
- Constant dialogue between the organization and the project team to ensure that the project brief is fully understood by the project team, i.e. that the project team knows what is required of it, and that the project is still relevant in the ever-changing competitive environment.
- Any changes required to the project are carefully evaluated and controlled.
- The completed project is carefully integrated back into the host organization with careful planning of training needs, for example.

The project manager can make errors which cause the project to fail but they will have been chosen, briefed and monitored by the Project Sponsor. It is the effectiveness of the Project Sponsor above all else that is critical to a successful project. If any of the above ingredients go seriously awry then the organization can be in big trouble.

In this chapter we have seen why projects are necessary to the growth and survival of organizations and the vital role that Project Sponsors play. In the next chapter we will look at how to identify the best people to become Project Sponsors.

CHAPTER 2

FACTORS IN THE SELECTION OF THE PROJECT SPONSOR

The purpose of this chapter is to help organizations identify the best people to be Project Sponsors. We have already seen how vital projects are to an organization's survival and growth and the key role that Project Sponsors play in the process. Choosing the right Project Sponsor is therefore the keystone for success.

An appropriate Project Sponsor is someone who can:

- Identify a business need, problem or opportunity.
- Ensure that the project remains a viable proposition and that benefits are realized.
- Resolve any issues outside the control of the project manager.
- Ensure that the project team and the organization communicate effectively.

I will now examine each of these in detail and draw out the underlying factors that make the difference between a good Project Sponsor and a poor one.

IDENTIFY A BUSINESS NEED, PROBLEM OR OPPORTUNITY

The Project Sponsor should have a good understanding of the area of the organization that the project is intended to improve. For example, if the project is an IT project intended to improve the organization's accounting system then the Project Sponsor should fully understand what the requisite improvements are, how the existing accounting system functions, what other systems it interfaces with, who uses it and for what purpose and what the benefits of the improvements are expected to be. If the project is the development of a new manufacturing facility then the Project Sponsor should have a clear understanding of how existing manufacturing facilities operate and how they could operate more efficiently and effectively.

Furthermore, the Project Sponsor should have a good appreciation of organizational strategy. At a minimum this will be an understanding of the elements that make up the organization's business strategy, why the strategy is important for the organization's survival and growth and how the project fits within that strategy. He or she should have the knowledge, experience and insight to develop effective strategies for the organization. This implies a working appreciation of the competitive environment within which the organization operates and the strategies being pursued by its competitors. A Project Sponsor with this level of competence will be able to identify and define valuable projects for the organization as well as promoting projects identified by others.

An effective Project Sponsor will also have a thorough understanding of the interfaces of the project with the various departments in the organization, and with customers, suppliers and other stakeholders outside the organization. This is important because the solution to a need or opportunity for one department may create a problem for another department or stakeholder. The Project Sponsor will need to understand these correlations in order to shape and define the best possible project.

ENSURE THAT THE PROJECT REMAINS A VIABLE PROPOSITION AND THAT BENEFITS ARE REALIZED

Before the Project Sponsor can ensure that the project remains viable they must have established its viability in the first place. There are several components of a project's viability which will be explored in detail later. In summary, however, the Project Sponsor must be able to:

- Define the project.
- Identify the benefits of the project, the costs of the project and the likely timescale for delivery of the project. The Project Sponsor is likely to need help with these and they will be progressively better defined during the project life cycle. However, the Project Sponsor should be able to lead on these issues.
- Assemble (with help from finance department) the business case for the project. This is explained in much more detail in Chapter 6. It will be necessary to demonstrate that the project has a positive NPV (net present value), in other words, that it adds value to the organization.
- Identify project stakeholders, all those having an interest in the project's success or failure, and maximize their support for the project.
- Present the project's business case to the board and obtain approval to proceed.
- Organize funding for the project, again with assistance from the finance department.

- Maintain a view of the project from the standpoint of the whole organization. They must ensure that all other necessary activities to reap the benefits of the project are proceeding satisfactorily, in parallel with the project. For example, it is easy to fall into the trap of assuming for an IT project that the development of the software is the project and forget that the training of staff on the new software and the migration from the old system to the new system are equally important in reaping the benefits.

The most common ways in which a previously viable project can become unviable are:

- The cost estimate increases and erodes the value of the project.
- The estimate of benefits decreases and erodes the value of the project. (The channel tunnel was justified on the basis of the estimated demand for rail journeys that it would create, however the estimates of demand proved to be very over optimistic.)
- The project becomes delayed such that the benefits are delayed and their value eroded by the financing costs.
- Changes in the external environment render the project unviable. For example there may be technological advances that make the technology on which the project is based obsolete. There may be changes in law which have a fundamental impact on project viability. There may also be changes in the competitive market place which warrant a rethink of the project.

There are a range of things that the Project Sponsor can do to help maintain the project's viability. These will be discussed in more detail in Parts 2 and 3. However, in terms of factors in the selection of appropriate Project Sponsors the main things to add to the list of what the Project Sponsor must be able to do are:

- Remain vigilant to the project business case. If it starts to move towards negative territory the Project Sponsor should investigate possible changes (perhaps via a value management study) that will make the business case viable once more.
- If, despite investigating all possible changes, the business case becomes unviable then the Project Sponsor must carry the organization's best interests above other considerations and should have the courage to recommend to the board that the project be stopped.

RESOLVE ANY ISSUES OUTSIDE THE CONTROL OF THE PROJECT MANAGER

These are likely to relate to interfaces within the organization or with the organization's key stakeholders. The main requirements of the Project Sponsor are that they should be:

- Well connected throughout the organization and its stakeholders and able to identify quickly who can solve a problem.
- Respected within the organization and by its stakeholders in order to secure a dialogue with stakeholders, garnering their support and commitment in resolving any problem.
- A capable negotiator able to persuade and influence stakeholders in the interests of the organization and its project.

ENSURE THAT THE PROJECT TEAM AND THE ORGANIZATION COMMUNICATE EFFECTIVELY

As we have already discussed in Chapter 1, industries, organizations, departments and projects all have a local jargon that is rarely understood by those outside of a given group.

The Project Sponsor must be able to translate. This means that the Project Sponsor must:

- Have the happy knack of being able to communicate effectively in plain English (assuming that English is the project language).
- Have the assertiveness to slow the conversation, question (repeatedly) and reflect back their understanding until a plain English translation is obtained and everybody understands the issues.

This requires tenacity.

I worked on a railway resignalling project in which the signalling engineers where effectively making their element of the project unintelligible to everyone else. The project director was Maurice McCracken, one of the greatest project managers that I have come across, and he was extraordinarily tenacious. When ideas were opaque, ambiguous or simply complex, he would slow the meeting down, ask detailed questions and reflect back in plain English each time to check his understanding. Many other non-specialists would have given up and resigned themselves to the fact that they were never going to understand, but not Maurice. Thanks to his tenacity everyone in the project team understood the signal engineering requirements and constraints. This element of the project then became manageable.

Project sponsors must be reasonably confident in the boardroom without being arrogant. The chair must be assured that sponsors know what they are doing and that they have a successful track record that supports this assurance.

Project sponsors should be able to communicate trust to the board. We have seen in Chapter 1 that projects involve risk. Project sponsors must be able to communicate clearly to the board both the benefits and the risks of projects. In return the board must feel confident that they can trust the sponsor to guard the interests of the organization.

Table 2.1 indicates the factors to be considered in selecting a Project Sponsor together with why each factor is important, how a potential Project Sponsor might be qualified to meet fulfil the requirement and the weightings that I would accord each factor.

In summary, Project Sponsors should be strategic thinkers with a good understanding of the project business case. They should be well connected and well respected within the organization and amongst its key stakeholders. They must also be good negotiators, communicators and tenacious enough to break down barriers to communication. The appointment of such a sponsor together with project governance controls outlined in the next chapter will go a long way to ensuring a successful project.

Table 2.1   Factors in the selection of project sponsors

Factor	Why	Qualification	Weight (%)
Experience in the main area which the project will impact upon.	The Project Sponsor plays the lead role in identifying and defining the project and then communicating it to everyone else. Thus it is highly important that the sponsor should have an intimate understanding of the main area affected. The Project Sponsor acts as an experienced buyer.	Work experience and qualification in the appropriate area.	13
Understanding of organizational strategy.	The sponsor should understand how the project is driven by and aligned with the organization's strategic direction. The sponsor should also have a good understanding of the competitive environment in which the organization operates.	MBA-qualified or equivalent practical experience, with an intelligent interest in business strategy and exposure to the development of the organization's strategy.	8
Well networked throughout the organization and its key stakeholders, understanding interfaces and the work of each.	The sponsor will need to understand the impact that the project will have on each part of the organization and its key stakeholders and vice versa. The sponsor will broker all the necessary discussions across the organization. Likewise the Project Sponsor must know that there is a support system to back them up and a good knowledge of the organization should mean that the sponsor knows where to get help when it is needed.	Ideally will have spent time working in many different environments.	10
An understanding of business case development and project appraisal theory.	The project is only viable if it adds value to the organization. The sponsor needs to have and maintain a good understanding of the business case, the value of the benefits and the costs.	Possibly an accounting, finance or business qualification. Understands discounted cash flow.	12
Keeps the big picture in mind at all times.	Must be able to keep the big picture in mind when all the day-to-day crises of project management are raging.	Strategic thinker and calm under pressure	11

Table 2.1   *Concluded*

Good relationships with the finance department.	The Project Sponsor will be a frequent visitor to the finance department and will require their help in developing the business case, arranging project finance and mitigating treasury risk. More than any other department except the main recipient of the project's output, finance department is key.	Previous successful dealings with finance department or with friends there.	5
Loyalty to the organization and the courage to bear bad news.	Must be able to put the organization's best interests above personal ambitions and relationships with colleagues and put a stop to the project if necessary.	Integrity, loyalty, courage and perhaps some ruthlessness.	11
Held in high respect throughout the organization and key stakeholders.	The Project Sponsor will need the support of numerous internal and external stakeholders. Often it will be necessary to persuade and change the minds of project opponents. Negotiations will also be necessary. All this will be much more achievable if the sponsor is well respected.	Integrity, competence in the day job and sufficient seniority to be well-known and respected	12
Good negotiator and communicator in plain language.	Every department will speak its own jargon and the sponsor must be able to communicate across departments. Plain language is the key to this. If the essence of the project and its business justification cannot be explained to and understood by a 5-year-old, it probably doesn't stack up! The sponsor should be a capable negotiator able to persuade and influence stakeholders to support the organization and its project.	Clear thinker and able to reduce complex concepts to their bare essentials. Able to communicate and speak plainly. Experience of contract negotiations an advantage.	11
Tenacity.	Many vested interests will seek to defend their turf by portraying their area as specialist and beyond the ability of others to understand. Projects have to reach across many of these boundaries and tenacity is often required to break down these barriers.	Ability to not worry about wasting the time of others and persisting until a straight answer is forced out.	7
			100

PART 2

CORE PROJECT SPONSOR DUTIES AND SKILLS

CHAPTER 3

GOVERNANCE, REPORTING AND MANAGEMENT STRUCTURES FOR THE SPONSORSHIP OF PROJECTS

Projects are departures from an organization's everyday business and represent significant risk for the organization. Corporate governance is a process, enshrined in law and accounting guidelines in many countries, designed to protect the owners of an organization from significant risks to the achievement of its business objectives. Because projects are often significant risk areas, project governance is an important and integral part of corporate governance for those organizations undertaking projects.

Good project governance requires:

- That the organization's portfolio of projects is aligned with its business objectives.
- That projects are sponsored such that a senior manager is responsible for ensuring that each project meets a business need, remains viable and that the benefits are realized.
- That projects are managed effectively and efficiently.
- That there is effective disclosure and reporting.

This book is dedicated to achieving the second bullet point. Chapter 5 will help Project Sponsors understand an organization's corporate strategy and select projects that contribute to its business objectives. Chapter 6 explains the business case for projects and the factors influencing project viability. Chapter 10, on commissioning and project close out, explains the process for ensuring that benefits are realized and despite the title, how this process starts almost from the very beginning. Chapters 11 to 19 cover the effective and efficient management of projects from the Project Sponsor's viewpoint and Chapter 13 specifically discusses reporting.

Therefore, if Project Sponsors follow the guidance contained in this book, good corporate governance will naturally follow. However, the organization needs assurance that this project governance is in place across its project portfolio. This assurance needs to be auditable and available to auditors of corporate governance.

In most companies and public sector bodies such assurance takes the form of a gateway review process.

A gateway review process is designed to check that the project is compliant with the project governance requirements listed above. These reviews are called gateways because they are scheduled at key stages of the project immediately before major risk decisions are taken, e.g. before contracts are let. The project can only get through the gateway if it is seen that the work done up to that point is compliant with project governance requirements and that all necessary plans are in place to ensure that the subsequent stages will also be compliant. Gateway reviews are either undertaken by a subcommittee of the board of directors or an independent reviewer appointed by and reporting to the board.

Gateway review processes differ slightly from organization to organization but generally have many elements in common. The OGC (Office of Government Commerce) Gateway review process is summarized here because this is a UK government-supported process and most other review processes are very similar.

The Project Sponsor should:

- Check that the organization's main board of directors have considered and decided upon the frequency and extent of reporting that it wishes to receive on projects, and the project approval powers that it wishes to retain or which it may wish to delegate to a subcommittee.
- Check that the organization's main board provide rules governing project approvals specifying criteria for approval and stages at which projects shall be approved for moving onto the next stage (whether such approvals are retained by the main board or delegated to a subcommittee).
- Keep the gateway review process within easy reach and ensure that all project activity is in compliance with delivering successful gateway reviews. In short, it is a checklist for project sponsorship. Where more detail is required consult the index of this book and re-read the relevant section.
- Ensure that gateway reviews are scheduled at the appropriate stages.
- Ensure that the project manager and project team are aware of the gateway review schedule and requirements and that these are built into their plans.

The rest of this chapter will comprise:

- A summary of the gateway review process
- Advice on management structures for a project
- Discussion of project portfolio risk

- Explanation of the context of corporate governance. I believe that it is important to understand the background to corporate governance and why this is a hot topic in order to appreciate the importance of project governance. However, this is placed at the end of the chapter so that the reader who already understands the context can skip on.

GATEWAY REVIEW PROCESS

The OGC is an office of HM Treasury and they set out some excellent guidelines for project governance, in particular the importance of a gateway review process.[1] There are six gateway reviews in the OGC process. At each stage, with the possible exception of the last one, the main questions are:

- Is the project still strategically important to the organization and a good fit with its strategy?
- Does the project make good business sense?
- What are the risks and are there satisfactory controls in place to manage those risks?
- What is the strategy for the next stage of the project?
- Should the project proceed to the next stage?

The stages identified for gate reviews in the OGC process and are as follows:

Gateway 0 – Strategic Assessment

At the earliest possible stage an assessment is made of whether the proposed project appears worthy of further assessment, probably using resources internal to the organization, before investment is made in initial feasibility studies.

Gateway 1 – Business Justification

Having passed Gateway 0 you will have spent some time and probably internal resources defining the project further and assessing what it will cost, how long it will take and what benefits it will bring.

You must try and estimate all the differences that the project will make to the organization and to its cash flow including capital expenditure on infrastructure, buildings and equipment (CAPEX), operating expenditure on salaries, leases, maintenance, materials etc. (OPEX) and revenue (how the money flowing into the organization changes).

---

1   http://www.ogc.gov.uk/what_is_ogc_gateway_review.asp.

This information, as you will see in Chapter 6, will enable you to put a project appraisal together. You will identify risks and you will also need to develop a clear plan for how you will develop the project to the point at which a decision can be made on whether or not the major expenditure on the project can be authorized.

For a project involving a significant element of design followed by implementation, passing gateway 1 will normally allow the design element to commence, often involving the appointment of external consultants.

Gateway 2 – Delivery Strategy

At gateway 0 you convinced the approval committee that the project looked as if it would be worth doing an initial assessment and seeing if it had a positive business case.

At gateway 1 you demonstrated (based upon preliminary investigation) that it does have a positive business case.

Now you need to show that everything you have demonstrated at gateways 0 and 1 is still valid (markets change and you have developed a much better understanding of the project between gateways 1 and 2), so you need to resubmit the business case for approval at a much more detailed level.

If you pass gateway 2 you will normally be authorized to commence the procurement for the implementation stage of the project. Therefore, you will need to be clear about what the procurement and delivery strategies are and the reasons for adopting those strategies.

Gateway 3 – Investment Decision

Gateway 2 authorized the commencement of the procurement process. You will therefore have selected potential suppliers to tender for the work through a pre-qualification process; put together tender documentation; sought tenders; received tenders back; reviewed tenders and selected the preferred suppliers.

Prior to placing orders with these suppliers it is necessary to check that any differences in cost, programme and the performance of the project between the estimates that informed the business case at gateway 2 and the tendered commitments arising from the tenders are either favourable to the business case or that any detrimental impact on the business case is not sufficiently detrimental to undermine the justification for the project.

It should be noted that the clue to the importance of gateway 3 is in the title – 'Investment Decision'. This really is the point at which the organization commits itself to major expenditure. It is quite often the case that a project will go through a gateway 3 several times if there are several major investment decision points. For example purchases of land, equipment and construction may be separated considerably in time and therefore justify three separate investment decision gateway reviews.

Gateway 4 – Readiness for Service

Once gateway 3 has been passed, then the delivery of the project moves into full swing. Any changes to the project scope will have major ramifications on cost and programme. The project manager has a job to do in managing and minimizing any change, coordinating any interfaces between different suppliers and generally keeping all suppliers delivering according to their commitments.

The Project Sponsor needs to cast his mind back to the early gateways 0 and 1. The project has by now assumed a life of its own and the Project Sponsor needs to check that as the project works its way towards being ready to deliver the hoped for benefits to the organization, the organization is equally ready to take advantage of those benefits.

For example, if one of the benefits of the project is to facilitate savings in manpower through increased automation, are plans in place and being implemented to reduce workforce through natural wastage, reassignment of employees or redundancy?

Are all training programmes in place to equip the workforce to deal with the operational and maintenance aspects of the new project deliverables?

Are there any supplier, customer or other stakeholder interests that need addressing?

Gateway 5 – Operational Review and Benefits Realization

The operational life of the facility delivered by the project may span many years or decades. The purpose of gateway 5 is to assess at various points how successful the project has been in delivering its expected benefits and feed back into the board of directors or the project approval subcommittee lessons that can be learned for the authorization of new projects.

It is worth noting that different types of benefits may become apparent (or not) at different points of the operational life cycle. For example, in a new factory energy and manpower savings will become apparent long before improvements in the product's long-term reliability. Similarly for a new teaching facility, any benefits in operational and maintenance costs will be felt long before an impact on academic achievement will become apparent.

It is important that gateway reviews are documented together with all available evidence given in support of the gateway review and that this documentation be retained for future audit purposes.

The OGC Gateway Review process has been designed with government projects in mind. However, the process is relevant regardless of whether the project is public or private sector. Indeed many private sector companies operate similar processes. Consideration should be given to the size of the project and, in particular, the risks to which the project exposes the organization when planning a structured review process. If the project and risks are small then such a formal review process is probably inappropriate. Even if the project and risk are assessed to be small it is still worthwhile having a 'sounding board' such as a colleague who can review what is being planned and offer advice on potential problems and solutions. Long before the OGC Gateway Review process was designed I worked in organizations where projects were selected for peer review where, essentially, colleagues would review each others projects. It has also been helpful in my experience to have an executive review group in which there is a small and experienced senior group who are not involved in the day-to-day sponsorship and management of the project who meet with the Project Sponsor and project manager on a regular basis to review project progress and strategy.

If a gateway review identifies deficiencies in the project then the reviewing authority can require that the deficiency be remedied before authorization of the next stage or cancel the project altogether. Where a gateway review raises serious concerns, these should be reported to the board of directors and the board of directors will need to decide whether other stakeholders need to be informed. It is very important that sound control systems be maintained throughout the project, whether a gateway review process is in place or not. There must be a system of reporting that ensures that any emerging problems with the project are reported to senior management promptly and accurately. Reporting in this context encompasses a meeting hierarchy structure and the format of written project reports.

MANAGEMENT STRUCTURES

We will now look in more detail at disclosure and reporting for project governance, because this is the key area arising from corporate governance requirements and applicable to project governance which is not covered elsewhere in this book.

I have a dilemma here. I feel almost duty bound in a chapter concerning project governance to prescribe a structure of meetings and advise on meeting frequencies, agendas and attendance requirements. Yet I am also too painfully aware that we live in a world where we have meetings about meetings, where good managers complain that they cannot 'do' any management because they spend their whole working lives in meetings. There are those who advocate meetings without chairs, keeping everyone standing so as to focus minds on getting the important issues across in the shortest period of time.

What I will say with respect to project governance, management structure and meetings is that the key things to bear in mind are:

- The project governance task of meetings is to aid the identification of risks to the organization arising from the project, advise senior management of those risks, formulate mitigation strategies for the risks and implement those strategies with the approval of senior management.
- Therefore, the sponsor will need to have regular meetings with the project team. Such meetings are often called project progress meetings. Typically they will be held monthly but that will depend on the duration and speed of the project. The sponsor will meet with the project manager and his or her key team members. Although they are called progress meetings these meetings should focus on past performance only in so far as to detect trends in performance on cost, time and quality. The important thing is to focus on what must happen over the coming period, what the risks are and plan to mitigate those risks.
- The Project Sponsor and project manager will usually attend Project Steering Group meetings. The steering group may be composed of senior level management entirely from within the organization or it may also include key project stakeholders, particularly if the stakeholders are part funders of the project or important supporters of the project (politically perhaps) who have a role in shaping the direction that the project should take. The Project Sponsor will update the steering group on how the project is progressing against the plan using reports described in Chapter 13. The steering group will also be updated on the project risks, the risk management plan and their endorsement of that plan should be sought. The frequency of steering group meetings will again depend on the duration and scale of the project, but once a quarter is probably about right in most circumstances.

PROJECT PORTFOLIO RISK

Organizations often have multiple projects active at any one time. Government agencies and infrastructure companies such as Network Rail may have several hundred or even thousands of projects to manage simultaneously. The collection of these projects represents the organization's project portfolio.

If we follow the advice in this book then each individual project will be well defined, address a need (or needs) of the organization, have a good business case and be well-sponsored and managed. If there are multiple projects it is because the organization has multiple needs in various areas of its operation.

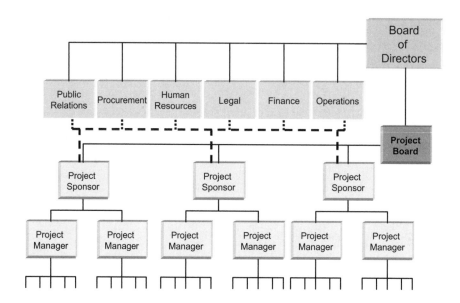

Figure 3.1   A project porfolio

At portfolio level, the organization needs to check regularly that it has the right balance of projects, that a new project is not rendering another project obsolete or competing with it for resources, that all projects can be financed and that the level of risk across the portfolio is manageable by the organization.

Portfolio theory tells us that if we wish to make an investment in stocks and shares then it is better to invest in a number of stocks and shares than to invest the same amount in the shares of one company. This is because as individual shares go up and down in value some will be going up as others go down and across the whole portfolio these effects will be smoothed out. There is less risk in a portfolio than in a single investment – in other words, don't put all your eggs in one basket! Wise Project Sponsors and project managers will always have a contingency fund, allowed for in the business case and available to cover unforeseen problems. However, we hope that not all projects will run into problems (particularly if they have Project Sponsors who have read this book) and that therefore we will not need the entire contingency that has been set aside. Tying funds up unnecessarily is a very bad thing for an organization, after all it is usually paying the bank a good rate of interest for its working capital and capital must do just that: work, not be put aside for a rainy day. Therefore it is entirely appropriate for an organization to allow individual projects a contingency but not to actually tie up as a contingency at organization level the sum of all projects' contingencies. Just as an individual project's contingency should be estimated based on a risk assessment, the contingency applicable to a portfolio of projects should be assessed as a result of a portfolio risk assessment. The important thing to be careful of here is to see if there are risks which will affect all projects in the same direction at the same time. Examples of this sort of risk include:

- Change of law
- Change of standards
- Change of technology
- Scarce resources
- Key supplier failure.

These are the sort of risks that can smash most of your eggs regardless of how many baskets you've put them in.

CONTEXT OF PROJECT GOVERNANCE

Corporate governance has been a hot topic since the early 1990s. It became an even hotter topic because a number of high-profile corporate failures coincided with the establishment of the Cadbury Committee, which had been set up to review and report on corporate governance.

As Sir Adrian Cadbury said in the preface of his 1992 report:[2]

> *When our Committee was formed just over eighteen months ago, neither our title nor our work programme seemed framed to catch the headlines ... It is, however, the continuing concern about standards of financial reporting and accountability, heightened by BCCI, Maxwell and the controversy over directors' pay, which has kept corporate governance in the public eye.*

The Cadbury report, or perhaps the coincidence of its birth alongside some very high-profile corporate failures, put corporate governance firmly on the management map. One of these failures was the Maxwell scandal[3] in which Robert Maxwell's Mirror Group Newspapers folded with debts of over £2 billion and a pension fund decimated by Maxwell's criminal attempts to keep the group solvent and shore up the share price. Another was the collapse of BCCI[4] (Bank of Credit and Commerce International) in which the bank's directors had manipulated international gaps in banking regulations and complex corporate structures to their own advantage. BCCI was raided in July 1991 by banking regulators from seven countries and

---

2   *Report of the Committee on The Financial Aspects of Corporate Governance,* December 1992, Gee & Co. Ltd, London, ISBN 0 85258 913 1.

3   http://news.bbc.co.uk/1/hi/business/1249739.stm.

4   http://www.erisk.com/Learning/CaseStudies/BankofCreditandCommerceIn.asp.

losses estimated at up to $17 billion were uncovered. Even now, that's quite a lot of money!

The fundamental problem which corporate governance seeks to address is the principal–agent problem in which the principals, those investing money (e.g. shareholders) necessarily rely on agents, e.g. company directors, to look after their investment for them. Sometimes agents can be quite reluctant to tell the principals if they're making a terrible mess of things early enough for the principals to do something about it, or, at worst, that they're making actually quite a good job of defrauding the principals out of their money.

Amongst the recommendations which emerged from the Cadbury report were a number which sought to:

- Guard against unfettered powers of decision making by one individual through separating the roles of chief executive and chairman and also by encouraging effective non-executive directors into the process.
- Provide greater transparency through encouraging the inclusion of balance sheet information and cash flow statements in interim reports.

These recommendations have been augmented, strengthened and clarified over the years by numerous committees, reports and guidance documents e.g. Greenbury, Turnbull, Higgs, Smith etc.

The collapse[5] of Barings Bank, the United Kingdom's oldest merchant bank, in 1995 demonstrated that you did not actually have to be at the head of an organization (like Robert Maxwell or the BCCI directors) to bring about its collapse. Nick Leeson was a trader with Barings, who was able to make phenomenal profits for the bank in a rising market but even greater losses in a contracting one. The bank's directors, eventually alerted by Leeson's calls for more and more funding for his desperate attempts to reverse his fortunes, discovered that Leeson had gambled away more than £800 million and the bank collapsed.

This lesson was clearly underlined more recently in January 2008 when another rogue trader, Jerome Kerviel, performed a similar feat for the French banking giant Société Générale, managing to lose around £3.5 billion of its money in depressingly similar circumstances.

In 2002 the one hundred and seventh congress of the United States of America introduced the Sarbanes–Oxley Act.[6] Sarbanes-Oxley (or SOX for short) was a

---

5   http://news.bbc.co.uk/1/hi/business/375259.stm.
6   http://frwebgate.access.gpo.gov/cgi-bin/getdoc.cgi?dbname=107_cong_ bills&docid=f:h3763enr.txt.pdf.

reaction to further scandals such as Enron and WorldCom. By 2001 Enron was one of the world's leading energy and communications companies employing 22,000 people and boasting profits of $111 billion. For six years in a row *Fortune* magazine had named Enron 'America's most innovative company'. It was certainly innovative in its accounting practices: the profits it posted were inflated and indeed fraudulent. With each passing year the accounting deceptions of the previous year grew larger to cover the gap between the ever-increasing profits that markets and shareholders want and the spiralling losses that were in fact occurring.

Arthur Andersen, which was one of the 'Big Five' accountancy practices and responsible for auditing Enron's accounts, virtually disappeared following lawsuits brought against it as a result. It had employed around 85,000 people worldwide. The concern which Cadbury had sought to address over the true independence of auditors who received consulting work worth far, far more than the audit fees was clearly still an issue.

If we set to one side the criminal, fraudulent behaviour of some parties in the corporate failures mentioned above there remain a few important truths:

- Investors do not like bad news.
- Managers do not like giving bad news and will go to extraordinary lengths to convince even themselves that actually things are not as bad as they seem and that they will get better.
- There really is a need for truly independent 'health checks' of business ventures.

This is the background to corporate governance, but what does it have to do with project governance? Well, the Financial Reporting Council makes clear in their *Internal Control: Revised Guidance for Directors on the Combined Code (The Turnbull Guidance)*[7] that:

> *A company's system of internal control has a key role in the management of risks that are significant to the fulfilment of its business objectives. A sound system of internal control contributes to safeguarding the shareholders' investment and the company's assets.*

We already know that projects are departures from the norm for most organizations and that they can be both vital for the organization's survival and growth whilst at the same time represent huge risks for it. If we need further proof of that consider the case of the ill-fated, privatized UK rail infrastructure company of the 1990s, Railtrack and the West Coast Route Modernization project. The initial

---

7   http://www.frc.org.uk/images/uploaded/documents/Revised%20Turnbull%20Guidanc e%20October%202005.pdf.

budget for the project was a staggering £2.4 billion. Now it should be borne in mind that Railtrack was floated on the London Stock Exchange in 1996 for £2.5 billion, so this was a 'bet the company' scale of project. However, costs escalated dramatically and by the time they reached £7 billion the government considered it time that Railtrack be refused further funding and placed into administration. Railtrack had bet the company on a project and lost. There were of course other accidents, errors of judgement and mistakes en route but one single project that got out of control essentially brought about the downfall of Railtrack, a seemingly low-risk utility company in which many thousands of employees and ordinary citizens were shareholders.

If we draw comparison again between the requirements of good corporate governance and good project governance we will recognize that gateway or stage reviews provide a good audit function for projects and that they, together with steering group meetings, also provide a route of transparency up through the senior management team who are then required by corporate governance to disclose risks to shareholders.

The one final word of caution that I would like to add is that one must beware of 'groupthink'. Although it is important to ensure that decision making is not solely invested in one person, it is a fact that groups of people will often take greater risks than individuals. If you are not the sole person responsible then you will not take all the blame if it goes wrong, and you may therefore be willing to take more risk. Also when individuals are members of a group they tend to avoid promoting viewpoints that differ from the consensus of the group. If you are the only person in the group opposing the project that can be a very lonely place to be. In these circumstances silence is seen as agreement. Therefore, I would always encourage Project Sponsors to consider if they would still recommend a particular course of action if it was their money that was funding it, and also to ensure that safeguards are in place to counter groupthink.

We discussed in Chapter 1 the Project Sponsor's key role in 'owning' the business case and that the business case will change throughout the lifetime of the project as estimates of cost, programme and benefits become further refined as the project is developed. We also said that it is vital that the Project Sponsor be prepared to recommend stopping the project if the project's business case turns negative. This chapter has concerned the processes that govern the Project Sponsor in the fulfilment of these duties and provide the assurance to the organization that this is being done. The next chapter will cover the Project Sponsor's duty in preserving health, safety and the environment, which is even more important than preventing corporate failure.

CHAPTER 4

HEALTH, SAFETY AND THE ENVIRONMENT

Health, safety and environment issues are of the utmost and ever-increasing importance. As a Project Sponsor whatever pride you expect to take in nurturing and delivering your project will be completely shattered if someone is killed or seriously injured in the process, or if the environment is damaged. The nature of projects is that they are different to the normal operations of the organization; they bring people together who haven't worked together before, in unfamiliar locations. Consequently projects do involve a degree of risk. This risk varies according to the type, the size and the complexity of the project.

LEGISLATION

In the United Kingdom, at present, legislation on health, safety and the environment relevent to project sponsorship falls into two categories. There is the Health and Safety at Work Act and other legislation governing how to do business safely. Then there is the Construction (Design and Management) Regulations (CDM) which addresses projects involving physical construction or alteration of premises. The CDM regulations place particular duties on clients, i.e. Project Sponsors, which we will look at shortly. First, however, we will review the requirements for working safely because these will be relevent to any type of project, whether it involves construction or not. I do not intend to quote the act verbatim, but rather convey the principles in plain language. I will also omit the 'so far as is reasonably practicable' test which occurs in most clauses. The definition of reasonably practicable set out by the Court of Appeal (in its judgment in Edwards v. National Coal Board, [1949] 1 All ER 743) is:

> *'Reasonably practicable' is a narrower term than 'physically possible' ...*
> *a computation must be made by the owner in which the quantum of risk is*
> *placed on one scale and the sacrifice involved in the measures necessary for*
> *averting the risk (whether in money, time or trouble) is placed in the other,*
> *and that, if it be shown that there is a gross disproportion between them – the*
> *risk being insignificant in relation to the sacrifice – the defendants discharge*
> *the onus on them.*

GENERAL CLIENT HEALTH, SAFETY AND ENVIRONMENTAL DUTIES

In other words there is a question of judgement involved. In the majority of cases, existing, recognized good practice represents what is reasonably practicable.

1. Every employer must ensure the health, safety and welfare of all employees.
2. Plant and systems provided for work must be adequate and maintained to be safe without posing risks to health or the environment.
3. Where articles and substances are to be transported, the arrangements for this transport shall be safe and without health or environmental risks.
4. You shall provide such information, training and supervision necessary for working safely.
5. The place of work shall be maintained in a safe condition and access to and from it shall be safe.
6. Adequate welfare facilities shall be provided.
7. You should ensure that people not employed by you are not harmed by your work, e.g. visitors, the general public, customers, suppliers, etc.
8. Your products shall be designed and constructed to be safe and without risk to health whether being assembled, used, cleaned, maintained or disposed of. You shall carry out tests and examinations to confirm this.
9. You shall ensure that your products are supplied together with sufficient information about the use for which it has been designed and tested such that it can be assembled, used, cleaned, maintained or disposed of safely. Ensure that revisions to such information are supplied if it becomes known that there is a serious risk to health and safety.

RISK ASSESSMENT PROCESS

There is a simple five step method for assessing risks that your project may give risk to:

1. Identify the hazards:
   - What hazards exist in the organization that may be exacerbated by the project?
   - What new hazards may the project introduce?
   - Typical workplace hazards include: slips, trips and falls, asbestos, hazardous substances, falls from height, musculoskeletal disorders (e.g. back injury through lifting), display screen equipment, noise, vibration, electricity, equipment and machinery, workplace transport, pressure systems, fire and explosion, radiation, stress.
2. Identify who might be harmed and how.

3. Evaluate the risks and decide on precautions:
   - Can the hazard be removed altogether?
   - If not how, can the risk be controlled?
4. Record your findings and implement them.
5. Review the risk assessment and regularly update it.

KEY SPONSOR DUTIES FOR HEALTH, SAFETY AND THE ENVIRONMENT

You will hire a project manager and a project team who should work with you to make the project as safe as it can reasonably be. They will be experienced in projects and the legislation in place. There are, I believe, just four fundamental duties of the Project Sponsor.

1. Any appointments that you make, e.g. the project manager, must be competent. You should pay particular attention to having a considered and documented process for ensuring this competence. You should request details of the project manager's health, safety and environmental management policies and their training, qualifications, experience and track record in these areas. Check qualifications are valid and take up references, asking previous clients about the project manager's general experience and particularly in the health, safety and environmental management area. Ensure that there is an audit trail of this and that your selection process is well documented. Competence in this area should have a pass/fail threshold set high with relative scoring above that to seek out excellence.
2. You must from the beginning make clear to the project manager that health, safety and environment are your top priorities.
3. You must ensure that sufficient allowance is made in the budget to fund the necessary health, safety and environmental management resources and you must allow sufficient time for the project to be executed safely.
4. Check that health, safety and environment issues receive the attention they deserve by the project team throughout the project life cycle. Ensure that project progress reports and meetings address them. There should be proactive action by the team to prevent accidents and near misses.

CONSTRUCTION DESIGN AND MANAGEMENT REGULATIONS (CDM)

We come now to those projects which involve some element of construction which fall under the Construction (Design and Management) Regulations. The duties of the client, i.e. the Project Sponsor, are in many ways an extension of the guidelines already covered. They are:

1. Appoint competent people. Check qualifications and references. Ask for proof of membership of a relevent trade association. Are there passport schemes which guarantee a level of competence or knowledge?
2. Allow adequate time. A rushed project is likely to be unsafe and of poor quality. Allow adequate time for design, planning, tendering, construction and commisioning.
3. Provide information to your project team. Your team will need to know what you want and how you will use and maintain it. They will also need to know about any hazards on the site e.g. asbestos, electricity cable routes, gas mains etc.
4. Communicate and cooperate with your team.
5. Ensure suitable management arrangements are in place.
6. Make sure there are adequate welfare facilities on site such as drinking water, toilets, washing facilities with warm water, storage for clothing and somewhere under cover for workers to rest and eat.
7. Make sure workplaces are designed correctly to the appropriate standards
8. Where construction work will last longer than 30 days or involve more than 500 mandays of work, you must additionally appoint a CDM coordinator. You should do this as soon as possible and certainly by the time initial design starts.The CDM coordinator will assist you with your duties by:
   - Advising you about selecting competent designers and contractors.
   - Helping to identify information required by the designers and contractors.
   - Coordinating the arrangements for health and safety during the planning phase.
   - Ensuring that the Health and Safety Executive (HSE) is notified of the project.
   - Advising on the adequacy of the initial planning.
   - Preparing a health and safety file which will contain useful information you need for operation and maintenance of the completed facility.
9. Appoint a principal contractor. The principal contractor is required to plan, manage and coordinate work and is usually the main or management contractor. Once again, the principal contractor should be appointed early enough to be involved in discussions about how the facility will be built, used and maintained.
10. Make sure that the principal contractor produces an adequate health and safety plan. This plan will outline the key arrangements for ensuring that work is carried out safely. Do not allow work to start until you and your team (especially the CDM coordinator) are happy with this plan.
11. Keep the health and safety file. At the end of the project the CDM coordinator will give you a file of useful health and safety information to help you manage health and safety risks during operation, maintenance, repair, alteration or demolition of the facility. You should keep this file safe and ensure that anyone who needs it has access to it. You should also ensure that it is updated if the facility is altered in any way.

CHAPTER 5

WHERE PROJECTS COME FROM – CORPORATE STRATEGY

In Chapter 1 we discussed the fact that projects are about implementing change and that change is necessary for every organization. The environmental changes affecting any organization may be competitive, technological, societal or a combination thereof, but address them it must if it is to remain competitive.

Because the Project Sponsor has a fundamental role in defining the change project they need to understand why the change is necessary, what change is necessary and how to achieve it. In this chapter we will explore several strategic tools that you can use. They are generally very simple frameworks to guide thought processes and are widely used and applied by leading companies.

As a Project Sponsor you may be asked to contribute to developing your organization's corporate strategy and perhaps even lead its development. If you are contributing, then reading this section will aid your understanding of the process and help you to contribute more fully. If you are leading the process then it will be your guide. Project sponsors may have no input to corporate strategy and simply be asked to own a project. In that case you should familiarize yourself with how the project fits with the corporate strategy. To do that you should obtain a copy of your organization's corporate strategy and five-year plan or similarly titled documents. Failing that ask your line manager or a board member what the strategy is. Knowledge of the material in this chapter will help you understand the process that has gone into developing the strategy and you should be able to identify how your project contributes towards it. If it isn't obvious then you must ask the board or the senior manager who is asking you to be the Project Sponsor. You cannot sponsor a project if you don't understand why the project is necessary.

If you are MBA qualified or already have experience of corporate strategy I suggest that you flick through the following pages quite quickly and move on. You are probably already well equipped to both identify projects which fit with your organization's strategy and understand how a project fits with the strategy.

However, if you are relatively new to corporate strategy read on. There are two main sections which follow. The first section contains tools for assessing changes to your operating environment. These are social, technological, economic, environmental, political, legal and ethical (STEEPLE), Porter's Five Forces, strengths, weaknesses, opportunities and threats (SWOT), The Ten Ps, scenario analysis. STEEPLE and Porter's Five Forces are frameworks to aid identification of external environmental influences for the opportunities and threats half of SWOT. Ten Ps is to help identify internal strengths and weaknesses for the other half of SWOT. Scenario analysis is a more sophisticated technique for identifying long-term environmental change.

The second section covers the development of strategies to exploit the anticipated future operating environment. This section includes Porter's generic strategies of cost leadership, differentiation and market segmentation with examples of each. It also includes the BCG Matrix which is a framework for understanding the life cycle of products or services and the Ansoff Matrix which considers the strategic options in terms of markets and products. I also include a review of mergers and acquisitions.

There are of course other tools of corporate strategy, but these are the main and most well-known ones. They provide a comprehensive set of frameworks which cover all of a Project Sponsor's corporate strategy requirements without too much overlap.

THE OPERATING ENVIRONMENT

Having said that projects implement changes necessary due to changes in the environment let us start with a simple corporate strategy tool for helping us to identify changes in our external environment. This tool is actually an acronym that has evolved over the years. I suggest the STEEPLE version but it has evolved through PEST, STEP, STEEP and PESTLE en route to STEEPLE: social, technological, economic, environmental, political, legal, and ethical. I offer no prizes for guessing which elements have been added to the previous models or which is the latest addition. If you sit down and think about what environmental changes are influencing your organization you may well think of two or three straight away and become fixated by those to the exclusion of other influences.

If you use the STEEPLE acronym to think through each possible category of environmental change in turn, you will capture a much wider range of relevant environmental influences. A few examples are given in Table 5.1.

Table 5.1   STEEPLE

Social	What demographic factors affect us, e.g. ageing population, smaller household groups?
Technological	How are technological changes affecting us, e.g. Internet shopping, digital revolution, nanotechnology?
Economic	At what point of the economic cycle are we? Where are interest rates going?
Environmental	How can climate change affect us and how will environmentally motivated consumer pressure change our marketplace?
Political	What political change could affect us?
Legal	What legal changes are on the horizon and how would they affect us?
Ethical	How do changing standards of ethics affect our business?

In terms of identifying the external environment of a business I like to use STEEPLE and Porter's Five Forces.[1] Whereas STEEPLE is a useful checklist for identifying influences and possible changes in the macro environment of a business, Porter's Five Forces model is useful as a checklist for looking at the factors affecting the business in its industry and market, i.e. its micro environment.

Porter's Five Forces model prompts us to think about:

1. The bargaining power of our suppliers.
2. The bargaining power of our customers.
3. The threat of new competitors entering our market.
4. The threat of substitute products.
5. The competitive rivalry within our market.

Later I will adapt this model to work in conjunction with the other relevant models and at that stage I will dispense with the fifth of Porter's forces, since I find the interplay between the first four forces to work more naturally with the other models.

There is clearly some overlap between these two frameworks or models. However, there is nothing in Porter's Forces that would trigger a consideration of say, the impact of a change in government with different political agendas or the effect on the market of global warming. Equally there is nothing in STEEPLE which would

---

1   Porter, M.E. (1979) How competitive forces shape strategy, *Harvard Business Review*, March–April, 137–45.

directly prompt you to consider the dynamics of the bargaining power of your customers and suppliers.

STEEPLE and the first four of Porter's Five Forces together provide the kind of checklist that guides our thinking through each of the areas of the external environment that influence our organization. As Project Sponsor you want to predict changes in the external environment and adapt your organization (via sponsoring projects) to make it organizationally as fit as possible to take advantage of the predicted change.

SWOT ANALYSIS

We now need a model to capture and analyse factors associated with the external environment and develop your strategic response. There are several models that provide useful perspectives, but we will start with what is undoubtedly the most widely used and that is SWOT analysis: strengths, weaknesses, opportunities, threats.

The strengths and weaknesses are our organization's strengths and weaknesses: the opportunities and threats are those opportunities and threats that we identify in the external environment through STEEPLE and Porter's Forces.

One of the most effective ways to undertake a SWOT analysis is via a workshop involving perhaps six to twelve colleagues who represent a reasonable cross-section of the organization. It is useful if you have some old hands as well as some colleagues relatively new to the organization who will have a different perspective. Secure a good size meeting room for a day. Arm yourselves with flipcharts and coloured marker pens, a suitable medium for securing flipchart pages to the walls, some coloured ribbon and a facilitator to guide you.

I suggest reviewing the external environment first using STEEPLE and Porter's Forces as a checklist. For each environmental category you should think about the changes that are occurring or expected to occur. Record these changes on a flipchart, and keep recording each change until you have exhausted your collective knowledge of that category and move onto the next category.

Now there is a dilemma. Is a predicted change in your external environment a threat or an opportunity? Some may be obvious but others may depend on how the organization reacts compared with how competitor organizations react. Don't worry at this stage, park the environmental changes and move on to strengths and weaknesses. These are internal to your organization. Brainstorm your organization's strengths followed by your weaknesses. If you have any customer feedback make sure that you bring it along. This is also an area where the relative newcomers to the organization can provide useful insight.

I have advocated STEEPLE and Porter's Five Forces as checklists for identifying external environmental factors. For internal strengths and weaknesses I recommend an adaptation of the four/seven Ps of Lilien, McCarthy and Kotler.[2] I call this Ten Ps.

Table 5.2   The ten Ps

Product	How do your products or services compare to the competition?
Price	How competitive are your prices?
Promotion	How good is your advertising, how strong is your brand?
Place	How effective and efficient are your distribution channels at getting your products or services to the customer?
People	Most companies say that their people are their biggest asset. Everything is relative. How do your people compare to the competition?
Process	How effective and efficient are your processes?
Physical evidence	What can customers see of your processes and how does this affect your standing, e.g. if you are servicing a customer's car are the reception and waiting rooms pleasant and comfortable? What can the customer see of the workshop? Does that view inspire confidence in the standard of service?
Pace	How fast can your organization change? How quickly can you get new products or services to market?
Profit	How profitable are you?
Power	What power do you have? Financial strength? Purchasing power? Power to influence key policy makers?

If you can, tidy up the results of your brainstorm to fit your organization's strengths on a single flipchart page and its weaknesses on another, then so much the better. If not, try and cluster the strength pages together on one area of the wall and place the weaknesses next to them.

---

2   Lilien, G.L., Kotler, P. and McCarthy, K.S. 1992. *Marketing Models*. Prentice-Hall International, Englewood Cliffs. NJ.

The understanding of your strengths and weaknesses should now resolve the dilemma over whether a predicted environmental change is a threat or an opportunity, at least in terms of the organization's current position. Therefore you should now be able to separate the external changes into a cluster of threat sheet(s) and opportunity sheet(s).

You should by now have a two by two grid with internal organizational *strengths* in one quadrant, internal organizational *weaknesses* in the second, external environmental *threats* in the third and external environmental *opportunities* in the fourth. It is at this point that many workshops slap themselves on the back for a job well done, record the SWOT analysis for posterity and move onto something else. And they were so close to getting something useful out of it! This is where the bits of ribbon come, in because you need to appropriately match each threat with a corresponding strength or weakness. Likewise you need to match each opportunity with a corresponding strength or weakness.

• *Strength–opportunity* connections suggest an aggressive strategy to exploit the opportunity using your strength.
• *Strength–threat* connections suggest a defensive strategy to counter the threat using your strength.
• *Weakness–opportunity* connections suggest that efforts to exploit the opportunity will be wasted unless you can quickly plug your weakness and turn it into a strength.
• *Weakness–threat* connections are certainly dangerous and may be a case of fix the weakness or die.

	STRENGTHS	WEAKNESSES
OPPORTUNITIES	Aggressively exploit opportunities using corporate strengths	Likely to be beaten by competition if weaknesses cannot be fixed
THREATS	Defensive strategy blocking threats using corporate strengths	Avoid exposure to threats where weak or fix weaknesses

Figure 5.1   SWOT analysis

Of course you should always be thinking about how you can enhance your strengths and mitigate your weaknesses, exploit your opportunities and counter your threats, but this process guides you much more effectively towards targeting action where it is needed.

That in essence is SWOT. It has the great virtue of being simple and easy to understand. It guides thinking in a useful way.

The drawback of SWOT is that it takes an assortment of external influences and matches them against an assortment of internal strengths and weaknesses without combining the influences, their outcomes and the organizational responses into a coherent scenario.

There may be many environmental influences that are contradictory. For example if one environmental influence is a sustained, significant rise in food prices and another is increasing disposable household incomes it is difficult to see how they can co-exist in the same scenario. Of course at the time of the SWOT analysis household disposable incomes may be rising and they may have been rising for some time. This may have been of great importance to the organization's success and used to bolster confidence within the organization in its continuing success. Suggestions of a rise in global food prices may be confined to news stories on page three of the broadsheet newspapers concerning poor rice harvests in India and China and heavy rains in the American Midwest. In other words the signals about disposable incomes are strong signals to the managers of the organization but the signals about food prices are weak signals. These weak signals may however be of cataclysmic importance for the medium- and longer-term future.

We discussed in Chapter 1 the impact of changing technology on the recording and film industries. With hindsight it is odd that those industries did not anticipate and react to the changes earlier. Research papers will have pointed to the possibilities years beforehand, but these were weak signals compared with the monthly sales results for vinyl records or film.

Figure 5.2 shows the models that we have looked at adapted and combined into a coherent model which can help us to think about and assess the organization's competitive position within its environment.

Around the perimeter of the diagram we have the STEEPLE forces which affect all organizations within the market sector. Inside that we have the power struggles between the organization, its customers, suppliers and competitors together with the threat of subsititute products, e.g. digital photography for film. At the core of the diagram we have the own organization's strengths and weaknesses, and it is the relationship between these strengths and weaknesses and the external forces bearing in on the organization that determine what the therats and opportunities are.

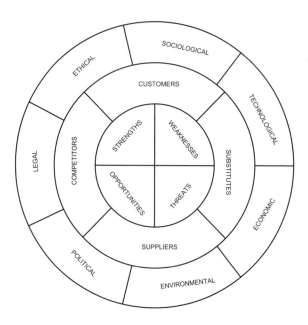

Figure 5.2   The organizational operating environment

SCENARIO ANALYSIS AND PLANNING

Most governments and military commands have a set of well-developed strategic plans with which they can respond to various crises. These have been developed from analysis of possible scenarios that have been played out in game environments (e.g. war games) to assess the possible moves and counter moves and hone the strategy. In the business world scenario analysis and planning has been perhaps most famously developed and used by the oil company Shell. They began using scenario planning in the early 1970s and very quickly found that the effort that they had put in had prepared them very well for the oil price shocks of the 1970s. Prior to that straight line forecasting had been very effective because the oil price had not changed in real terms between 1950 and 1970. Then, between 1971 and 1973, the oil price doubled. Between 1974 and 1978 it quadrupled. It doubled again between 1979 and 1981. It then stabilized and began falling in the 1980s. Shell accredited much of their success in adapting better than competitors to these dramatic events to the scenario planning that they had done.

An oil company needs to plan many years, if not decades, in advance because the activities of oil exploration and construction of drilling platforms and refineries is a lengthy process. Needless to say the price of oil is a key factor in determining strategy and Shell's developed scenarios helped to make their decision making robust in the face of surprising changes.

Before we look at how to go about scenario analysis and planning, you may get a better idea of what scenarios look like if you browse the following website where many scenarios are publicly available:

- Shell http://www.shell.com/home/content/aboutshell/our_strategy/shell_ global_scenarios/dir_global_scenarios_07112006.html

These are a little out of date and have lost their commercial advantage, but they do give a good picture of what well-researched scenarios look like.

The process of scenario analysis and planning has been well researched and documented by Mercer[3] and is designed for the strategic level and a time horizon of about 10 years.

1. Identify the Drivers for Change

You need to identify those things that are going to have an important influence on our organization in the future. The trick here is to detect those drivers for change which are currently only weak signals. My advice here is to start a process of scanning the media. You probably already read a daily newspaper and the trade press relevant to your industry. You watch television, dine with friends and browse the Internet. Make it work for you. Try and find items of interest for each of the STEEPLE areas that could have an impact on your organization. Create a file (I use a concertina file with a labelled pocket for each of the STEEPLE areas) and save press cuttings or scribbled notes from TV programmes or dinner table conversations in the file. Over a month or so you will build up a useful body of information.

If you are going to embark on a scenario planning exercise you will need a team of six to twelve colleagues (as for the SWOT analysis), but you will also need several sessions and this may take some time to arrange. Therefore try and identify the appropriate colleagues, discuss it with them and encourage them to practice this environmental scanning too. You will read different newspapers, watch different TV programmes and have different dinner party friends therefore collectively you will build up a much more comprehensive file of environmental drivers for change.

For your first workshop you need a large meeting or conference room with a wall suitable for sticking Post-it™ notes to. Ask everyone to begin writing their drivers for change on the Post-it™ notes and sticking them on the wall. If you can arrange enough different colours of Post-it™ notes it can be useful to have a different colour

---

3   Mercer, D. 1998. *Marketing Strategy: The Challenge of the External Environment.* Sage Publications. London.

note pad for each STEEPLE area. Initially the Post-it™ notes should be placed on the wall fairly randomly.

Unlike a brainstorming there can and should be some debate of the drivers as they are put on the wall. It is important that everybody understands what is meant by each driver. There should also be a test of importance and uncertainty for each driver. If it is agreed that a driver is not important, i.e. if it came to pass it could not have any significant effect on the organization, then it should be removed. If it is agreed that a driver is important but also certain, then it should be placed in a special marked out area of the wall. This is because something that is important and certain will affect all scenarios whereas we are really trying to find the key turning points where a driver may send our world off in different direction.

2. Assemble Drivers into a Coherent Framework

The next stage involves the group moving the Post-it™ notes around on the wall, clustering together drivers that seem to fit together, i.e. where one driver could plausibly lead to another. This is a difficult but important stage and should not be rushed. The group should be allowed to debate the possibilities at length.

3. Produce 7–9 Mini Scenarios

This is an extension of the previous activity. The aim at this stage is to continue merging the drivers until they form around 7 to 9 mini scenarios. Each mini scenario should be debated and the group should discuss and agree how the drivers are connected and what chain of influences, turning points and events they represent.

4. Reduce to 2–3 Scenarios

Now the challenge is to further merge the mini scenarios, grouping them together until they represent just two or three main scenarios. Again these groupings may merge and diverge and merge again. They should be debated at length until the group is agreed that each grouping of drivers is connected in a logical way and that they can tell the story represented by the scenario.

The reason for reducing to two or three scenarios? Shell found that when managers were asked to use the scenarios to plot their business strategy, they could not cope with more than three scenarios.

5. Write up the 2 or 3 Scenarios

It is now time to write up the scenarios as essays describing the drivers, events, reactions, counter reactions and so on that lead to the organization's world in around ten years time.

It is very important at this stage that the scenarios should be complementary, i.e. together they should encompass all conceivable outcomes. After all we are trying to anticipate, as best we can, all the conceivable futures so as to plan for them. It is also very important to write them and to title them objectively so that you don't introduce any bias as to the likelihood of their realization. If they are not written in this way then managers will be encouraged to favour specific scenarios and will neglect to plot robust strategies against each eventuality.

In the Shell website referenced above, Shell have published their *Global Scenarios to 2050*. In this they present two scenarios:

- Scramble
- Blueprints.

These scenarios reflect different possible balances between the forces of:

- Surging energy demand
- Supplies struggling to keep up
- Stresses increasing on the environment.

There is published evidence to support a tendency towards each scenario and both are entirely plausible. Shell has been in the vanguard of scenario planning for a long time and it regularly updates its scenarios in order to direct business planning. Consequently, by the time you read this the scenarios may have changed in detail although the general principles should remain.

The process of researching and thinking through the scenarios or just reading the scenarios prepared by colleagues does much to prepare managers to plot their business strategy for the long-term future.

6. Develop Robust Strategies

Having identified two or three complementary scenarios the organization's managers should then prepare strategies that are robust, in other words that will enable the organization to survive all of the scenarios and preferably that it will prosper in them. A strategy in which the organization is highly profitable in one scenario but wiped out in the other two is less robust than one in which it is moderately profitable in two and break-even in the third.

Of course, the world is dynamic and the market situation must be monitored. Strategies can and should be changed if events are moving in one particular direction. The scenario planning should also be updated. Shell began by renewing their scenarios every three years but now do so annually.

WHICH STRATEGY?

A simple approach to developing strategy is to answer these three questions:

1. Where are we now?
2. Where do we want to be?
3. How do we get there?

The answers might be:

1. The public like our product: all the market research and customer feedback is very positive but our competitors are outselling us with inferior but much cheaper models.
2. We want to be market leader, retaining our quality but reducing our cost per unit by 25 per cent.
3. We need to move our manufacturing to the Far East.

It is very important that you take every possible opportunity to gather feedback from your customers and when you recruit staff from competitors, de-brief them on how things are done there.

I now need to amend the three strategy formulation questions because as we have discussed, the world is a dynamic place and we sponsor projects to produce change relative to the changes in our operating environment.

1. Where are we now?
2. Where do we want to be in the future environment, as we predict it will be?
3. How do we get there?

Business consists of selling a product or service in a market. There are therefore two main fronts that a business strategy can work on i.e. the product/service and the market.

Porter[4] identified three generic strategies:

1. Cost leadership
2. Differentiation
3. Market segmentation.

Cost leadership is a strategy by which an organization aims to be successful by selling its product or service at a lower cost than its competitors, thereby achieving

---

4   Porter, M.E. 1979. *Competitve Strategy*. The Free Press, New York.

large volume of sales. Stack them high and sell them cheap! If an organization can achieve large sales volumes that results in economies of scale which further reinforces the cost leadership advantage. The low-cost airlines are a good example of the cost leadership strategy in practice.

The second of Porter's generic strategies is differentiation. The differentiation strategy seeks to find attributes for the product or service which the customers value and are prepared to pay extra for. A differentiation strategy attempts to make the product or service better in some way than the competition. For example, if you value generous leg room on a flight then you might be prepared to pay the extra and fly with one of the 'flag carrier' airlines rather than a low-cost airline. At the time of writing Singapore Airlines are using the new A380 aircraft to offer the only double bedrooms on a commercial airline. This is a clear differentiator for them.

Market segmentation is a strategy in which you identify a particular niche in the market and focus on that. For example a construction company might decide to focus its attention solely on the railway sector, acquiring the expertise necessary for that specialism.

Porter identified that the most profitable companies fall into one of two categories: they either have large market share or low market share. The large market share companies he found to have pursued a cost leadership strategy and the low market share companies had pursued either differentiation or market focus strategies. He argued that companies must stick to one strategy otherwise their processes, brand and culture become confused and they fall into the gap in the middle where the lower profit companies live.

I think it is fairly clear that cost leadership and differentiation are incompatible. You cannot offer sumptuous double bed airline suites at low-cost airline prices. However, it seems to me that there is an overlap between differentiation and market segmentation. If you are focused on one particular market niche then you will develop the differentiation factors that most appeal to the customers in that niche. Do we believe that Rolls-Royce follow a differentiation strategy playing on unique qualities of their luxury motor cars or are they focusing on the small market segment of customers who can afford them and adapting their motor cars to provide the attributes that those customers most value? The end result is the same.

There has been some debate and criticism of Porter's theory, with others suggesting that 'hybrid' strategies can be successful. However, the great success and indeed greater resilience of the leading low-cost airlines to the economic turmoil of 2008 supports his point. The low-cost airlines are able to be very focused on the processes that deliver low cost, e.g. fast turnarounds, no meals, high utilization etc.

The 'flag carrier' airlines, with their economy, business, and first class sections, cannot be as focused.

A factor influencing the aircraft turnaround time and hence cost is the time taken to load and unload hold luggage. Consequently low-cost airlines introduced additional charges for hold luggage to deter passengers from taking hold luggage with them. This further deepens the cost advantage and is consistent with the cost leadership strategy. However, a recent development has been low-cost airlines adding speedy boarding options whereby you can jump the queues at check-in for an additional charge. Low-cost airlines are also offering airport lounge access again for an additional charge. These priority boarding and lounge options might appear to be a move back towards the service offered by the flag carrier airlines, but they are not services that add any cost to the airline. The speedy boarding and lounges do not slow down aircraft turnarounds. It is the customer's option to take it or leave it. In fact the low-cost airlines are gradually identifying differentiating attributes which their customers will value, e.g. not queuing, but which do not impact the basic low-cost offering.

So generic strategies for business success are about:

1. Your products or services and how you either:
   - Structure your business to deliver them more cheaply than your competitors, or
   - Differentiate them with attributes that customers value and for which they are prepared to pay a premium.
2. The markets in which you sell your products or services, identifying segments of the market on which you should focus that suit you particularly well, either because your products or services are or can be particularly well adapted to that niche or because the level of competition is lower.

BRANDING

A subject intimately connected to differentiation is branding. Branding is the art of representing an organization through symbols and slogans which become associated in the mind of the consumer with positive experience of the products or services. The brand is likely to be built using both genuinely good products/ services together with advertising to:

- Enhance or reinforce the perception of quality amongst those who have tried the product or service.
- Persuade potential consumers to buy the product/service.
- Create awareness of the brand amongst a wider public.

The benefits of building a brand for the organization are that:

- A brand fosters loyalty amongst consumers and they are less inclined to sample competitor's offerings.
- Followers of a brand will pay more for the branded product than a non-branded product. For example a supermarket's own brand of a foodstuff will almost always be cheaper than the branded product even though the contents of the packets are often virtually identical.
- Through 'brand extension' the brand can be used to enter new markets or establish new products or services.

There are thousands of examples of brands. The brewer Bass lays claim to its red triangle being the world's first trademark. Coca-Cola, McDonald's, Disney, and Ford are other obvious examples. Their brands are easily recognizable through the font in which their names are written, their slogans, songs, tunes, symbols etc.

In fact if the task was to match the above list of brand names with the following:

- Golden arches
- The tune to '*When you wish upon a star*'
- 'It's the real thing'
- Blue oval.

I bet that over 70 per cent of the world would score 100 per cent.

Virgin is a good example of branding. Once again the font used to write Virgin is very identifiable as is the slight sloping up from bottom left to upper right. The colour red is also prominent. Richard Branson takes every opportunity to reinforce the brand through his personality and public persona. Virgin plays upon a sexy image. Virgin have used the brand to enter a multitude of markets from records to airlines, credit cards, railways, holidays, books, cruises, cola, phones – you name it, they seem to be there.

The benefit to the consumer of branding is that being loyal to a brand avoids confusion when making a purchase. Consumers feel that they can trust the brand. Apple has an incredibly loyal following which has crossed from its Macintosh computers to iPods.

There are two other models that are worth knowing about which address in a simple way these key issues of products/services and markets. The first is the Boston Consulting Group (BCG) matrix.[5]

---

5   Stern, C.W. and Stalk, G. 1998. *Perspectives on Strategy from The Boston Consulting Group*. John Wiley & Sons, New York.

This examines the product life cycle, recognizing that new products take time to develop and establish market share and that eventually products become obsolete or in some other way unmarketable. The product life cycle may also apply to some services. Of course there are products which may simply go on for ever, e.g. tins of baked beans, loaves of bread, bricks, cement, paper etc. But cars, aircraft, records, CDs, cameras, computers and countless other products certainly go through a product life cycle. Many generic services such as legal services, medical services etc. will similarly go on for ever, but legislation, technological advances and new academic theories are constantly emerging which give rise to new and changing services within those generic services.

The BCG matrix looks at two dimensions for products which are growth and market share. It defines four stages in the life cycle of a product:

1. Problem child or question mark – low market share and high growth. High growth often goes hand in hand with high investment. This is a product at the beginning of its life cycle when there is high investment in production, marketing and distribution yet market share is still low so there is relatively little revenue.
2. Star – high market share and high growth. It sounds fabulous doesn't it? The problem child is becoming successful and has achieved a good market share. However, the high growth is still fuelling high investment perhaps as production facilities expand and marketing extends to new markets. The high market share is generating significant revenues which may be sufficient to payback the investment.
3. Cash cow – high market share and low growth. The star has reached its zenith and has captured a high market share. It is not growing any further which means that further investment to fuel this growth is not required. It is highly profitable and a big cash generator.
4. Dog – low market share and low growth. The dog may be a problem child whose growth has decayed before it ever achieved significant market share, or a star that suddenly became eclipsed by a competitor's superior product, or indeed a cash cow that has become obsolete.

The BCG Matrix is useful because it helps you to:

1. Identify which category each of your products or services fit into.
2. Realize that you should kill off any dogs as quickly as possible.
3. Understand that your portfolio of products or services needs a mixture. You need cash cows to generate a profit and to fund the development of problem children and stars. You need stars because cash cows don't appear out of thin air and you need problem children for the same reason.

The next model that looks at products and markets is the Ansoff[6] Matrix. Ansoff considered that the options for growth of a company could be analysed along the dimensions of existing or new products/services and existing or new markets.

This analysis results in four generic growth strategies:

- *Market penetration* is all about expanding market share of existing products in existing markets. In other words selling more of what we sell in our existing markets.
- *Product development* can be likened to a food retailer like McDonald's, e.g. who whilst remaining in the fast food market are constantly launching new products. This is finding new things to sell to our existing marketplace.
- *Market development* is where an existing product or service is sold into new markets. For example Lucozade was an energy drink originally marketed to aid the recovery of (predominantly) sick children. Many years later this was launched as an energy drink to sportsmen and sportswomen.
- An example of *diversification* is the exploitation of the Virgin brand across music, cola, airlines, railways, telephones etc. It is selling new things in new markets.

There is no doubt that if you are seeking a strategy to grow your organization, thinking through the Ansoff matrix helps to ensure that you consider all options. The Lucozade example is a good one. It betrays my age if I reveal that when I was young Lucozade was a fizzy drink containing glucose syrup, sold in pharmacies and marketed with the slogan 'Lucozade aids recovery'. The sick were the target market. The only compensations of being sick in my childhood were days off school and Lucozade.

Then in 1983 Lucozade's owners Beecham, a pharmaceutical company which subsequently became SmithKline Beecham and then Glaxo SmithKline, identified the possibility of market development as a growth strategy. The same fizzy glucose syrup drink was rebranded with the slogan 'Lucozade replaces lost energy' and the advertising campaign featured Daley Thompson, the Olympic champion decathlete. In five years UK sales of the drink tripled.

Alternative strategies could have been to promote Lucozade more vigorously in pharmacies, doctor's surgeries and hospitals in the UK and overseas, or to develop new products or services, perhaps Lucozade lozenges or Lucozade powders for the health care market. Another would be to develop Lucozade lozenges for a different market, e.g. sportsmen and sportswomen.

---

6   Ansoff, I. 1957. Strategies for diversification, *Harvard Business Review*, 35(5), September–October, 113–124.

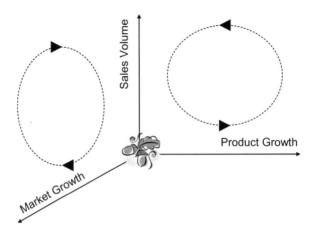

Figure 5.3   Project nursery

In my opinion the Ansoff matrix helps us to think of both markets and products and how we might develop across products or market whilst the BCG matrix reminds us that products have a life cycle and that young products need nursing and nurturing. 'Adult' products which have ceased to grow can bring in the cash to help the new products grow. These models are both two-dimensional, whereas it seems to me that markets also need development. For example breaking into a new country takes time and the fledgling market will need support from existing markets until it is established.

MERGERS AND ACQUISITIONS

Mergers and acquisitions are frequently used as part of an organization's corporate strategy. They are not really a strategy in their own right but instead should form part of one of the generic strategies. If an organization buys another organization it should be because that purchase allows it to:

- Make cost efficiencies and extend its cost leadership, or
- Better differentiate its products or services, or
- Gain access to new markets or extend its market share in existing markets.

Mergers and acquisitions generally fall into two types:

1. Vertical integration
2. Horizontal integration.

Vertical integration is where an organization buys or merges with another organization that is or can be a part of the value chain in which it operates, for example a travel agency buying an airline or an airline buying a travel agency. Another example may be a car manufacturer buying one of its key component suppliers. Oil companies have long been vertically integrated owning the drilling, shipping, refining and retailing parts of their supply or value chain.

The advantages of vertical integration are said to be lower transaction costs between the different parts of the supply chain, better communication of demand and supply and better control for the organization over its business. Downsides are that the organization is committed to its suppliers and discouraged from buying from other perhaps more efficient suppliers.

Horizontal integration is when an organization buys another organization at its own level in the supply chain. Examples would be one oil company buying another, when BP bought Amoco, or a pharmaceutical company merging with another, e.g. Burroughs Wellcome merged with Glaxo Laboratories to form Glaxo Wellcome. Beecham merged with SmithKline Beckman to become SmithKline Beecham and SmithKline Beecham merged with Glaxo Wellcome to become GlaxoSmithKline.

The advantages or horizontal integration are economies of scale and the efficiencies that can be made by sharing resources, perhaps only needing one marketing or accounts department instead of two. The merged organization also has increased market power over its suppliers. There may also be reduced costs of international business if it has merged with an organization with a complementary geographical spread of operations.

A disadvantage (for the consumer anyway) is that horizontal integration reduces the number of competitors. Consequently such a merger or acquisition will often come under the scrutiny of government and may be prohibited.

A third type of merger and acquisition is when it contributes to diversification, i.e. buying or merging with companies delivering different products or services in different markets. An example in the US would be General Electric which acquired businesses in aviation, financial services, health care, railways and many other industries. In the UK Hanson was another example of a conglomerate. It bought businesses in chemicals, mining, tobacco, batteries, timber, toys, golf clubs, jacuzzis, cranes and cod liver oil. Both GE and Hanson operated by buying companies that could be managed better and applying their skills to doing that. Another benefit claimed by conglomerates was that of spreading risk for their shareholders. In other words if one of a conglomerate's businesses suffered a downturn then the others, being in totally different markets, probably would not. Another advantage of buying companies was that the conglomerate became larger and more powerful with more earnings. The stock market is interested in the price/

earnings (p/e) ratio and generally speaking as the conglomerate acquired more earnings its share price went up, recognizing those acquired earnings in line with the conglomerate's original p/e ratio even if the company it bought had had a lower p/e ratio which might have been expected to dilute the conglomerate's p/e ratio.

Conglomerates started to go out of fashion with the stock markets from the 1970s when rising interest rates hit conglomerates' profits and investors found that the companies within conglomerates were often not growing faster than they had been before acquisition. It was also difficult to dispute the fact that it is much easier and effective for a shareholder to spread their risk by buying shares in a portfolio of companies than by a company buying lots of companies. You can buy shares with a telephone call or a few clicks of the mouse, whereas for a company to buy another company a small army of lawyers and bankers will be required. The fashion changed to one of companies sticking to their core competencies and not spreading themselves thinly across too many industries. If the City wants to invest in, say, telecommunications it does not want to buy a conglomerate in which the telecommunications business is diluted with construction, shipping, mining and tobacco. I worked for Bovis Construction for nearly 18 years and experienced at first hand the City's distaste for conglomerates. Bovis had been owned by P&O (the Penninsular and Oriental Steam Navigation company) since 1972, but Lord Sterling the chairman of P&O came under pressure to divest P&O's conglomerate interests and focus on ports. The P&O share price was simply not reflecting the underlying value of the individual businesses. The reason that P&O bought Bovis in the first instance is rather interesting. P&O in 1972 was a much larger company than Bovis yet was subject to an aggressive take over bid by Bovis. The then Bovis chairman Frank Sanderson had identified that there was a synergy for the combined group. Bovis specialized in management contracting whereby it managed many subcontractors but employed very little labour and owned very little plant itself. Bovis would have vast amounts of cash in the bank overnight, or perhaps slightly longer, between being paid itself and paying its subcontractors. On the other hand P&O required vast amounts of capital to support its ship buying. The synergy that Bovis could see was in the difference between the interest it would receive on its cash overnight from the bank (and this represented a large part of its profits) and the interest that P&O had to pay its banks for the enormous loans needed to buy and operate its ships. Effectively Bovis saw value in becoming a banker for P&O. As the much larger party in this takeover battle P&O not only saw off the bid from Bovis but saw the value in the strategy and bought Bovis instead. This was therefore a strange sort of vertical integration in so far as banks were a supplier of capital to P&O and P&O bought a quasi bank, i.e. Bovis, in order to capture some of the banking profit in its value chain.

Mergers and acquisitions are very difficult to make work. In normal times (I write this during the credit crunch of 2008 in which banks are being thrust together by governments trying to avert worldwide economic collapse) the buying company will need to pay a premium to acquire its target. This premium might be between 10 and 50 per cent, perhaps more. In 2008 Microsoft offered to buy Yahoo at a 61 per cent premium to its market value. The very rumour of an acquisition pushes a target company's share price up. If you pay 30 per cent premium above market price to buy your target company then you will have to find 30 per cent of efficiencies or added value emerging from the marriage and pay off your own and your acquisition's advisors before you begin breaking even on the deal. You'd better have a very clear vision of where the value is in buying the company. You may believe that the acquisition gives the combined company more power over suppliers or that costs can be reduced because two marketing departments for example are not necessary in the combined company. You may believe that the target company's management is poor and you can manage it much better.

CONCLUSIONS

This has been a very quick canter through the basics of corporate strategy. Its implications for the Project Sponsor are that projects may be born out of:

- The need of an organization to exploit an opportunity through capitalizing on its strengths.
- The need of an organization to counter a threat through using its strength or fixing its weakness.
- The need of an organization to create a new product or service.
- The need of an organization to find efficiencies in its processes and reduce costs.
- The need of an organization to expand its volume of production and sales.
- The need to improve product or service quality and therefore differentiate itself.
- The need of an organization to enhance the perception of its brand, perhaps through a marketing campaign.
- The need of an organization to accelerate the first phase of the product life cycle, bringing new products to market earlier and getting them established as cash cows as quickly as possible.
- The need of an organization to buy or merge with another organization.
- The need of an organization to identify new markets for its products or services and to exploit those markets.

I hope that this chapter gives the Project Sponsor who finds themselves in the situation of sponsoring such a project some insight into why they are doing so. I also hope that it will help sponsors to identify and promote new projects within their organizations.

CHAPTER 6

THE PROJECT BUSINESS CASE – WILL THE PROJECT BE WORTH IT?

Project appraisal or investment appraisal is the structured process for identifying whether or not a project is worth doing. It weighs the capital and operating costs of the project against the expected revenues to see whether the value of the revenues will exceed the costs and therefore justify the project.

DISCOUNTED CASH FLOW ANALYSIS

What complicates this weighing exercise somewhat is that for many projects the capital investment is large relative to either the revenue or the operating costs, and the capital investment is required up front with revenues arriving perhaps years later and continuing perhaps for decades.

If I put it to you that if you invest £1,000 now in my project I guarantee to pay you back £1,100 in ten years time, representing a whopping 10 per cent clear profit, would you fall for it? No, of course you wouldn't. If I had guaranteed to pay you back the £1,100 in 1 year rather than 10 then you might have given it some consideration. You know that there is a time value of money and that you could invest your £1,000 in a bank and at only 5 per cent annual interest (half the total profit that I offered) it would be worth £1,629 in 10 years time. The miracle of compound interest! The clear message is that money now is worth more than the same amount of money in the future.

Therefore we need some way of adjusting future cash flows to their present value so that we can compare them with money we are asked to invest now on a like for like basis. The answer to this problem is discounted cash flow analysis (DCF).

Let's track that £1,000 that you invested in the bank at 5 per cent p.a.

Year 0 i.e. now = £1,000
Year 1 £1,000 × 1.05 = £1,050
Year 2 £1,000 × 1.05 × 1.05 = £1,103

Year 3 £1,000 × 1.05 × 1.05 × 1.05 = £1,158
Year n £1,000 × (1 + 5%)^n
Year 10 £1,000 × (1 + 5%)^{10} = £1,629

From this we can say that the future value (FV) of £1,000 invested over 10 years at 5 per cent discount rate is £1,629. Working this in reverse we can also say that the present value (PV) of £1,629 in 10 years time at a 5 per cent discount rate is £1,000.

In general we can say that where 'd' is the discount rate the present value (PV) of an amount (FV) n years in the future is:

$$PV = FV \frac{1}{(1+d)^n}$$

The part of the calculation $\frac{1}{(1+d)^n}$ is known as the discount factor. Clearly the discount factor varies with d and n. Once upon a time tables of discount factors were published which helped with the manual calculation of the discounted cash flow analysis. However, spreadsheets have made this all incredibly easy.

The spreadsheet shown in Table 6.1 analyses a new proposal that I have for you. If you give me £1,000 now (year 0) then I will pay you £150 every year for ten years, starting next year. The total repaid to you is £1,500, an impressive 50 per cent profit, and you start getting your money back as early as next year. Now what this is telling us is that the net present value (NPV) of this project, i.e. the result of the present value of revenues minus the present value of costs, is + £158. So we have converted the future revenues to present values and weighed them in the balance with the present value of the costs, so as to compare like with like, and we have found that the PV of the revenues outweighs the PV of the costs by £158. There is a NPV of £158. All other things being equal you should accept my proposal.

All other things aren't equal:

- What if the taxman wants a slice of the action?
- Are you sure that this seedy-looking fellow you met in front of the bookshop will honour his promise to pay you back? What's the risk that I'll default? Will your money be safer in the bank than with me?
- Isn't inflation nibbling away at the present value of your future revenues as well?

We will address these issues soon, but first I have another proposal for you.

Table 6.1   An initial business proposal

Year	0	1	2	3	4	5	6	7	8	9	10	Total
Discount rate	5%											
Discount factor	1.000	0.952	0.907	0.864	0.823	0.784	0.746	0.711	0.677	0.645	0.614	
Cost	1,000											1,000
Revenue		150	150	150	150	150	150	150	150	150	150	1,500
PV of costs	1,000											1,000
PV of revenues	0	143	136	130	123	118	112	107	102	97	92	1,158
PV of cash flow	−1,000	143	136	130	123	118	112	107	102	97	92	158

SUNK COSTS

I will offer to sell you an envelope for £350. Inside the envelope there is a really outstanding financial proposal that knocks spots off the previous one. However, I'm not going to give you the envelope until you give me the £350.

You decide that I'm an honest-looking chap, not half as seedy as you first thought. You pay me the £350 and I give you the envelope. In the envelope is the proposal that you give me £1,000 now and I will pay you £170 every year for 10 years. That's £1,700, an even more impressive profit of 70 per cent, and you start getting your money back next year. Do you invest?

Which is the correct project appraisal A or B?

In project appraisal A the proposal is set out exactly as found in the envelope. It results in a NPV of + £313. That's a heck of a lot better that the previous deal. What's more the NPV is positive so the PV of revenues outweighs the PV of costs, so you should undertake the project. Shouldn't you?

In project appraisal B we have added in the £350 that you had to spend to get the envelope. So the investment is really £1,350 rather than £1,000. Unfortunately the NPV is now –£37. The PV of costs outweighs the PV of revenues. So you shouldn't undertake the project, or should you?

So which is right? A or B?

Please send £500 in a sealed envelope to me at my publishers address on the back cover and I'll send you the answer. Only kidding ;-). It's appraisal A, surprised? You may have thought that appraisal B more accurately represents all the cash transactions taking place and therefore overall you've subtracted value of £37 from 'Dear Reader plc'. You have paid out £1,350 as per appraisal B, not £1,000 as per appraisal A. And you'd be right about that. However, you're forgetting the purpose of the appraisal. An appraisal is undertaken at a point in time to assess whether or not, at that time, to invest in the project. At the time that you undertook the appraisal you had already spent the £350 to get the envelope. It was history! I wasn't going to give it back to you if you didn't like what was in the envelope. It was what we call a *sunk cost*. Having sunk that cost you need to forget it and get on with life. Appraise the project on the table. That project would add value of £313 to 'Dear Reader plc'. Admittedly there was a previous project called 'Envelope Gamble' that subtracted value of £350 from 'Dear Reader plc' but you didn't run an appraisal on that project. The project in the envelope allows you to get back most of the money that you lost on project Envelope Gamble. If you decided not to go ahead then you would be £350 down instead of just £37.

Table 6.2   Project appraisal A

Year	0	1	2	3	4	5	6	7	8	9	10	Total
Discount rate 5%												
Discount factor	1.000	0.952	0.907	0.864	0.823	0.784	0.746	0.711	0.677	0.645	0.614	
Cost	1,000											1,000
Revenue		170	170	170	170	170	170	170	170	170	170	1,700
PV of costs	1,000	0	0	0	0	0	0	0	0	0	0	1,000
PV of revenues	0	162	154	147	140	133	127	121	115	110	104	1,313
PV of cash flow	−1,000	162	154	147	140	133	127	121	115	110	104	313

Table 6.3   Project appraisal B

Year	0	1	2	3	4	5	6	7	8	9	10	Total
Discount rate 5%												
Discount factor	1.000	0.952	0.907	0.864	0.823	0.784	0.746	0.711	0.677	0.645	0.614	
Cost	1,350											1,350
Revenue		170	170	170	170	170	170	170	170	170	170	1,700
PV of costs	1,350	0	0	0	0	0	0	0	0	0	0	1,350
PV of revenues	0	162	154	147	140	133	127	121	115	110	104	1,313
PV of cash flow	−1,350	162	154	147	140	133	127	121	115	110	104	−37

Appraisal B would have been the valid appraisal if you had X-ray vision (I'm guessing that you don't) and had been able to see inside the envelope before parting with your £350.

A real life analogy is drilling for oil. You drill for oil in various locations at considerable expense. You don't know whether you will find oil on the first attempt or the hundredth. It's the hundredth. You then do a project appraisal to see whether or not to progress with extracting the oil. In the appraisal do you add the cost of all that exploratory drilling to the costs of setting up the extraction wells, pipelines etc? No! It's a sunk cost. You've spent it looking for the oil. You won't get it back, it is sunk cost! Having found the oil you now need to decide if it's worth extracting it or not.

Another analogy is feasibility study cost. You carry out a feasibility study for that new car plant so as to examine various options and assess the costs. Do you add into the appraisal the small fortune that you spent on consultants doing the feasibility study? No, it's a sunk cost. Basically at the time of doing the appraisal look forward and don't try to add in costs that you've already spent and lost for ever.

Of course overall your business needs to have a handle on all the costs. If you spend all your profits on feasibility studies you'll go broke, but at the time of doing an appraisal sunk costs are irrelevant. The same is true if you re-run an appraisal when a project is half complete. If either the future costs have gone up or the future revenues have gone down such that a previously good business case needs revisiting, you must forget about the costs spent that you can't get back. You must focus on present and future cash flows. However, you do need to take account of opportunity costs.

OPPORTUNITY COSTS

Let's imagine that you are the Project Sponsor for the construction of a new factory. The project investment appraisal on which the board authorized the project is as shown in Table 6.4.

The cost of land purchase was £6,000,000. Design, construction and all tooling and fit out costs were estimated at £6,000,000 spread over 2 years, £1m in the first year for design and £5m in the second year on construction. The factory then costs a total of £100,000 per annum to operate and maintain. It brings in revenues of £1,500,000 per annum. It is expected to continue operating for nine years by which time it will be obsolete. You will then redeploy the workforce and sell the land and equipment from which you expect to net £6,500,000 after all associated sale and redeployment costs. The NPV was positive at £1,515,606.

Table 6.4 Factory original appraisal

	Year	0	1	2	3	4	5	6	7	8	9	10	11	Total
Discount rate	5%													
Discount factor		1.000	0.952	0.907	0.864	0.823	0.784	0.746	0.711	0.677	0.645	0.614	0.585	
Costs														0
Land purchase		6,000,000												
Design and build costs		1,000,000	5,000,000											
Operating and maintenance costs				100,000	100,000	100,000	100,000	100,000	100,000	100,000	100,000	100,000		
Total costs		7,000,000	5,000,000	100,000	100,000	100,000	100,000	100,000	100,000	100,000	100,000	100,000	0	12,900,000
PV of costs		7,000,000	4,761,905	90,703	86,384	82,270	78,353	74,622	71,068	67,684	64,461	61,391	0	12,438,840
Revenues														
Revenue from product sales				1,500,000	1,500,000	1,500,000	1,500,000	1,500,000	1,500,000	1,500,000	1,500,000	1,500,000		13,500,000
Residual value from sale of land and equipment													6,500,000	
Total revenues		0	0	1,500,000	1,500,000	1,500,000	1,500,000	1,500,000	1,500,000	1,500,000	1,500,000	1,500,000	6,500,000	20,000,000
PV of revenues		0	0	1,360,544	1,295,756	1,234,054	1,175,289	1,119,323	1,066,022	1,015,259	966,913	920,870	3,800,415	13,954,446
PV of cash flow		-7,000,000	-4,761,905	1,269,841	1,209,373	1,151,783	1,096,937	1,044,702	994,954	947,575	902,452	859,479	3,800,415	1,515,606

Table 6.5 Revised appraisal incorporating higher year 1 costs

Year	0	1	2	3	4	5	6	7	8	9	10	11	Total
Discount rate 5%													
Discount factor	1.000	0.952	0.907	0.864	0.823	0.784	0.746	0.711	0.677	0.645	0.614	0.585	
Costs													0
Land purchase	6,000,000												
Design and build costs	1,000,000	8,000,000											
Operating and maintenance costs			100,000	100,000	100,000	100,000	100,000	100,000	100,000	100,000	100,000		
Total costs	7,000,000	8,000,000	100,000	100,000	100,000	100,000	100,000	100,000	100,000	100,000	100,000	0	15,900,000
PV of costs	7,000,000	7,619,048	90,703	86,384	82,270	78,353	74,622	71,068	67,684	64,461	61,391	0	15,295,983
Revenues													
Revenue from product sales			1,500,000	1,500,000	1,500,000	1,500,000	1,500,000	1,500,000	1,500,000	1,500,000	1,500,000		13,500,000
Residual value from sale of land and equipment												6,500,000	
Total revenues	0	0	1,500,000	1,500,000	1,500,000	1,500,000	1,500,000	1,500,000	1,500,000	1,500,000	1,500,000	6,500,000	20,000,000
PV of revenues	0	0	1,360,544	1,295,756	1,234,054	1,175,289	1,119,323	1,066,022	1,015,259	966,913	920,870	3,800,415	13,954,446
PV of cash flow	-7,000,000	-7,619,048	1,269,841	1,209,373	1,151,783	1,096,937	1,044,702	994,954	947,575	902,452	859,479	3,800,415	-1,341,537

You have bought the land and are at the end of year 0. Design works have cost the £1m predicted. However, unforeseen problems have occurred which means that next year costs to construct the factory will be £8m rather than the £5m predicted. You make this change to the spreadsheet that you presented to the board and it looks like Table 6.5.

Unfortunately the positive NPV has turned an angry shade of red. Should we stop the project? You remember about sunk costs. We have already bought the land and spent the first-year design costs. So you revise the spreadsheet as shown in Table 6.6.

Wow! It looks like we should press on with the project after all. The design costs and land costs were history and they more than compensate for the increase in construction costs. It just goes to show that we were too far into the project to stop. It would be madness to stop now. There was no way of getting the design costs or the land purchase costs back ... Oh! Hang on! Don't circulate the revised paper to the board yet. We could get the land value back by selling the land and not building the factory. We nearly missed an opportunity cost. In other words, even though at this point in time we already own the land on which we will build the factory, the act of building the factory denies us the opportunity of selling it now. We need to recognize this cost of a lost opportunity.

So, revise the board paper as shown in Table 6.7. Abort project is the recommendation. Selling the land is the right decision. It is a close run thing though, so expect a heated debate at the board meeting. And it does mean that the hired in project manager is out of a job, so you can see why ownership of the investment case or business case belongs with the Project Sponsor rather than the project manager.

INFLATION EFFECTS

The next issue that I think we should cover is inflation. You will notice that in order to keep the factory investment appraisals relatively simple I showed the operating and maintenance costs steady at £100,000 per year each year and the revenues also steady at £1,500,000 per year each year. Likewise, the residual value of £6,500,000 reflected no increase in land value but with depreciation in the value of equipment. What I was doing was representing everything in real terms. Real means after adjusting for inflation. You have probably heard economists say something like *'in the last 50 years salaries have risen by 50 per cent in real terms'* What they mean is that the purchasing power of salaries has risen by 50 per cent. Salaries themselves have gone up by much, much more than 50 per cent, but inflation has affected the cost of goods too, so in real terms, after inflation has been factored out the real increase is 50 per cent.

Table 6.6 Revised to remove sunk costs

Year	0	1	2	3	4	5	6	7	8	9	10	11	Total
Discount rate 5%													
Discount factor	1.000	0.952	0.907	0.864	0.823	0.784	0.746	0.711	0.677	0.645	0.614	0.585	
Costs													0
Land purchase													
Design and build costs		8,000,000											
Operating and maintenance costs			100,000	100,000	100,000	100,000	100,000	100,000	100,000	100,000	100,000		
Total costs	0	8,000,000	100,000	100,000	100,000	100,000	100,000	100,000	100,000	100,000	100,000	0	8,900,000
PV of costs	0	7,619,048	90,703	86,384	82,270	78,353	74,622	71,068	67,684	64,461	61,391	0	8,295,983
Revenues													
Revenue from product sales			1,500,000	1,500,000	1,500,000	1,500,000	1,500,000	1,500,000	1,500,000	1,500,000	1,500,000		13,500,000
Residual value from sale of land and equipment												6,500,000	
Total revenues	0	0	1,500,000	1,500,000	1,500,000	1,500,000	1,500,000	1,500,000	1,500,000	1,500,000	1,500,000	6,500,000	20,000,000
PV of revenues	0	0	1,360,544	1,295,756	1,234,054	1,175,289	1,119,323	1,066,022	1,015,259	966,913	920,870	3,800,415	13,954,446
PV of cash flow	0	-7,619,048	1,269,841	1,209,373	1,151,783	1,096,937	1,044,702	994,954	947,575	902,452	859,479	3,800,415	5,658,463

Table 6.7 Opportunity cost of land added

Year	0	1	2	3	4	5	6	7	8	9	10	11	Total
Discount rate	5%												
Discount factor	1.000	0.952	0.907	0.864	0.823	0.784	0.746	0.711	0.677	0.645	0.614	0.585	
Costs													0
Land purchase		6,000,000											
Design and build costs		8,000,000											
Operating and maintenance costs			100,000	100,000	100,000	100,000	100,000	100,000	100,000	100,000	100,000		
Total costs	0	14,000,000	100,000	100,000	100,000	100,000	100,000	100,000	100,000	100,000	100,000	0	14,900,000
PV of costs	0	13,333,333	90,703	86,384	82,270	78,353	74,622	71,068	67,684	64,461	61,391	0	14,010,269
Revenues													
Revenue from product sales			1,500,000	1,500,000	1,500,000	1,500,000	1,500,000	1,500,000	1,500,000	1,500,000	1,500,000		13,500,000
Residual value from sale of land and equipment												6,500,000	
Total revenues	0	0	1,500,000	1,500,000	1,500,000	1,500,000	1,500,000	1,500,000	1,500,000	1,500,000	1,500,000	6,500,000	20,000,000
PV of revenues	0	0	1,360,544	1,295,756	1,234,054	1,175,289	1,119,323	1,066,022	1,015,259	966,913	920,870	3,800,415	13,954,446
PV of cash flow	0	−13,333,333	1,269,841	1,209,373	1,151,783	1,096,937	1,044,702	994,954	947,575	902,452	859,479	3,800,415	−55,822

The alternative is to work in nominal terms. That means that all the values entered into the spreadsheet will be at the values we actually expect them to be in the year that we expect them to accrue.

So which is best, real or nominal? As long as you are absolutely consistent and work the whole appraisal in either real or nominal terms there is no difference. You must remember that the discount rate must also be either real or nominal (i.e. after the effect of inflation is removed, or including inflation). However, there is an argument which favours working in nominal terms, and that is that there is more than one rate of inflation. The rate of inflation that applies to your staff wages is probably different to the rate of inflation that applies to your material costs, which will in turn be different to the rate of inflation of your energy costs. The rate of increase in your finished product prices will be different again. It is probably simpler to work in nominal terms and represent each of these cost and revenue lines with their own row in the spreadsheet and their own rate of inflation.

Particularly in public sector projects the issue of project lifespan can be quite complex. Aircraft, ships, trains and infrastructure will all have a very long life but in addition to operating and maintenance costs there will be major refit, overhaul or renewal required perhaps once, twice or even three times during the asset's working life. These must not be forgotten in the appraisal.

CAPITAL ASSET PRICING MODEL

Now it is time to talk in more detail about the discount rate. We saw earlier that there is a time value of money and we used the bank interest rate of 5 per cent p.a. to represent what you could have earned with your money if you hadn't given it to me. Most interest rates quoted by banks are nominal rather than real, and I used the same 5 per cent in my 'real' factory investment appraisal. So that looked like a mistake. If say inflation is running at 3 per cent p.a. then the equivalent nominal discount rate was $3 + 5 = 8$ per cent p.a. The fact is that most companies have better things to do with their money than put it in the bank. Investors want a higher rate of return than the return they can get from the bank. Despite the odd scare, banks are relatively low risk places to put your money, but the downside is that low risk equals low rate of return. Equity shareholders buy a share in a company and put their investment at risk. There is no guarantee that they will get their money back. If the company goes bankrupt then the banks will be first in the queue (after the receiver) to recover their money, then will come the suppliers who are owed money by the company and finally the shareholders will get a share of what is left. In return for the risk of losing their money, equity investors expect a higher rate of return from dividends and growth in share price. The question is what rate of return should a shareholder expect? If the shareholder could get 5 per cent by putting their money in the bank then they will certainly want more than that by investing in risky shares. The answer to this question lies in the capital asset pricing model, also known as CAP-M. This is a model for which William Sharpe, Harry Markowitz and Merton Miller jointly won the Nobel Memorial Prize in Economics in 1990. A detailed study of CAP-M is beyond the scope of this book but what it boils down to is:

$$Ri = Rf + \beta \times (Rm - Rf)$$

In which:

Ri is the rate of return that is expected from the equity investment.

Rf is the risk free rate of return, i.e. the return that can be generated without taking any risk. No investment is entirely risk free but government bonds come close enough.

Rm is the rate of return from the market as a whole, say the FTSE All Share Index for example.

Consequently $(Rm - Rf)$ is known as the risk premium or the average return that an investor in the stock market expects over and above government bonds. The equity risk premium varies over time and over which market you are looking at. It is currently estimated as 3.75 per cent for London's FTSE.

β (beta) is the sensitivity of the investment returns relative to the market returns. In practice we measure β as being the movement in a company's share price relative to the market index.

When I worked for Bovis Construction they were owned by P&O and since I was incentivized with share options in P&O I took a keen interest in their share price. Over a period of about four months I recorded P&O's share price as well as the FTSE100 index each morning from the newspaper. In Figure 6.1 you can see that there was quite a close correlation between the movement of the FTSE100 index and the movement of P&O.

Beta figures are published in the financial press. They can be calculated by drawing the line of best fit through a graph similar to the one for P&O shown in Figure 6.1 and working out the slope, or you can use the statistical functions in a spreadsheet such as Excel to calculate the correlation. In simple language if a share has a beta of 2.0 then a 10 per cent movement one way or the other by the market as a whole will on average produce a movement of 20 per cent in the share whose beta is 2.0. If a share has a beta of 0.5 then a 10 per cent movement one way or the other by the market as a whole will on average produce a movement of 5 per cent in the share whose beta is 0.5. Now I am not saying that shares all move in perfect harmony

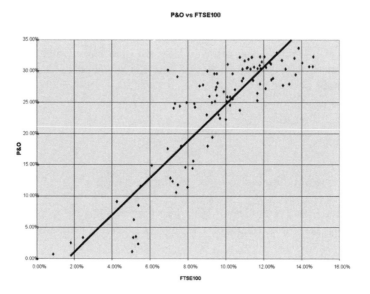

Figure 6.1   P&O's beta

with each other to different degrees. Of course not! If ACME Kiddies Toys Ltd have to withdraw all their toys because they are found to contain harmful toxins for example then you would expect their share price to suffer even if the market as a whole is booming. However, on average, movements in market sentiment and macro economic factors like growth, interest rates, unemployment, oil price etc. affect all companies but to varying degrees. It should be apparent that the market as a whole has a beta of 1.0 by definition because it moves in perfect harmony with itself. A utility company for example usually has a beta of less than 1.0 because it has a steady business relatively unaffected by the vagaries of the market. People still need electricity even if unemployment is rising. However, a cruise company will often have a beta of greater than 1.0 because when times are hard people will still pay their electricity bills but they will cut back on that expensive Caribbean cruise and go camping instead. Consequently we may expect the cruise company to be more affected by the economy as a whole than average. While I'm on the subject of share price movements and having cited the fictitious ACME Kiddies Toys Ltd, it often seems odd that companies come out with bad news such as poor annual results and their share price goes up whilst they release good news like record profits and their share price goes down. This is because market analysts and other commentators are watching companies throughout the year and have already anticipated such news. There will have been buy, hold or sell recommendations made and target prices suggested by pundits. When a company releases record profit figures and its share price goes down this is because the market had expected the profits to be even better and the anticipated rise had already been factored into the price. Consequently the market is a little disappointed and the share price falls.

For an equity investment we can look up in the financial press what the current market premium is, what the risk-free rate is (e.g. for government bonds) and the beta for our companies shares and can then calculate the required equity rate of return Ri.

Let's assume that our beta is 1.1, the risk-free rate offered on government bonds is 4.8 per cent (nominal *not* real) and the market premium is 3.75 per cent. This means that our required equity rate of return is 4.8 per cent + $(1.1 \times 3.75\%) = 8.925$ per cent nominal.

Most companies will be funded by a mixture of equity (shareholders' capital) and debt from lenders such as banks. The discount rate that we use in our project appraisal should be based on the *weighted average cost of capital* (WACC). Let's assume that 25 per cent of our funding is from equity shareholders (at the 8.925 per cent required return that we calculated above) and 75 per cent is from bank debt at an interest rate of 5.1 per cent. Thus our WACC is $(0.25 \times 8.925\%) + (0.75 \times 5.1\%) = 6.056$ per cent

If the project being considered is absolutely standard business for the company, it is small in size compared to the company and it does not change the capital structure of the business then the discount rate that we should use in the project appraisal is 6.056 per cent. However, it is quite likely that the project under consideration is more or less risky than the company's whole business. In that case we should apply a project risk factor to the WACC to produce a *risk-adjusted discount rate* (RADR). If we do this I'm afraid that estimating how much more or less risky than your average business the project is becomes a matter of judgement. Everything I have said about projects (i.e. that they are different to your normal business and unique in many ways with teams brought together that haven't worked together before etc.) should suggest that projects are more risky than most organizations' normal everyday business. Should you add 10, 20 or 100 per cent to the WACC for this project? You might be able to look at other companies who undertake a lot more of the type of project that you are appraising and see what their beta is. However, you should bear in mind that the very nature of their doing more of this sort of project will mean that they are more adept at them and that consequently your risk will be bigger than theirs.

An alternative approach is to use WACC as the discount rate and make the allowance for risk elsewhere. If we make careful and prudent assessment of the risks that may affect our project costs and our project benefits, and if we account for these in our appraisal then we do not need to make another risk allowance on the discount rate. We can make allowances for risk within the appraisal in simple or sophisticated ways. A simple way would be to increase costs and project duration by a risk percentage based on judgement and experience. A more sophisticated way would be to represent our project costs and benefits by probability distributions which reflect the range and likelihood of possibilities. This can be done using Monte Carlo simulation. which I will talk about at more length in Chapter 15. There are reasonably priced Monte Carlo add-ins for spreadsheets such as Microsoft Excel which provide this functionality.

The allowance that you make for risk is a matter of judgement, however you might like to consider that in the UK Her Majesty's Treasury requires an allowance to be made for 'optimism bias' in project appraisals for public projects. Allowances that they recommend vary according to type of project and whether it is standard or non-standard. Allowances can also be reduced if mitigation actions have been put in place against specific risks. However, if no mitigation actions have been put in place then the optimism bias (risk allowance) to be applied to the capital cost ranges from 24 per cent for a standard building project through 66 per cent for a non-standard civil engineering project to 200 per cent for an equipment development project. It also states risk allowances to be applied to project duration and these are 4 per cent for standard buildings, 25 per cent for non-standard civil engineering and 54 per cent for equipment development projects. Don't forget that for the project appraisal, a longer project duration will extend the benefits further into the future, consequently making them less valuable due to the time value of money.

Earlier I said that the WACC would be used for the discount rate if the project being considered is absolutely standard business for the company, it is small in size compared to the company and it does not change the capital structure of the business. We have examined the allowance for project risk in the appraisal but we do need to think about how the project is being financed. If new debt is being taken on to finance the project then that will alter the capital structure of the business, particularly if the project is quite large in relation to the business. Equally if new shares are being issued to raise finance then that too will need to be taken account of in calculating the appropriate WACC for the appraisal. We will look at project finance in more detail in Chapter 9, but it is worth noting here that if the project is large then the organization may well consider creating a special purpose vehicle (SPV) to deliver it. The purpose is to create a separate legal entity that will undertake the project such that if the project runs into severe financial trouble it does not bring the organization down with it. For this very reason, and because of the corporate scandals that we mentioned under project governance in Chapter 3, this area of project finance is one that is subject to change as regulators seek to enforce transparency for shareholders. SPVs can be created for projects in which one or more other organizations finance the SPV along with the organization if the organization wants to spread its risk for a share of the benefits. If this is the case then the WACC will need to be calculated based on the ratios of debt to equity within the SPV and taking account of the probably different equity returns of the parties participating.

ASSESSING THE APPRAISAL RESULTS

I think it's time for a recap of where we are. We have learned that there is a time value of money and that discounted cash flow analysis is the way to analyse the situation where we have large costs in the short term and a long stream of benefits in the future. We have learned to ignore sunk costs but to account for opportunity costs. We have also learned how to calculate the discount rate that we should apply, and to make allowance for risk. We learned that the result of the discounted cash flow analysis is the NPV and that, if this is positive, that is theoretically the amount of money in today's terms that the project will add to the organization. Therefore if the NPV is positive we should embark on the project and if it is zero or negative we should not.

However, there are other ways to use the discounted cash flow analysis to make investment decisions. One is to look at the *internal rate of return* (IRR). The IRR is defined as the value of the discount rate that makes the NPV equal to zero. Consequently you can either calculate this by trial and error making adjustments to the discount rate until the NPV is zero and noting what the discount rate is, or you can use the goal seek function in your spreadsheet to speed up the trial and error or you can use the built-in IRR function.

I have resurrected overleaf as Table 6.8 the car plant DCF that we did earlier. I have adjusted the opportunity cost for the land downwards so that the project does have a positive NPV and I have used the 6.056 per cent discount rate based on our WACC. I haven't at this stage made any allowance for risk or optimism bias because I want an appraisal that is positive simply to demonstrate the IRR calculation.

In Table 6.9 I use goal seek to find the IRR which is 9.24 per cent.

Table 6.8   Car plant DCF adjusted for opportunity cost and WACC

Year	0	1	2	3	4	5	6	7	8	9	10	11	Total
Discount rate	6.06%												
Discount factor	1.000	0.943	0.889	0.838	0.790	0.745	0.703	0.663	0.625	0.589	0.555	0.524	
Costs													0
Land purchase		3,000,000											
Design and build costs		8,000,000											
Operating and maintenance costs			100,000	100,000	100,000	100,000	100,000	100,000	100,000	100,000	100,000		
Total costs	0	11,000,000	100,000	100,000	100,000	100,000	100,000	100,000	100,000	100,000	100,000	0	11,900,000
PV of costs	0	10,371,879	88,906	83,829	79,042	74,529	70,273	66,260	62,477	58,909	55,545	0	11,011,649
Revenues													
Revenue from product sales			1,500,000	1,500,000	1,500,000	1,500,000	1,500,000	1,500,000	1,500,000	1,500,000	1,500,000		13,500,000
Residual value from sale of land and equipment												6,500,000	
Total revenues	0	0	1,500,000	1,500,000	1,500,000	1,500,000	1,500,000	1,500,000	1,500,000	1,500,000	1,500,000	6,500,000	20,000,000
PV of revenues	0	0	1,333,585	1,257,435	1,185,633	1,117,931	1,054,095	993,904	937,150	883,637	833,180	3,404,283	13,000,835
PV of cash flow	0	−10,371,879	1,244,680	1,173,606	1,106,591	1,043,402	983,822	927,644	874,674	824,728	777,635	3,404,283	1,989,186

Table 6.9   Car plant DCF adjusted to find IRR

Internal rate of return (IRR)

Year	0	1	2	3	4	5	6	7	8	9	10	11	Total
Discount rate	9.24%												
Discount factor	1.000	0.915	0.838	0.767	0.702	0.643	0.589	0.539	0.493	0.452	0.413	0.378	
Costs													0
Land purchase		3,000,000											
Design and build costs		8,000,000											
Operating and maintenance costs			100,000	100,000	100,000	100,000	100,000	100,000	100,000	100,000	100,000		
Total costs	0	11,000,000	100,000	100,000	100,000	100,000	100,000	100,000	100,000	100,000	100,000	0	11,900,000
PV of costs	0	10,069,887	83,804	76,718	70,231	64,292	58,856	53,879	49,324	45,153	41,335	0	10,613,479
Revenues													
Revenue from product sales			1,500,000	1,500,000	1,500,000	1,500,000	1,500,000	1,500,000	1,500,000	1,500,000	1,500,000		13,500,000
Residual value from sale of land and equipment												6,500,000	
Total revenues	0	0	1,500,000	1,500,000	1,500,000	1,500,000	1,500,000	1,500,000	1,500,000	1,500,000	1,500,000	6,500,000	20,000,000
PV of revenues	0	0	1,257,057	1,150,766	1,053,462	964,386	882,841	808,192	739,855	677,296	620,026	2,459,598	10,613,479
PV of cash flow	0	−10,069,887	1,173,253	1,074,048	983,231	900,093	823,985	754,312	690,531	632,143	578,691	2,459,598	0

Many people find it easier to compare projects by their IRR than by their NPV because the IRR is a percentage. You will then authorize projects which have an IRR higher than the hurdle rate which you set. The hurdle rate should be set based upon your WACC and any remaining risk allowance that you think appropriate to add to the WACC. We can understand some peoples' preference for IRR if we look at a situation in which you have several projects to choose from. Consider the following projects:

	Capital outlay (£)	NPV (£)
Project A	11,000,000	1,989,186
Project B	160,000	84,646
Project C	14,300,000	2,076,472

Projects A, B and C have positive NPVs so you should do them all. But what if you need to prioritize? Project C adds the most value: should that be first?

	Capital outlay (£)	NPV (£)	IRR (%)
Project A	11,000,000	1,989,186	9.24
Project B	160,000	84,646	14.41
Project C	14,300,000	2,076,472	8.77

On the basis of IRR Project B looks quite attractive and Project C no longer looks like the best one.

The reason to prioritize might be because we have limitations on the capital we can raise. The way to approach this is to prioritize in terms of NPV/k where k is the capital outlay. You then proceed with projects in descending order of NPV/k such that you get the most NPV added to your organization per unit of capital used.

	Capital outlay (£)	NPV (£)	IRR (%)	NPV/k
Project A	11,000,000	1,989,186	9.24	0.181
Project B	160,000	84,646	14.41	0.529
Project C	14,300,000	2,076,472	8.77	0.145

By using a capital rationing approach we have found that we should undertake Project B first, then Project A and finally Project C.

ESTIMATING INCREMENTAL COSTS AND BENEFITS

The next important principle that I want to state is that we should always think in terms of incremental costs and revenues, by which I mean that we are assessing the impact of the project on the organization and therefore the cash flow to be analysed is the difference in cash flow between the organization with the project and the organization without the project.

Estimating the costs that a project will incur is difficult. At the point when the appraisal is done you must ignore sunk costs, i.e. those costs that you have incurred to get to this point. You should also ignore costs which you will incur whether you continue with the project or not. The costs that you do need to take into account include:

- Development costs for designing the project.
- Project management costs.
- Fees.
- Capital expenditure, e.g. on land, equipment, infrastructure, buildings etc.
- Increases in operating costs, e.g. labour, energy, other utilities, maintenance, management, materials etc.
- Incremental tax liabilities (more on this subject later).
- Opportunity costs – the value denied to the organization by the project, e.g. the value of land on which the organization is building a new facility.

Although the project costs are difficult to estimate the capital costs, which are often the largest part, will at least be incurred in the relatively near future (assuming that the project goes ahead). They are therefore less subject to the vagaries of market forces. Estimating the project benefits is at least an order of magnitude more difficult. If your project was something simple and of a domestic scale, like laying additional insulation in your loft, you will be running a project appraisal to compare the cost incurred now of paying for the insulation and perhaps someone to install it versus the reduction in heating bills in the future. You can measure up your loft, wander down to your local DIY shop and ascertain the price now of insulation. You can get a builder round and ask for a quote to lay it. How do you know exactly how much the insulation will save you on your heating bills? I could get my old thermodynamics textbook off the shelf, and perform some calculations involving temperature gradients, U values and areas, and would at best come up with an estimate of heat loss saved which I could convert into the cost of providing that heat today. I would more likely conclude that I had forgotten most of the engineering I'd learned at university and had better ask an expert. Even that expert however would be clairvoyant if they could predict energy prices in one year's time, let alone five or ten. For loft insulation I understand that the savings usually pay for the investment in one winter, and you may be able to get a government grant, so it's an easy investment decision, a 'no brainer'. However, the capital cost of a wind turbine and generator is a much more difficult decision with a payback period of many years.

The above is a simple domestic example of the relative ease of calculating costs now versus future benefits. The decision whether to invest in bringing out a new model car will hinge on how well the new model sells, and how much people will pay for it. You can do market research and run focus groups but it will be difficult to predict how the market will look by the time your new model is in the showrooms. There may have been a recession and your customers may have much less disposable income. Your competitors may have brought out a new model far better than yours.

If you are appraising an improvement to a public transport system you will have many benefits to assess. These will include:

- The additional fares that will be collected due to the improvement. This additional revenue may be as a result of higher ticket prices that can be charged as a result of the improvement or more likely because more passengers will be attracted to use the service because of the improvement. This increased demand may be as a result of faster journey times, increased service frequency or less inconvenience such as changing trains.
- The social and environmental benefits, for example:
  - The reduction in carbon emissions due to the passenger journeys made by public transport rather than private car. However, you will have to offset this against the proportion of people who will make journeys that they otherwise would not.
  - The value of time saved by the working population who get where they need to go more quickly, both because they are travelling on a faster train and because those who have elected to travel by train rather than car have eased congestion on the roads and therefore those who continue to use the roads can also benefit from faster journey times.
  - The value of lives saved because people who were travelling by relatively dangerous road transport are now making those journeys by train. This must be offset by the increased danger to those still travelling by road who are travelling faster due to reduced congestion and are therefore at greater risk.

As you can see this is a complex science (or perhaps art). The social and environmental benefits of a project are given a monetary value. This is necessary in order to distribute limited government money where it will do the most good. For example, when I was closely involved in sponsoring railway projects in the UK, a life saved due to railway safety improvements was valued at around £2,000,000. This enabled the decision to be taken on whether to invest or not based upon the cost of the scheme and how many lives it was likely to save. Now you might think this is callous and believe that your own life or that of a loved one is worth more than £2 million. However, the government has other uses for that money if it does not invest in the rail safety improvement. It may decide to invest in road safety improvement instead. Social and environmental benefits of public sector projects are given due weight in investment appraisals but where a public–private partnership (PPP) is created to deliver the project and there is a mixture of public and private investment, the social and environmental benefits will usually only be of interest to the public sector.

I hope that your projects deliver benefits that are easier to assess but I think the rule is to make the best assessment of all the many benefits that may arise, value them in monetary terms if you possibly can but draw a line between the hard cash and the softer benefits giving much more weight (in private industry at least) to the hard cash benefits.

TAXATION ISSUES

I've postponed talking about tax almost as long as I possibly can, but first I shall digress onto the subject of universal truth. Some things in life are universally true, by which I mean that they are true regardless of which country you are working in and which year it is. The laws of gravity are the same whichever country you are in and, although Einstein revolutionized gravity as far as physicists understand it, for the rest of us Newton and Galileo had it right enough. Psychology and human nature don't change and nor does the art of leadership. What I am trying to do in this book is stick to areas of universal applicability, so that it will be useful to you wherever and whenever you read it, but there are two important areas where I cannot. One of these areas is health and safety legislation. The principles of health and safety do, by and large, fall into the area of universal truth. Falls from height, hard fast-moving objects, sharp blades and fire have always been dangerous and always will be. However, our knowledge does improve in many ways. For example asbestos was once thought to be harmless and cigarettes were even thought to be good for you. As far as project sponsorship is concerned the principles of health and safety don't pose a problem, but legislation will vary country by country and year by year. The other area is tax. Tax law changes even more radically, country by country, and probably more frequently too. So you definitely need to consult your finance department about tax implications on the project or investment appraisal. I will however try to point you in the direction of how tax implications commonly affect the appraisal.

The first effect of tax can be on the WACC and the discount rate. It is quite common for governments to allow interest payments to be written off against tax. If this is the case then it affects your effective cost of debt. I emphasize again that you must consult with a tax expert or your finance department because this is not a universal truth, but if it is the case then:

$$\text{WACC} = (Pe \times \text{Re}) + (Pd \times Rd) \times (1 - Rt)$$

Where Pe = proportion of equity funding

Re = return required on equity

Pd = proportion of debt funding

Rd = return required on debt funding

Rt = tax rate

Therefore in this type of tax regime debt financing is considerably cheaper than equity financing and leads to a lower WACC and hence hurdle rate. Hurdle rate is effectively the minimum IRR which an organization requires in order to approve a project.

The other common tax implication for project appraisal is capital allowance. Currently in the UK there are a bewildering assortment of different capital allowances depending on the size of company and the type of investment being made. They are structured to incentivize certain types of investment (e.g. energy efficiency) and to encourage small companies in particular.

You will need to carefully discuss with your finance department, accountant or tax advisor which allowances are available for your proposed investment and then take these allowances away from the costs in the pre-discounted part of the cash flow. Note that the cash flow should aim to represent post-tax cash flows. Also note that a common mistake is to include interest payments on debt as a cash flow. The cost of interest has already been accounted for when calculating the WACC and hence the discount rate so it would be incorrect to account for interest payments again, to do so would be double counting interest payments.

In the following example we shall look at a project in which an investment is to be made in a factory. The factory will comprise an industrial building costing £10,000,000 in year 0 and plant and machinery costing £6,000,000 also in year 0. Also in year 0 we will need to invest £1,400,000 in inventory. We expect to operate the factory for five years at the end of which we will be able to sell the factory building for £10,000,000 and the plant and machinery for £4,000,000. We expect inflation to be 2.5 per cent per annum on both our revenues and expenditures. Corporation tax is payable at 28 per cent on profit after interest is paid on debt. There are capital allowances available which are 4 per cent straight line on industrial buildings (designed to write off the value of these assets over 25 years) and 6 per cent reducing balance on plant and machinery. We are funded by 15 per cent equity with a calculated return on equity of 10.0 per cent and 85 per cent debt with an interest rate of 5 per cent. Our revenues are expected to be £X in year 1 increasing by inflation thereafter and with zero growth in sales. Our expenditures (excluding interest payments) are expected to be £Y in year 1 increasing by inflation thereafter.

Table 6.10   Factory DCF with tax allowances included

Year	0	1	2	3	4	5	6
Investment flows							
Industrial building	−10,000,000					8,000,000	
Plant and machinery	−6,000,000					4,400,000	
Inventory	−1,400,000						
Total	**−17,400,000**	–	–	–	–	**12,400,000**	
Inflation rate	0						
Operating flows							
Revenues		1,600,000	1,640,000	1,681,000	1,723,025	14,166,101	
Expenditure		800,000	820,000	840,500	861,513	883,050	
Total		800,000	820,000	840,500	861,513	3,283,050	
Corporation tax		–	−11,200	−22,848	−34,273	−45,501	−3,528,555
Net cash flow	−17,400,000	800,000	808,800	817,652	827,239	25,637,550	−3,528,555
Discount rate	4.56%						
Discount factor	1	1	1	1	1	1	1
Present value	−17,400,000	765,111	739,793	715,273	692,100	20,513,919	−2,700,246
NPV	3,325,949						
Capital allowances							
Building allowance	0	Straight line					
Assessed value	10,000,000	9,600,000	9,200,000	8,800,000	8,400,000	8,000,000	
Allowance for year		400,000	400,000	400,000	400,000	400,000	
Plant and machinery allowance	0	Reducing balance					
Assessed value	6,000,000	5,640,000	5,301,600	4,983,504	4,684,494	4,403,424	
Allowance for year		360,000	338,400	318,096	299,010	281,070	
Tax							
Corporation tax rate	0						
Revenues		1,600,000	1,640,000	1,681,000	1,723,025	14,166,101	–
Operating costs		800,000	820,000	840,500	861,513	883,050	–
Capital allowances		760,000	738,400	718,096	699,010	681,070	–
Taxable profit		40,000	81,600	122,404	162,502	12,601,981	–
Corporation tax		−11,200	−22,848	−34,273	−45,501	−3,528,555	–

As described previously, the discount rate we shall use is:

$$(15\% \times 10\%) + ((85\% \times 5\%) \times (1 - 28\%)) = 4.56\%$$

This takes account of the tax efficiency of debt as interest payments are deducted as an expense before profit is calculated.

Note that corporation tax is shown paid in the year after the taxable profit is made. I emphasize again that taxation is a very specialized subject and changes from year to year and by country. Therefore this example is illustrative only and you need to take specialist advice in this area.

PREPARING THE BUSINESS CASE

By now you should have a good idea of the financial elements of the project appraisal. If the appraisal says that the project should go ahead then it is time to put the proposal before the company board or its nominated investment committee. Each organization will usually have a standard format in which it likes to see project proposals but the following structure is fairly typical.

1. Executive summary – you need to summarize the key points of the proposal on one page for the busy executive.
2. The project opportunity – describe the project. Include any technology issues and partners who can be involved. Clearly define the benefits that the project is aimed to secure and the major areas of investment required. Identify changes that the project will require in existing organizational operations, staffing, management or procedures. Identify any alternatives to the proposed project and why these have been ruled out.
3. Strategic context – describe why the project is necessary and how it fits with the existing corporate strategy.
4. Competition – describe what rival projects your project will compete with and what the organization's established competitors are doing in the context of your project.
5. Stakeholders and approvals – identify key stakeholders who will need to be involved in the project and their likely position on it. Identify any statutory or other approvals that the project will require.
6. Financial appraisal – include the financial appraisal with NPV, IRR and NPV/k highlighted.
7. Assumptions – set out all assumptions that you have made
8. Risk register – identify the risks that you have identified together with your quantitative assessment of the risks and your proposed action plan for managing the risks

9. Schedule – set out the timescale for key activities in the project. Identify key milestones, and in particular, further authorization points, approval stages and points at which the project could be aborted if necessary.
10. Project organization structure – set out your proposed structure for sponsoring and managing the project.
11. Funding requirements – state the proposals for funding the project both:
    – In total
    – For the next stage.
12. Next stage – identify when you intend to return to the board/investment committee for the next stage of approval and to what level of detail and financial certainty you expect to have developed the project.

CHAPTER 7

DEFINING THE PROJECT

Project definition can mean either of two things:

1. It can be the document in which the project is described such that the project can be clearly communicated to the project management team and other stakeholders. This is also sometimes referred to as the project charter, project initiation document or project scope document.
2. It can be the process by which a project which has already been conceived and authorized is further developed, options are analysed, a preferred option identified and a Project Management Plan (PMP) or Project Execution Plan (PEP) produced.

They are both valid 'definitions' of project definition, therefore I will cover both in this chapter.

Let's start with the process for developing and defining a project and then look at documenting that definition.

CREATING THE PROJECT VISION

In Chapter 5 we looked at corporate strategy, which should be the birthplace of most projects. There should be a reason for the project and documenting the steps that you went through to formulate the strategy is a good start. Write up, if you haven't already done so, your SWOT, STEEPLE, scenario analysis etc. and any strategy that arose out of it. If you haven't yet received board approval to develop the project now is a good time to critically review the analysis that you have produced.

- Was there any key information that we would have liked but didn't have at the time? Can we get it now? Does it affect our analysis?
- Have events moved on? What has changed?

The STEEPLE, SWOT and Porter's Five Forces analysis work that you did answers the 'where are we now?' question of strategy development. The work that you did to make connections on the SWOT analysis, the scenario analysis, and the generic strategies all focus on the 'where do we want to be?' question. The 'where are we now?' is useful context setting for the project definition. The answer to 'where do we want to be?' is the vision, the objective for the project. Describing this in a way that everyone subsequently involved in the project can understand, support and sign up to is vital, and is probably the single most important thing the sponsor can do for the project. The answer to 'how do we get there?' is in fact what defines the project and forms the body of the project charter/project initiation document/project scope document. However, as the project team grows and work is done, plans will be revised and improved. The answer to 'how do we get there?' will almost inevitably change. What should not change unless absolutely necessary is the objective and the vision. In 1962 John F. Kennedy set the vision that America would put a man on the moon and return him safely to earth before the end of the decade. It was achieved. However, if the vision had been changed in 1964 from the Moon to Mars I think I can guarantee that it would not have been achieved. Partly because we still haven't achieved that, but also because all the planning and development work done up to that point would, in the main, have had to be redone. Mars is a totally different ball game. The *Saturn V* rocket did not have the range.

Another example of project vision comes from one of my company's current clients. This client enjoyed his stay in a London hotel so much that he wanted exactly the same design built on his site in the Middle East and employed my firm (who had done the engineering design of the London hotel) to do so. Now that is a fine project vision, there can be no doubt over what is required. It is possible to take any member of the project team around both the existing hotel and the new site and everyone can see what is needed. The reason I use this example is that the client could not understand why we needed time to design the new project. In his mind he wanted us to repeat exactly the same design and to reuse the same drawings. Why should we need any time to redesign it? Because London is not an earthquake zone and his Middle East site is. The structure will look similar but the new design will have to be stronger and more resilient. Because the Middle East is a lot hotter than London and consequently the air conditioning will need to be much more powerful. Because the local utilities are differently located on the site and will be brought into the building from different directions. Because the road system is different and access arrangements will be different. There are many other reasons but it remains a clear vision. Imagine though if we had been nearing the completion of the design of the original London hotel and the original client had said 'I've changed my mind, the hotel is not going to be in London, it's going to be in Cairo instead'. We would really have had to go back almost to square one and a lot of time and money would have been wasted.

It is unlikely that you will have anything as visible as an existing building to use in order to communicate your vision, so how do you create a vision that will communicate what you want to achieve and that works? I have the following advice for creating a vision:

1. Envision an article written in the future about the success of your project. What does it say?
2. Describe your desired future in a sketch, model or photo-montage.
3. Imagine yourself receiving an award for your project, what is the person presenting the award saying about you and your team?

The purpose of creating our vision for the project is to communicate what it is that we are trying to achieve through the project. Communication can take many forms: music (e.g. bugle calls tell the army when to get up, when to eat, when to fight, when to stop fighting and when to go to bed); pictures (still or moving) and drawings; the written or spoken word and even smell (supermarkets communicate that they have freshly baked bread by ducting the smell of the bread from their bakery and exhausting it at the supermarket entrance).

In order to work I believe that a vision should SERVE.

Succinct

Evocative

Resonant

Values

Excellence

Figure 7.1   The SERVE mnemonic for vision

Quite early in the project you will probably get the vision translated into pictures, for example a concept sketch of a new motor car, airplane, or building, a process flow chart for a new chemical plant, a diagram illustrating a new departmental structure etc. However, unless you are a talented artist yourself you will have to communicate your vision initially in words. Going back to my mnemonic SERVE, what I mean by this is:

- *Succinct* – you need to get your vision across in as few words as possible if people are going to remember it. Think of John F. Kennedy and Martin Luther King and how they communicated their visions.

- *Evocative* – your words must evoke strong images, memories or feelings if they are going to inspire people to deliver your project.
- *Resonant* – your words must all work together to reinforce the vision, they must be in harmony. If one word is suggesting something that runs counter to your actual vision or subtracts from it is some way, change it.
- *Values* – your vision must be in line with the organization's values and your team's values if it is going to be really successful.
- *Excellence* – you will not inspire a team by asking them to do something quite dull and ordinary.

DEVELOPING THE PROJECT VISION

Now you have a vision for your project. You should also give your project a name. It can be a name that describes the project in some way or you could name your project after, say, a Greek god or goddess. I have worked on projects named after cheeses and US presidents. If the project is confidential avoid a name that gives the game away. Now let's assume that you are in the stage between having identified through the strategy development of Chapter 5 where you need to get to, you have a vision but you haven't approached the board for authorization or funding yet. How do you get to the stage where you are confident enough to approach the board with a proposal? Basically you need to go through a microcosm of what you will do after you have board funding but with no resources other than yourself and what you can beg or borrow.

Step 1: Find Friends

Approach colleagues, perhaps those that you worked with in the strategy workshop, and ask for their help in developing the project to the point where you can seek board approval to develop it fully. Tell them that there is no funding to cover their time at this stage but it is a really exciting project and they can be in at the ground floor of changing the organization for the better. You really value their input and you're going to need to bounce ideas off them.

Step 2: Identify Options

This is where having friends to bounce ideas off is really helpful. If you have found friends that you didn't work with on the strategy then you need to bring them up to speed with where you have got to so far and why. Next ask yourselves what options you have for fulfilling the vision.

You should aim to identify between three and seven workable options. Start by trying to identify radically different ways of achieving your vision. Bear in mind that the way to have a good idea is to have 100 ideas and throw away the 99 bad ones. Consequently, all ideas should be welcome in the beginning because ridiculous ideas often prompt you to think along a different track and come up with something good.

After you have come up with a few options to fulfil the vision, look at whether the vision can be broken down into parts. Perhaps it consists of stages or perhaps it contains a number of functions that the project must provide. If it does, then break it up and consider different options for each part. When you have got as far as you can evaluate the options that you have come up with and select the ones that you are going to move forward with. I recommend that you have two options that are radically different ways of achieving the vision and several variations on a theme. The variations on a theme allow you to optimize and the radical option allows you to look at something totally different.

Step 3: Estimate Benefits

For each of your selected options write down a list of all the benefits that will accrue to the organization. If you still have your friends, do this with them or do it separately and compare notes afterwards. Next, estimate the value of the benefits. I once worked with a colleague who was sponsoring a project involving the upgrade of an automated railway signalling system. One of the benefits was that it required less signalmen to operate it and therefore there would be a cost saving arising from a reduction in workforce. He needed to estimate the saving so he phoned the signal box and asked the signalman how much he earned. This may seem barely credible, but is true nevertheless. The signalman quite reasonably asked who he was and why he was asking and you can imagine the result. A more subtle way might have been to ask the HR department. Another good reason for sounding out friends is that my ex-colleague had plenty of colleagues around him and any one of us could have told him that there was a better way.

Ways that can help you to estimate benefits include:

- Asking any experts that you can trust being sure to avoid the error mentioned above.
- Looking at any projects or organizations that might have done something similar.
- Search the Internet for anything similar. I don't know how I used to function without it.
- Making an educated guess. If there isn't anyone more expert than you (see first bullet above) then your guess is probably quite good.

Step 4: Estimate Costs

Remember we are at the stage here where we are developing a proposal to obtain the board approval to develop it further. If we get board approval we should have funding and can then hire a team to develop feasibility designs and cost estimates. But for the moment you are on your own, apart from your friends.

ESTIMATING METHODS

For each option we now need to estimate both capital costs and operating and maintenance costs. I always approach estimating from two directions:

- Benchmark
- Breakdown.

With benchmarking you are seeking to find a similar project, convert to present-day costs by factoring in inflation between when your benchmark was completed and today, and then scaling in proportion to the 'size' of your project relative to the benchmark. It is useful if you can find several benchmarks so as to average out errors.

For example, several times I have had to estimate the cost of developing a new city. On each occasion I started out simply with a location and a proposed population. I then tried to find benchmark cities in similar locations and either their cost or their estimated cost. This is not as difficult as it sounds. A Google search for 'new city Saudi Arabia' will lead you to discover that there are several new cities being built there. From a simple statistical analysis of four cities we can see several things:

Table 7.1   Estimating the cost of a city

	Prince Abdulaziz Bin Mousaed Economic City	Jazan Economic City	Knowledge Economic City	King Abdullah Economic City
Projected cost (US$)	8,000,000,000	33,000,000,000	7,000,000,000	27,000,000,000
Population	80,000	250,000	200,000	2,000,000
Area (m²)	156,000,000	100,000,000	4,800,000	168,000,000
Cost per head of population (US$)	100,000	132,000	35,000	13,500
Cost per m² (US$)	51	330	1,458	161
Cost correlation with population	0.46			
Cost correlation with area	0.36			
Cost per head correlation with population	−0.68			
Cost per head correlation with area	0.09			
Population	80,000	200,000	250,000	2,000,000
Cost per head of population (US$)	100,000	35,000	132,000	13,500

1. Cost correlates more closely with population than with area. That is because expensive items like hospitals, schools, universities, power consumption, water consumption etc. are dependant on the size of the population rather than the area of the city.
2. There is quite a good inverse correlation between cost per head of population and population size (–0.68). In other words the larger the population the lower the cost per head.

From this information I created a simple rule of thumb for calculating city costs in the Middle East from population size (see Figure 7.2). It will not be perfectly accurate but it gives me a guide.

It is possible to rely just on benchmarking like this to estimate the cost of your project, and it is quick. In about 30 minutes using an Internet search engine you can estimate the cost of building a new city. However, it is always better to approach a problem from two or more viewpoints and see how close the results are. If you reach a similar result from two distinctly different approaches then you can have some confidence in the result. If the results are very different then you should investigate further.

The other approach is what I call breakdown. This means breaking your project down into its component parts and estimating the cost of each part. The smaller the component, the better chance you have of getting the cost of that component right. However, making sure that you have identified all of the parts becomes more difficult as you increase the degree of breakdown. Once you have a team in place your project will probably be broken down into detail right the way down to cost of materials, labour, equipment, management, fees etc. If your project is relatively small it may be possible for you to get quite close to this degree of breakdown. The degree to which you break your project down depends on the time that you have available to do it.

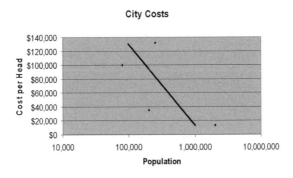

Figure 7.2   Estimating the cost of a city per head of population

To continue the earlier example of estimating the cost of building a city, clearly I would not have the time to break the city down into volumes of concrete, steel, asphalt etc. However, I have constructed a spreadsheet model which based upon both land area and population will calculate the cost of all the major components. For example a typical unitary development plan in the UK provides a formula for calculating financial contribution from developers for education. The one I used to construct my model in 2001 stated an average child yield of 25.7 from 37 houses. Children spend seven years in primary school at a cost of £4,007 p.a. and five years at secondary school at a cost of £5,318 p.a. From this information I was able to estimate the cost of primary and secondary school provision based upon estimates of demographics. A parliamentary question and answer reported in Hansard gave me the information that there is a total of 15 linear metres of road per hectare in the whole UK and that the average cost per mile of dual carriageway construction was reported as £12m per mile. This would equate to £3,730/linear metre for two-carriageway roads which enabled me to estimate the cost of roads required for a city based upon area. I continued this process for hospitals, universities, offices, housing, power, water, sewerage treatment, parks, leisure facilities, libraries, shops and so on. It took me about two weeks but I ended up with a model that gave me a good comparison with the benchmark.

I hope you agree that estimating the cost of a city is a fairly extreme example. It is the method of estimating costs by benchmarking and breakdown that I want to illustrate.

Step 5: Estimate the Time Required for Completing the Project

I advocate the same process for estimating time requirements as for estimating costs, i.e. benchmarking against other similar projects and breaking the project down into components then thinking about the sequence and duration of each component. See also Chapter 12 on project planning.

Step 6: Identify Risks

Risks should include those that might be possible to describe but difficult to quantify, such as competitor action in response or failure to gain stakeholder approval and also risks that are easier to quantify. For example in Figure 7.2 a line of best fit was drawn through four points to establish a rule of thumb for estimating cost per head of population for developing a city. Some idea of risk could be estimated by parallel lines drawn to the right or left representing pessimistic or optimistic views respectively. Any assumptions made represent risks and should be clearly documented.

Step 7: Conceptual Project Appraisal

For each option that you have identified run a simple project appraisal as illustrated in Chapter 6. This should enable you to clearly identify a preferred option (i.e. the option with the highest IRR or NPV) and show whether or not the project is likely to have a positive business case when it is further developed.

Step 8: Identify the Resources that you Need to Develop the Project through to the Next Stage

In terms of the gateway process this will probably be from gateway 0 to gateway 1 (see Chapter 3). You will almost certainly need internal resources from operations, finance, marketing and possibly others. You will probably require external resources such as designers and cost consultants, and of course you will need a project manager. If you work for the public sector or other large organization and you do not have internal project managers for this role then you talk to your procurement department the opportunity to discuss your project with external project managers. If you are not constrained by regulations against doing this it will allow you to get some advice about the size and shape of team required to develop the project to the next stage and the budget necessary to do so. It is best to get several project manager's views if you can, then you can average out their suggestions or tend towards whoever appeared best informed.

DOCUMENTING THE VISION

With all of this information in place you will be in a position to write a good definition of your project. If you are approaching gateway 0 then you can structure all this information in accordance with the proposal layout suggested at the end of Chapter 6 and fix an agenda item for the next board meeting. You might like to also start lobbying board members in advance on the vision for your project.

If you are approaching gateway 1 then you will have been doing much the same thing except with a project manager and a project team supporting you. All the way through a project until your organization actually commits to implementation of the project, you are trying to:

- Better define what the project deliverables are.
- Identify and examine options.
- Examine and gain a better understanding of the benefits, costs, timescales and risks associated with each option.
- Choose a preferred option or options.
- Check that the business case is still positive.

Whichever stage you are at you will be able to define the project in a 'Project Charter' document in which you will describe:

1. Project name
2. Vision for the project
3. Project context:
   - competitive environment
   - social, technological, environmental, economic, political, legal and ethical background
   - organizational context and fit with the organization's strategy.
4. Objectives – what benefits the project must deliver
5. Deliverables – what products does the project deliver which enable the objectives to be met?
6. Constraints:
   - budget constraints
   - time constraints
   - quality constraints
   - authority constraints.

This project charter will enable you to communicate to the project team what is required. In the next chapter we will review how to go about selecting the project team.

CHAPTER 8

THE PLAYERS: SELECTING AND LEADING THE TEAM

TEAM SELECTION

The Project Sponsor should be involved in the selection of all the key players in the team, either by being present at interviews or by having recommendations referred to him or her. However, the responsibility for leading the project team and making sure that it delivers the project as defined by the sponsor rests with the project manager. Unfortunately, on many projects the project manager is appointed after some other team members. For example, on a building project the architect and quantity surveyor may already have been appointed because the sponsor wanted to have a better idea of building layout and cost before proceeding further. This seems perfectly reasonable except that it is the project manager's job to *lead* the team and get it to deliver. People also usually have a sense of loyalty to the person who appointed them and often a sense of resentment towards anyone who comes between themselves and their master. You can see how difficult this makes things for the project manager arriving after the project has started. Therefore I urge Project Sponsors to make sure that their first appointment is the project manager. Of course Project Sponsors have every right to influence the selection of the project team, I am only saying that the project manager has this right too.

WHAT ARE THE OPTIONS FOR SELECTING A PROJECT MANAGER?

- Select someone internally within the organization to be project manager.
- Recruit someone into your organization to be the project manager.
- Recruit a freelance project manager into your organization.
- Appoint a project management company as your project manager.
- Appoint a company or more likely a consortium of companies to develop the project, possibly all the way through testing and commissioning.

Some of the advantages and disadvantages of these approaches are listed in Table 8.1. This is a general list and you should feel free to add your own pros and cons as they apply to your project. There are sometimes organizational preferences for a particular procurement route and these should be considered.

There are, of course, many variations on a theme. For example you may want a fixed price for the management of the project in either of the last two options above. A company will be reluctant to take this sort of risk without a great deal of information about the project. Many project management companies will be happy to develop the project to an intermediate stage under a reimbursable arrangement before committing to a fixed price. In this way they learn on the job and have a much greater idea of the risk they are taking. However, they can also submit low prices at the beginning knowing that it may be difficult to change horses at the later stage and they can make up their lost profit then. Competition is good at driving prices down but project management staff are very mobile. Therefore project management companies in competition have to find ways to make their prices competitive. One way to do this is to assume that they can delegate functions that you might expect them to fulfil, down to other suppliers that they will appoint later.

Table 8.1   Factors in the selection of a project manager

	Pros	Cons
Internal appointment	• Loyalty to the organization • Knows way round the organization • Knows the organization's business and industry	• May have limited project management experience • No professional indemnity insurance to cover costly project management errors • No project management systems, procedures, software, support, holiday cover
Recruit	• Can choose someone with good project management experience • Loyalty to the organization	• No professional indemnity insurance to cover costly project management errors • Takes time to find feet in organization • Will you have continuity of employment for the project manager? • Will they be fully employed? • No project management systems, procedures, software, support, holiday cover

Table 8.1 *Concluded*

	Pros	Cons
External freelance	• Can choose someone with good project management experience • Can end contract if project is cancelled relatively easily	• Takes time to find feet in organization • Will they be fully employed? • No project management systems, procedures, software, support, holiday cover • Higher day rates than permanent staff • Do they have their own professional indemnity insurance?
External project management company appointment	• Company can provide project management systems, procedures, software, support, holiday cover • Professional indemnity insurance cover • Opportunity to transfer some risk to the project manager • Can absorb peaks and troughs of project management workload	• Profit required by the project management company on top of the individuals providing the service • Takes time to find feet in organization
External consortium appointment	• Total responsibility for delivery and transfer of risk • Can seek lump sum price	• Any one consortium is unlikely to include the best of each discipline required • Loss of control over delivery • May try to offset cost risk with reduced quality and benefits particularly if benefits were difficult to define contractually and/or will not become apparent until after contract completion • Contract negotiations may be long and difficult

We will now look at things to consider when appointing a project manager. We will assume that you have chosen to follow the route of appointing an external company as project manager, but most of the considerations apply, to a greater or lesser extent, whatever your choice.

1. If you are a public sector or large organization consult your procurement department. You will probably have statutory procedures to follow such as advertising the opportunity in the *Official Journal of the European Union*. Your organization may have already selected a framework of service providers from which you can form a tender list. Either way it will be able to guide you through the appropriate process.

2. If the above does not apply draw up a shortlist of, say, three to six possible candidates. You can do this by asking around those you know who have used project managers in the context of your project, checking the trade journals to see what successful projects there have been recently and find out who project managed them. Try an Internet search with some keywords associated with your industry and project together with project manager.

3. Prepare an invitation to tender (ITT) document. Send this to your shortlisted candidates. It should include:

   – Brief details of your organization.

   – As full a description of the project as possible as developed during the project definition stage (see Chapter 7).

   – Clarification of the scope of service that you require from the project manager. This may exclude certain services that you are able to provide in-house. It may also specify certain break points in the service at which you could either cancel the project or change procurement route and wish to change project manager role.

   – Conditions of contract to be used. These of course vary according to the nature of the industry and country. In the UK construction industry suitable contracts are available from various sources including the GC/Works5 from Her Majesty's Stationery Office (http://www. tsonline.co.uk); or the Professional Services Contract from the New Engineering Contract suite of contracts (http://www.neccontract.com) amongst others.

   – A list of the information which you want the tenderer to provide in the tender. This normally includes:

   – background on their company and their relevant corporate experience on similar commissions; a method statement describing how they intend to manage your project safely, efficiently and effectively; an organization chart of the team that they will use; curriculum vitae of the staff that they will use; their health and safety policy; their environmental management policy; copies of their insurance certificates (e.g. professional indemnity and employers liability); references; pricing schedule.

   – Definition of how you want the tender priced, for example daily and hourly rates for staff, fixed lump sum price, expenses included in rates or paid separately. How you intend to deal with inflation if the project management task may last several years.

– The criteria that you will use to assess tenders including the weighting that you will give to each of the things you have asked them to supply. You should pay particular attention to scoring their competence in health, safety and environmental management because if anything goes wrong in these areas you must be able to produce your documented process for appointing a competent project manager. You should also tell them if there is to be an interview and the relative weightings that will be given to the tender document and the interview.

– Whom to return the tender to, where and by what date and time.

– Tender validity period, that is for how long you require their tender offer to remain open.

– Approximate time when you expect to hold interviews and date by which you hope to be able to make an appointment.

4. Note that the time you allow for tenderers to prepare and submit their tender depends on a number of factors. If the project managers can provide all the services that you need in-house and if the project is not too complicated then two weeks is a reasonable period. If, however, you are looking for a consortium appointment then project managers will need to assemble a team and coordinate the writing of the proposal amongst the consortium members. You should allow at least four weeks and preferably six to eight for this.

5. If practicable, it is useful to schedule a tender conference during the tender period. This should allow the tenderers to meet with the Project Sponsor and ask questions. It will also be useful if they can see at first hand the relevant aspects of the client's existing operation and the site.

6. When tenders are returned take up references. Contact the tenderers' previous clients and ask them how the project manager performed, what were their strengths and weaknesses. You would be amazed how many people do not take up references and how often references are less than flattering.

7. Set up a spreadsheet with a column for each tenderer and a row for each of the criteria you will score against. Apply weightings and then read and mark each tender. Ideally the tenders should be read and scored by a tender committee.

8. You (or as noted above, the tender committee) need to interview the project managers. There is little point interviewing just one because you will have nothing to compare them against. Aim to interview at least the top two from your tender assessment. If possible, before the interview you should visit the tenderers in their own working environment. This will help you to validate claims that they make in the tenders

9. You should decide how much weight you give to the interview and how much to the tender assessment. Personally I would weight as follows:

– 50 per cent interview – the chemistry between Project Sponsor and project manager is so important and this can't come through on paper.

  - 10 per cent method statement.
  - 15 per cent CVs of team, especially project manager.
  - 10 per cent price – you are buying experience, skill and intelligence. The best project manager will be worth their weight in gold.
  - 15 per cent the other criteria.
10. Make your choice, secure whatever internal approvals you need and appoint the project manager.
11. Congratulations, you are no longer alone. You can develop the project with an experienced and successful project manager.
12. Now that you have a project manager appointed they will spend some time getting fully familiar with the project and will then advise on and begin selecting the rest of the team as necessary. The project manager will lead and manage the team of consultants, suppliers and contractors required to deliver your project. Your leadership role will be mainly leading the organization with respect to its role in procuring and absorbing the project into its operations, as well as assimilating and exploiting the planned changes that the project brings into effect. As can be seen from the hourglass in Figure 1.3, the project manager manages the lower part of the hourglass and the Project Sponsor manages the upper part. This requires considerable leadership skill because whereas the project manager usually leads a team that he or she has selected, and therefore one that owes the project manager loyalty, the Project Sponsor has to lead the existing organization. Much of the organization may see the project as a distraction from the day job. Some departments may feel threatened by the project and the changes that it will bring about. It may be that some members of the project team will be drawn from within the organization. Careful consideration should be given to how they are managed. They may resent being managed by an external project manager. Nevertheless, if they are seconded into the project full time this may be necessary.

THE PROJECT SPONSOR AND LEADERSHIP

There are currently 199,877 books on leadership available from Amazon, so it's clearly a big and important subject. In Chapter 11 we will discuss the aspects of the project manager's leadership that the Project Sponsor needs to be aware of and keep an eye on. For the remainder of this chapter I will summarize the key leadership skills that the Project Sponsor needs for this subtle and sometimes difficult business of leading the upper part of the hourglass.

Vision

The first key skill that equips the Project Sponsor for leadership is vision. Having a compelling vision for the project is a very powerful tool for getting people on board and aligned with the project. We covered developing a vision and the SERVE model in Chapter 7, so I will simply remind you of it and move onto the next key skill, managing expectations.

The old adage of how to please people – 'under-promise and over-deliver' – is as true today as it has ever been. The following is an example provided by Stephen Bennett, friend and colleague, from his career with British Rail.

> When I was implementing new finance computer systems for British Rail, my sponsor was the Director of Finance. My boss was aiming to provide the financial infrastructure behind the Chairman's change from functional management to sector management. It was one thing to say that from now on the new Director Inter-City would make all the decisions about his business, it was another to provide him with regular four-weekly accounting information across all five regions and seven functions in enough detail and in a timely manner sufficient for him to exercise his authority. My boss went through a predictable cycle with each development. It started with enthusiasm for the new project, followed by elation as the mission was sketched out and impossible promises made to the Chairman about how wonderful things would be. Then as I wrote the functional specification and reported back what could actually be done, doubts began to creep in. As time wore on things went from bad to worse. Why was it taking so long? Then real anger as various forces of reaction fought back and did their best to sabotage the project (real power was being transferred and some people really didn't like it). Then there were setbacks when we tested the new system. The mainframe couldn't cope with multiple users entering information at the same time (difficult to simulate in advance). Eventually things got sorted out and implemented and with that his temper improved, so such so that we were heroes by the end.

I think this illustrates very well how sponsors can be tempted to oversell the vision in order to secure backing for the project 'impossible promises made to the chairman', and how that makes managing expectations very difficult. Fortunately Stephen is extremely good at building trust with key stakeholders. He also knows how important it is for the sponsor to shield the project team from the politics and power struggles raging overhead and give them the breathing space to implement the project effectively.

In order to manage expectations the sponsor must establish a good rapport with the key stakeholders in the top half of the hourglass. Individually and in private the sponsor must establish what each stakeholder's expectations of the project actually are. The sponsor must then tread a delicate path between maintaining the vision for the project whilst educating the stakeholder in the risks the project must overcome and the enormous amount of work that will be needed to deliver the vision. The sponsor must tackle this early on in the project because the longer that those unrealistically high expectations are held, the more difficult they are to manage.

The Project Sponsor must bring stakeholders to see that he is aiming really high, but that the road ahead will be fraught with difficulty. The sponsor is unlikely to achieve all of his own expectations but, by working so hard at ambitious goals a very good outcome will be achieved in the end.

NEGOTIATION

The next skill that will be invaluable to the sponsor is the ability to negotiate effectively. Negotiation means both reaching an agreement or compromise by discussion and finding a way over or through a difficult path or obstacle. If your project vision is not sufficiently compelling to motivate a colleague or other stakeholder to support the project as you require then you will need to either pull rank (in your own right if possible or by engaging the help of a superior) or negotiate. Pulling rank may work but you will not win any friends (quite the opposite) and any support obtained will be given grudgingly. It is much more effective and sustainable to negotiate for the support you require.

The first principle of successful negotiation is preparation. If you want to negotiate something from someone you need to think through the value of what you are asking for, both to yourself and to the person you are asking and also the value of what you have to offer in return, to yourself and to the other party. Teachers of the negotiating arts insist that you should know what your 'best alternative to a negotiated agreement' (BATNA) is, and that you should estimate the other party's BATNA. An understanding of your own and the other party's BATNA suggests the point in a negotiation at which the other party will yield no further and also the bargaining zone. You should know what your long-, medium- and short-term objectives are. Where are we vulnerable and where is the other party vulnerable? What are the most and least important issues for us and for them? What can we trade? Don't forget that a minor point for us might be a major point for the other party. What are the disadvantages for them and how can we overcome them? What are the personalities involved and who should we engage in the negotiation? Is there, or should there be a deadline to the negotiation? Negotiations often go right up to the wire and then get agreed at the deadline. It is often deadlines that make negotiations work. However, we want deadlines that put pressure on the other party rather than ourselves.

Next comes the desirability of win–win over win–lose. In competitive situations most people like to win and in sport or combat that usually requires that the opponent lose. If you win and they lose, they will not be very helpful next time. If you value the working relationship you should look for an outcome which works both for yourself and the other party, a win–win. Actually whether or not you value the working relationship is worth a bit more exploration because negotiation impacts other aspects of the Project Sponsor's role, e.g. stakeholder management. Game theory has some interesting light to shed on this subject. There is a famous game called '*Prisoner's Dilemma*'[1] in which two suspects are held by the police. The police lack hard evidence and need a confession in order to convict. They keep the prisoners separate and individually offer them a deal. If one prisoner offers evidence for the prosecution against his accomplice (who remains silent), the prisoner who has betrayed his partner in crime will go free and the silent accomplice will serve the full ten-year sentence. If both remain silent, both prisoners are sentenced to only six months in jail for a minor charge. If each betrays the other, then they both get five years. Each prisoner must choose to betray the other or to remain silent.

This is a game that depends on repetition. If both prisoners betray each other they both have five years to work out a better strategy. If one betrays the other then if there is another bank job the prisoner who kept silent won't do so again. However, if they did both keep silent they will realize that the strategy worked quite well and will be prepared to try it again. The more they collaborate (even without being able to communicate) the more they will trust each other. I have played simulations of this game (I hasten to add that I have never robbed a bank) and the problem comes if it is known that the last game has arrived. At this point one or both of the prisoners may choose to betray their accomplice and go for the outright win. It can come to blows in management schools, be warned!

The moral is that collaboration, i.e. win–win, is often the best policy as long as you are going to have the opportunity of collaborating again. If you are not then you may be tempted to go for win–lose at the other party's expense. Therefore think carefully about the future relationship with the party with whom you are negotiating and also their perception of the longevity of the relationship. They may be tempted to go for win–lose against you.

There are issues of human psychology that can heavily influence your chances of successful negotiation. These are described by Malhotra and Bazerman[2] and summarized below:

- People prefer to receive gains in instalments but losses in one lump. This is probably because although both gains and losses are finite and equal, a drip-feed approach suggests that there may be more to come. For negotiation therefore you should try and package all of the losses to the other party together but disaggregate and drip feed the gains.
- Losses loom bigger than gains. For example in a study two videos were made promoting HIV testing to young women. In one version the video

---

1   Poundstone, W. 1992. *Prisoner's Dilemma*. Doubleday, New York.

2   Malhotra, D. and Bazerman, M. 2008. Psychological influence in negotiation: an introduction long overdue. *Journal of Management*, available online at www.hbs.edu/research/pdf/08-058.pdf.

explained the benefits of being tested. In the other version the costs and risks of not being tested were explained. Only 23 per cent chose to be tested as a result of the first video but 63 per cent did as a result of the second even though the information was the same. Similar results have been found with selling loft insulation on the basis of how much money you will save if you insulate compared with how much money you will lose if you don't. Therefore you should pitch a proposal in terms of what the other party has to lose by not accepting your proposal.

- People try to justify their past behaviours and choices. The willingness to agree to one request leads to a greater propensity to agree to other requests which are consistent with the first. Expert negotiators will try to win small concessions to begin with and gradually work towards bigger ones. Likewise the more time the other party has invested in negotiations the more they will need to justify to themselves having invested that time. It becomes increasingly difficult to walk away from a lengthy negotiation and the pressure to find an agreement increases.

- People are biased towards the status quo and will be more concerned with the risk of change than with the risk of not changing. This is rather unfortunate for Project Sponsors but I thought I'd better tell you. Probably the most powerful illustration of this effect is organ donation. In countries where you have to opt out of a donation assumption donation rates are around 90 per cent, whereas in countries where you opt in by for example carrying a donor card donation rates are around 15 per cent. The effect can be used to the advantage of the negotiator because whoever creates the first draft of an agreement has power over its terms and establishes a quasi status quo that the other party will need to negotiate against.

- People feel compelled to reciprocate the concessions of others even when it goes against their own interests. They feel obliged to meet halfway. In an experiment researchers posed as representatives on a youth counselling programme. They then interviewed people in the street asking them to sign up to escort a group of youth offenders on a two-hour visit to a zoo. They achieved a 17 per cent sign-up rate. In another trial they asked people to sign up as a youth counsellor for a two-year period. Nobody agreed to this but when the researchers then modified the request to the two-hour zoo escort duty they achieved a 50 per cent success rate. It was the negotiators concession that prompted a move by the other party. At no time was anyone in the street obliged to take on either duty, so the relaxation of the request by the researcher was not a real concession, nevertheless the other party felt a compulsion to move their own position. The lesson for the negotiator is that if their initial proposal can be extreme without causing the other party to walk away immediately, backing down from that extreme position is likely to result in reciprocal behaviour from the other party.

- People do not evaluate costs objectively but by comparison to reference points. In an experiment people were given two scenarios. In the first they are about to buy a calculator for $50 when the salesperson informs them that the calculator is on sale at another branch 20 minutes away. They are then asked what the minimum discount is that they would need to drive the 20 minutes. The second scenario is the same except that they are trying to buy a $2,000 computer. On average people needed at least a $20 discount in the first scenario and a $200 discount in the second. Both scenarios are effectively asking 'what is 20 minutes of your time worth?' but people do not assess this objectively they refer to the reference point of the item under consideration. Salesmen use this to great effect by persuading purchasers of relatively expensive items to add lots of expensive extras which don't seem so expensive in relation to the main item. Any concessions you are negotiating for are more likely to be made when put in context of a much larger number, for example the size of the project or the other party's annual budget.
- In the absence of objective means of evaluation people place undue weight on the opinion of other people. A TV 'infomercial' concluded its sales pitch with 'operators are standing by, please call now'. There was very little response. However, when this was changed to 'if operators are busy, please call again' sales shot up. Even though the sales information was identical the first ending created an image of operators waiting by silent phones whilst the second conjured the image of busy operators and busy phone lines. This illustrates the pack mentality – if everyone else is doing it perhaps I should too. This tactic is used by estate agents who limit viewing times of properties to ensure that those viewing are there with lots of other buyers too. You may choose to emphasize how many other people are supporting the project in your negotiations.
- The final psychological aspect of negotiation will not, I think, apply to your negotiations, although I include it for completeness and as part of your defence against those trying to negotiate concessions from you. Simply stated it is that if a negotiator's case is strong then they are most likely to succeed by speaking slowly when the other party is free from distractions, avoiding overly technical jargon and providing a written explanation of the proposal. Conversely if the negotiator's case is weak then they are more likely to succeed by speaking quickly when the other party is distracted, using technical jargon and evading requests for written explanation. Don't be bamboozled!

There are more tactics to be employed in negotiation, but let us first place some of these psychological techniques in context with the sort of negotiation a Project Sponsor may encounter on a daily basis. We will assume that you need help from the finance department to work on updating your investment appraisal. You think about two mandays should be sufficient; however the finance department is very busy at the moment. Before meeting the head of finance think through what his position is likely to be and what you have to offer. When you meet you will open with an extreme request for perhaps twenty mandays of input to the project in order to update the investment appraisal and half-a-dozen other things (that will be useful to the project but which you don't need right now). You explain the benefits that the project will bring for the organization and the finance department in particular. You note that both the marketing and operations departments are providing enormous assistance with the project. Unfortunately, although he would love to help he simply cannot spare anyone at the moment. Somewhat disappointed you ask if he could at least just spare two mandays to help you get the investment appraisal updated. You note that two mandays is such a small proportion of his budget. He feels compelled to agree. What is more, having agreed to this request he will be inclined to comply with future requests in order to justify having complied with this one.

For the more formal negotiations that the Project Sponsor is likely to have with other departments, funders, regulators or other stakeholders there are other negotiating behaviours and tactics to be aware of.

The behaviours that are routinely employed in negotiation are discussed in Table 8.2.

Negotiating styles broadly fall into two groups, *push* and *pull*.

- Push relies on proposing; giving information; shutting out.
- Pull relies on seeking information; testing understanding; building.
- Push styles work in the short term when you have power but are high risk. They are win–lose and do not get commitment.
- Pull styles work without power and are low risk. They get high commitment and are effective in the long term.

Good negotiation skills are really important for a Project Sponsor. The best way to acquire them is gradually through practice. The next time you are in a negotiation, whether it is for someone's help, buying a new car or over your child's pocket money, think about the psychology and behaviour styles that you and the other person are using. Try out the different techniques and see if you can find the win–win.

Table 8.2   Behaviours in negotiation

Proposing/initiating	Putting forward a suggestion or course of action: 'I think that we could bring the completion date forward if you could reduce your space requirement'
Building	Extending or developing a proposal made by another person: 'and your plan would be even better if we added a guarantee clause'
Testing understanding	Establishing whether or not an earlier contribution has been understood: 'So can I just check that we're talking about the same thing here?'
Summarizing	Summarizing or restating concisely previous events. 'Ladies and gentlemen, we have agreed: to accelerate the schedule by one month to reduce the storage area by 10% to add a guarantee clause in the equipment supply contract'
Seeking information	Seeking facts, opinions or clarification from another party: 'which page is that on?'; 'what are you current annual maintenance costs?'
Giving information	Offering facts, opinions or clarification to other people: 'On my last project that ended up costing us half a million'
Supporting	Declaration of agreement or support for another's opinion: 'That sounds fine to me'
Disagreeing	Direct disagreement or the raising of objections or obstacles: 'That wouldn't work, we'd never get it through planning approval'
Defending/attacking	Attacking another directly or being defensive. This is similar to disagreeing but often more emotional. Language can get quite heated. 'Don't blame me, it's not my fault'; 'that's either a lie or incompetence!'
Bringing in	Inviting views or opinions from a party not currently participating: 'Tom, do you have anything to say on this?'
Shutting out	Excluding another person or reducing their opportunity to contribute. Richard: 'Tom, do you have anything to say on this?' Karen: 'What I feel is important here is that …' Karen has shut out Tom by interruption, which is the most common form of shutting out.

CONFLICT MANAGEMENT

Sometimes negotiation can turn into conflict. Where conflict arises between departments or between your project team and a department or another stakeholder it will be invaluable if the Project Sponsor can resolve it quickly and effectively before it becomes destructive to the project. Therefore the remainder of this chapter is dedicated to the other key skill in the Project Sponsor's armoury, conflict resolution, which is itself closely related to negotiation.

The pressure cooker of project work is pretty much bound to generate conflicts of one sort or another. People are brought together often from different departments, companies, disciplines and cultures with tight timescales to be met.

In fact, conflict is often necessary. It helps to raise and address problems and energizes people. It helps people to identify their differences and recognize how they can work together most productively.

It is acknowledged that good teams go through a forming, storming, norming, performing process, and storming involves conflict. Ever heard of 'creative conflict'?

However, conflict that isn't resolved can affect productivity, quality, morale, relationships and even health.

Conflict can be of several varieties. It may be:

- Within one person, when that person is:
    - not living according to their values, or
    - feeling that their views and values are threatened, or
    - fearing change or failure.
- Between two people in the same team
- Between two people in different teams
- Between groups
- Between companies
- Technical, commercial or emotional (or all three).

The root cause of most conflict is a communications failure. As Winston Churchill said 'To jaw-jaw is always better than to war-war'.

Issues to be aware of which contribute to communications failure include:

Misunderstanding. Communication involves the sender composing and sending the message, the carrier of the message and the recipient receiving and understanding the message. Errors can creep in at each stage leading to misunderstanding.

Transactional analysis[3] is a theory of psychology which describes humans as existing in three ego states – parent, adult and child. In the parent state people behave, feel and think in response to an unconscious mimicking of how their parents (or other authority figures) acted. In the adult state people behave, think and feel in response to an objective appraisal of reality using all their experience and power of thought. In the child state people revert to behaving, feeling and thinking as they did in childhood. The nature of transactions is important to understanding communication. Complementary transactions occur when both parties are addressing the ego state that the other is in, for example:

A – 'Have you been able to write the report?' (adult to adult)
B – 'Yes – I'm just about to e-mail it to you.' (adult to adult)

Or

A – 'Would you like to come and watch a film with me?' (child to child)
B – 'I'd love to – what shall we go to see?' (child to child)

Or

A – 'Haven't you produced that report yet?' (parent to child)
B – 'Will you stop hassling me? I'll do it eventually!' (child to parent)

Communication failures are typically caused by a crossed transaction where parties address ego states other than that which the other party is in, for example.

A – 'Have you been able to write the report?' (adult to adult)
B – 'Will you stop hassling me? I'll do it eventually!' (child to parent)

Clearly harmonious working is best served by transactions of the adult to adult type. However, when trying to be creative and innovative it might be useful to visit your child state. This is because as adults we have become conditioned by rules. We lose the sense of wonderment and curiosity. Children think 'why not?' whilst adults think 'because'.

Other aspects of conflict are *feelings* and *escalation*. Conflict starts when disharmony is felt within any one of the participants. The longer that this feeling is allowed to fester without resolution the worse the conflict will get, i.e. it will escalate.

The symptoms of conflict are:

---

3   Berne, E. 1964. *Games People Play*. Grove Press, New York.

- Suppressed anger
- Aggressive behaviour
- Factions and gossip, people campaigning behind others' backs
- Resentment
- Withdrawal
- Misinterpretation of motives
- Unwillingness to listen.

Conflict usually builds up (escalates) between people through the following stages:

1. Discomfort – the suspicion that something is not quite right, but nothing that you can put your finger on.
2. Incident – usually a minor incident, words are exchanged but nothing to dwell on. Perhaps you are left feeling a little annoyed, but it is soon forgotten.
3. Misunderstanding – you start to suspect dark motives for other actions that would otherwise seem ordinary. You develop a negative perception of the other person.
4. Tension – a distinct and fixed negative perception of the other person is established. All interaction is heavy and strained.
5. Crisis – the situation becomes all consuming and it is difficult to function normally.

The following are effective strategies for minimizing conflict:

1. Good briefing. Ensure that everybody in the team knows what the objective of the project is and what the strategy is for achieving it. Also ensure that everybody is fully briefed on and understands their role and the roles of those that they will interact with.
2. Meet regularly with your key stakeholders to ensure that they are happy with the performance of your team and that no surprises emerge.
3. Meet regularly with your project manager and project team. Be sensitive to their feelings and watchful for conflict situations arising.
4. When conflict does arise, help the participants to resolve it.

Unless they have had training in this area, at best most people are going to cope with conflict, they are not going to resolve it. The strategies that people use to cope with conflict are:

- Fight it out. They work to get their way.
- Yielding. Although there are occasions when this is wise, if a person feels continually obliged to give in to another then they will cease to care and become withdrawn.

- Avoidance. Often people will avoid conflict with the other party and instead persuade others that they are right. Once a person has the support of a friend they will feel justified in their view and not invest energy into solving the conflict.

There are four reasons why we do not naturally (i.e. without training, acquired knowledge or mediation) resolve conflicts.

1. We feel the need to explain our side first. We think that if they understand our perspective then they will naturally agree with us.
2. Our inability to listen properly. Surprisingly listening is not just being quiet whilst awaiting our turn. You have to really understand the other person's perspective.
3. Fear. We fear losing face, being made to look foolish, embarrassment, losing status, being wrong.
4. Our assumption that it is a win–lose situation.

Actually the first three and perhaps also the fourth stem from our emotions. For example, it is very difficult to listen properly when adrenaline is coursing through your veins and you are rehearsing your arguments. If, however, we were all Vulcans like Mr Spock from *Star Trek*, we would probably be able to work through the conflict resolution process quite logically.

For conflicts between two or more people the stages in resolving conflict are:

1. Negotiation
2. Mediation
3. Arbitration.

Negotiation is the process through which the parties in conflict explore each others' positions, feelings and needs and explore options which meet all or most of both parties needs. Negotiation looks for a mutually acceptable solution, hopefully a win–win.

Mediation is the involvement of a third party in assisting the conflicting parties to negotiate a solution. It remains essential that the parties in conflict own the problem. The mediator will help them reach a solution, not impose one upon them.

Arbitration is when a third party listens to the arguments of the two parties and reaches a fair and impartial decision that (hopefully) both parties will accept. Arbitration can be at several levels depending on the situation. For example, it may be a respected colleague settling a conflict between two parties in the same firm over a technical issue or it may be formal arbitration between two companies in a construction dispute. The word arbitration is normally applied to the process of finding a fair resolution of disputes by an impartial tribunal, without unecessary delay or expense, i.e. the delay and expense that litigation would impose. However, within the context of solving conflict by negotiation, mediation or arbitration litigation is the extreme form of arbitration, i.e. the use of an independent body or person officially appointed to settle a dispute. The trouble with any sort of arbitration is that there will be at least one loser. If matters have got bad enough for arbitration to be involved then you will by now have involved HR for interpersonal conflict or legal for inter-company conflict. The rest of this chapter will be about negotiation and mediation.

There are three really useful keys for unlocking and resolving conflict:

1. The first of these was highlighted by Steven Covey[4] and it is 'Seek first to understand, then to be understood'. This is designed to break through the first two blockers, you remember – wanting to speak first and not being able to listen. If we encourage others to explain their side first and really listen and show that we understand them, then they will be more inclined to listen to our side.

2. The second key was found by Ury, Fisher and Patton[5] and is that people in disagreement should focus on their needs rather than their positions. By focusing on our positions we tend to reinforce our disagreements. When we focus on our needs we tend to find that we have more in common than we had assumed. We reach a solution by trying to satisfy the sum of both our needs and the other party's needs. The light goes on and we realize that it is not a win–lose situation but can be a win–win.

3. The third key is provided by Winslade and Monk,[6] who found that if they asked individuals how they might have felt forced by the conflict to do or say things that they wish they had not, then they could place the blame on the conflict and allow the parties concerned to save face and slowly distance themselves from the emotions of the conflict. Such a technique can allow parties to detach themselves from the conflict long enough to see that each has a choice as to whether he wants to continue feeding the conflict or not.

It may be that either one or both parties are not very experienced at using these keys and perhaps they need a mediator. It is vital that the parties involved have respect for the mediator's integrity, impartiality and mediation ability.

---

4   Covey S. 1989. *Seven Habits of Highly Effective People*. Simon & Schuster, London.

5   Fisher, R., Ury, W. and Patton, B. 1991. *Getting to Yes: Negotiating Agreement Without Giving In*. Penguin Books, Harmondsworth.

6   Winslade, J. and Monk, G. 2000. *Narrative Mediation: A New Approach to Conflict Resolution*. Jossey-Bass Publishers, San Francisco.

The mediator will usually hold a pre-mediation meeting with each party separately. As previously explained, the primary barrier to conflict resolution is the desire of each party to express their position first. Once the party feels understood by the mediator at least, a giant emotional burden is lifted and mediation can continue. It is important, however, that the mediator makes clear at the outset that it is mediation rather than arbitration and that the power to resolve the conflict lies with the parties, not with the mediator. Otherwise each party will be suspicious that the other party is affecting the neutrality of the mediator.

Figure 8.1 describes the process for applying the understanding of conflict and conflict management to a conflict using the tools identified in the next section.

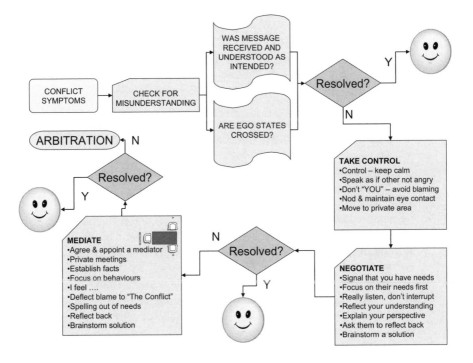

Figure 8.1   The conflict resolution process

TOOLS

Managing your own Internal Conflict

1. Give the conflict a name. Write down your thoughts on it and see if you can reach a solution. Consider whether or not the conflict is worse because you are tired or angry.
2. Get a different perspective by talking it through with a trusted friend.
3. Find at least two positive courses of action you can take to resolve the conflict. Write down the pros and cons for each. Select the best option and talk it through with your friend. Listen to their advice.
4. Have a cooling off period of at least a day.
5. Implement your plan. Doing something positive will be medicine in its own right.

Managing Conflict with Another Person

1. Control yourself. If you and/or the other party are becoming agitated or angry, calm yourself!
   - Speak to the other person as if the other person is not angry or agitated. This will have a calming effect on them.
   - Don't use the word 'you', this will help to avoid blame.
   - Nod to show that you are listening.
   - Maintain eye contact.
2. Move the discussion to a private area.
3. We need to signal that we have needs (so that it doesn't come as a shock when they emerge) but we also need to listen to their needs first. Try a formula like 'We clearly have different perspectives on this. I want to share my needs with you later, but let's focus on your needs and feelings first. Please help me to understand what your needs are concerning ...'
4. Really listen. *Don't* interrupt to inject your needs, feelings or perspective.
5. Reflect back your understanding of their needs and perspective by way of a tentative statement or question.
6. Refine your statement/question until the other party agrees that you have understood their needs and perspective.
7. Now explain your needs and perspective.
8. Ask them to reflect back their understanding of your needs.
9. Move on to brainstorming a solution that meets all needs or most needs of both parties.

Mediation Skills

1. As mediator take control of the process, but not the problem.
2. Describe the process and ground rules:

- You will not arbitrate, they will reach a resolution which you will help them find.
- You will have private meetings with each of them in turn to understand their needs and perspectives.
- You will not take sides.
- You will then bring them together to discuss in turn their needs and perspectives.
- You will help them explore the issues and their feelings and seek solutions.

3. Pre-meetings:
   - Take notes. These will help you during the actual mediation meeting.
   - Focus on behaviours not personality. You can change the former but not the latter.
   - Establish objective facts. Clarify words used ... e.g. when you say that Mary is disrespectful, what do you mean? Give me an example of her being disrespectful.
   - Encourage them to talk about their feelings by using 'I feel' statements to describe their feelings about the conflict, the events and the behaviours.
   - Get them to spell out their needs.
   - Get them to identify some positives about the other person.

4. The mediation meeting.
5. Use a seating arrangement as shown in Figure 8.2. This is a very powerful way of emphasizing that they are here to talk to each other.
6. Get each party in turn to describe their needs.
7. As each is finished ask the other party to reflect back to show that they have understood the other's needs. This is most usefully done on a flipchart.
8. Help them to start working towards a solution that meets all needs. The flipchart pages of needs can be displayed side by side.
9. Diffuse any heat by getting them to blame the conflict rather than the people.

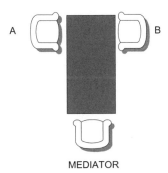

MEDIATOR

Figure 8.2   The role of a mediator

In this chapter we have looked at how to appoint a project manager and the key leadership skills that the Project Sponsor needs to deal with stakeholders namely negotiation and conflict resolution.

CHAPTER 9

PROJECT FINANCE

WAYS TO FUND PROJECTS

Projects can be funded, broadly speaking, in three ways.

1. From retained earnings. If an organization is making good profits and generating lots of cash, then it may be able to retain profits in order to finance new projects. By retain profits I mean not distribute them in dividends to the shareholders. If the projects have an IRR (see Chapter 6) greater than the expected return on equity, then the shareholders should find this acceptable.
2. From borrowings secured against the organization's assets.
3. From borrowings secured against the assets and revenues of the project.

The term project finance is used to describe the method of securing finance against a project's revenues and assets rather than against the organization as a whole, i.e. option 3 above. The funding of projects from retained earnings is a perfectly practicable way of funding projects. In the UK the Office of the Rail Regulator (ORR) is ring fencing a portion of Network Rail's earnings in order to fund new projects.

Large corporations do issue corporate bonds (we will talk about bonds later) in order to fund projects without actually specifying which projects. They may also issue new equity for similar purposes.

Option 3, i.e. project finance has advantages for the organization in that it is insulated, to a considerable extent, from failure of the project. If the organization had borrowed from the bank directly to fund the project and the project failed, the bank would have recourse to the organization for recovery of the money that they had lent. Consequently, another name for project finance is non-recourse financing.

PROJECT FINANCE

Project finance is normally only suitable for very large projects or a series of similar projects because the time and money spent on lawyers, bankers and other professionals in setting up the contractual arrangements would not make sense on a small project.

Other than the project being very large there are several other requirements that make a project suitable for project finance. Both the costs and revenues must be dependent on the project alone. Success must depend on clearly understandable factors such as the cost of construction or the value of a mineral. Note that these factors must be understandable but not necessarily certain. There will be a great deal of risk but the ability to understand these factors leads to the next key requirement which is that there must be clear understanding and apportionment of risks and excess cash flows.

An early example of project finance is BP's Forties oilfield in the North Sea, which illustrates these principles quite simply.

In 1972 BP established this structure to secure US$945 million of finance from a syndicate of 66 banks to develop the Forties oilfield. A Special Purpose Vehicle (SPV) or Special Purpose Company (SPC) called NOREX was established as a legal entity. The banks made the loan to NOREX, which in turn made an advance payment for agreed quantities of oil to BP Development. BP guaranteed that BP Development would develop the field as agreed, thereby taking on the construction risk. NOREX had an agreement that BP Trading would buy the agreed quantities of oil at a pre-agreed price. In this way BP took the risk of fluctuations in the oil price. NOREX repaid the loan and interest to the banks.

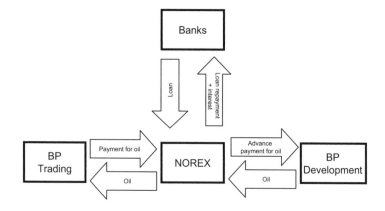

Figure 9.1　An early private finance project – BP

The banks took on the risk that the oil reserves in the Forties field might be insufficient to repay the loan. BP guaranteed that in each year of production the market value of oil produced less the debt service charge would be paid into a 'reclaim account' which would be available to NOREX if future oil flow fell below the quantity needed to make the required payments to NOREX. In other words if early oil revenues exceeded the specified loan repayments they were ring fenced in case future flows were insufficient.

The advantages for BP were that it was able to raise the finance to develop this oil field without, effectively, mortgaging its other assets. The additional debt did not show up as a debt on BP's balance sheet, rather it was a deferred liability against future deliveries. BP also got the banks to take the risk that the oil reserves might be less than predicted.

This 'off balance-sheet financing' proved to be very popular with a great many private and public sector organizations. It was a perfectly legal (at the time) way that could be used to disguise borrowing. The potential for misuse was great and in 2001 this became obvious through the Enron scandal. Enron, a US utility company, had used hundreds of SPVs to disguise its debts and mislead investors. After the Enron collape, regulators around the globe moved to tighten accounting standards and prevent liabilities being held off balance sheet.

Unlike other types of loan where repayments begin as soon as the loan is made, in project finance the first payments are designed to match the ability of the project to generate cash. Therefore it is normal to agree that the first payment will be made a certain number of months after completion of the facility. These grace periods are particularly common on projects in the developing world.

Project financing has been very widely used for projects involving the extraction of minerals and also for the construction of power stations. In the latter case, advance payments are made for agreed quantities of electricity rather than oil. The model is otherwise very similar. The model has been used for road construction where revenues arise either through tolls or shadow tolls. What's a shadow toll? If a government wants to use project finance to build a road but does not want to alienate motorists through imposing a toll, it can pay tolls to the SPV on behalf of the motorists who use the new road and fund this through general taxation. In fact the use of project finance to fund government projects has grown dramatically to include hospitals, schools, railways, prisons, government buildings and other infrastructure via public–private partnership (PPP) or private finance initiative (PFI) arrangements. Typically the public sector will invite bids from the private sector to design, finance construct and operate a facility for a number of years. A number of consortia will form, involving banks, contractors, designers and operators which then bid for the project.

Governments, particularly of the more stable and wealthy countries, are usually considered a fairly low credit risk and can raise finance at lower rates of interest than the private sector. Why therefore would a government wish the private sector to raise finance for a public sector project?

ADVANTAGES OF PROJECT FINANCE

Before answering this question I suggest that we look at the general advantages of projects undertaken via the project finance route. We have already discussed:

- Protection of the organization's other assets from the banks.
- Clear allocation of risk and excess cash flows.
- Clear success factors.

The clarity of success factors and the isolation of the project from the rest of the organization mean that the project manager has nowhere to hide. Project managers are normally very exposed to scrutiny, but the nature of PFI projects, and perhaps a certain degree of political controversy that they continue to attract, enhances the spotlight. Success or failure is clearly visible. Normally managers do have some control over the information that they release to shareholders and the banks. There is a name for this – agency cost. Funders accept that they cannot manage an organization themselves and they employ management to do this as their agent. The agent has a better knowledge of what is going on in the organization than the funder does and manipulates this to their benefit. Usually governance arrangements restrict this, but it does occur. So called 'empire building' is an example of the inefficiencies that can occur and that go to make up agency cost.

The public sector has long been encumbered by a problem with major projects in that government departments are set budgets annually and this constrains their ability to clearly commit funding to a project in a way that is efficient. If a department is spending below budget as it approaches the year end it runs the risk of having its budget for the next year reduced. This leads to all sorts of game-playing between treasury and departments. There are advantages of paying for major infrastructure investment in deferred known annual payments rather than less predictable and fluctuating sums. Although there have been attempts to solve this problem through clearly differentiated capital and revenue budgets, when cuts have to be made in difficult times, it proves far easier for government departments to cut capital project budgets rahter than revenue budgets. If a project is committed contractually as a PFI project then it becomes considerably more difficult to cancel, as the following recent example illustrates.

The Scottish Government is promoting a railway project called the Edinburgh to Glasgow Improvement Programme (EGIP), where the frequency of trains between the two major cities is increased, and journey times significantly reduced. There are environmental benefits in both the conversion from diesel to electric traction and the opportunity to transfer journeys from private cars to public transport. The project had a good outline business case with benefits well in excess of costs – the benefit–cost ratio (BCR) test, which gave the Scottish Government confidence that project was worth doing and that it also fitted well with the government's wider strategic objectives. The sponsor had two main options for financing this £1.2 billion pound project. The first was through the government's own capital budget where payments would be made to the railway as each stage of the capital outlay was incurred. Alternatively the government could ask Network Rail, a private sector public interest company that owns the railway infratructure, to borrow the money from the international capital markets by issuing long, index-linked bonds and then remunerating the company over the life of the assets (30 years).

In order to determine the best option, the terms of the second option had to be ascertained. This was done in the first half of 2009 by detailed negotiation with Network Rail and the active participation of the independent rail regulator, the Office of Rail Regulation (ORR). Detailed financial analysis was conducted to ensure that Network Rail could raise and service this amount of debt without risk to its core activities. This proved that it was possible, but also highlighted that when this project was added to others that were being promulgated in England, the company was close to the ceiling of what could be safely undertaken in the medium term. Helpfully the ORR formally set out the negotiated terms that would apply to the financing deal and the main Board of Network Rail accepted them.

Now that the Scottish Government knew not only the terms of the second option, but also that it was a viable realistic option to be overseen by the rail regulator, it was in a position to decide which financing option, or combination thereof, to choose. A detailed report was prepared contrasting the two options. Perhaps the most important consideration was the spreading of the government expenditure over a long period. The discounting over a long project life compensated, to a large degree, for the higher cost of capital of the private sector compared to the public sector. There were, for this project, other factors to consider, an important one being that in the second option the rail regulator was prepared to oversee the efficient implementation of the project and use extensive powers of regulation to ensure an efficient outcome. This meant that there was a very real risk transfer from the public to the private sector.

On the other side of the argument were concerns that committing to payments for 30 years limited the options open to ministers. This is an important aspect of all PFI-type public expenditure projects that is not always openly discussed, but is likely to be of concern in circumstances where public expenditure comes under heavy pressure to make cuts. In the past ministers have been reluctant to sacrifice day-to-day recurrent expenditure (resourse in government accounting parlance), because it directly impacts upon the quality of service provided to citizens. Traditionally it has been capital projects that have been cancelled or deferred, but this is very difficult in the PFI context where a legal contractual framework exists to protect against these sorts of changes. An example in the Scottish context was the draft budget for 2010–11 presented to the Scottish Parliament at the end of 2009 which contained only one major sacrifice: the Glasgow Airport Rail Link project. It was not the whole project that was cancelled, only the half of the project sitting in the Government's capital budget. The half that had been contracted with the railway under a PFI-type arrangement was to be retained. The result is that the EGIP project will be largely financed by the second, PFI-style option.

The UK National Audit Office (NAO) published a report in October 2009 which looked at the performance of PFI contracts.[1] This review contained many caveats, particularly relating to data collection. Nevertheless it found that 69 per cent of PFI projects were completed on time and 65 per cent to the contracted price. This compared to 63 per cent of non PFI projects being delivered on time and 54 per cent to contracted price. A large majority of PFI projects were given good quality ratings. The main reasons identified for the good PFI project performance were:

- The nature of the PFI contract with its clear output specification.
- The deferment of payment until completion.
- Clear communication between partners to the contract.

It is a military principle that time spent in reconnaissance is never wasted. Likewise, time spent at the beginning of a project clearly defining the project, the success factors and risks is never wasted. Because the contractual process involved in PPP/PFI is necessarily rigorous, it forces the public sector to define the project very tightly or, commonly, the service outputs that it wants from the project. Once these are set the contract arrangements ensure that it far more difficult to make changes.

The typical PPP contract in which the private sector is contracted to operate and maintain the facility for a number of years provides an incentive to the private sector to pay due heed to the long term operating and maintenance costs of the facility. This contrasts with tendering to provide a facility at the lowest price which just meets the specification and represents another important advantage of PPP over the traditional design and build procurement route.

The NAO also published a paper for the House of Lords Economic Affairs Committee in October 2009.[2] In addition to the findings already noted, this report

---

1   *NAO Review: Performance of PFI Construction*, October 2009. www.nao.org.uk.
2   Private Finance Projects, A paper for the Lords Economic Affairs Committee, October 2009, www.nao.org.uk.

found that institutional incentives had encouraged the use of private finance and that funding and budgeting mechanisms had made on balance-sheet projects less attractive. Although the financial reporting standards which followed Enron were beginning to be applied to the public sector, the debts and assets of PFI projects would still not necessarily be included in departmental budgets or in statistics of government debt.

The subject of PFI attracts strong political views both for and against. Nevertheless public–private partnership which uses private finance and management to deliver public infrastructure has become an important procurement option.

Let us now look at the key issue of finance. Inevitably the financial world is a dynamic one, and certainly, at the time of writing, it is difficult and uncertain. Much of what I say in the next few pages about finance is based in the world of financing projects during the decades before the credit crunch. Because many banks are receiving massive injections of public money to remain solvent, the line between public and private finance has become somewhat blurred. However, there appears to still be intent, on all sides, to continue with PFI, albeit with some, as yet, unclear changes. I will endeavour to set out some of the principles of project finance, whilst drawing attention to those aspects which are currently uncertain.

There are, essentially, three components of finance: bank debt, bonds and equity.

EQUITY

Equity bears the highest level of risk. That is if it comes to the situation in which those providing finance will lose money, the equity providers are last in the queue of those recovering money. Consequently equity is the most expensive form of funding in that equity providers look for a high return on their capital. However, in order to achieve an acceptable transfer of risk to the private sector, some degree of equity is normally a prerequisite of PFI agreements. The proportion of equity is generally quite small, typically around 10 per cent of the total funding requirement. There are two types of equity involved. The first is 'pure' equity, or ordinary shares which the investors buy in the project company. The second is subordinated debt, also known as junior debt. This junior debt is less at risk that the 'pure' equity but more at risk than senior debt or bonds, and commands a commensurate return. Since interest payments on debt are generally tax deductible, there are tax advantages to using subordinate debt over pure equity and it often represents the majority of the equity in the project finance package.

The remainder of the funding can be either bank debt (senior debt) or bond financing. It is possible for larger projects to be funded via a mixture of bank finance and bond finance. However, this means that the issue of who gets paid first in the event of a default must be resolved, and this can be quite complex. There are advantages and disadvantages to both bank finance and bond finance. However, before we go on to look at bank finance I would like to return to the issue of the high cost of equity. Equity in the form of ordinary shares conveys partial ownership of the company and voting rights at shareholder meetings. The shareholders own the business and the management run it on their behalf. Therefore one cost of equity is the surrender of control, particularly to large, institutional shareholders. However, a company does not have to pay dividends. If it does not, then the share price will suffer and the options for further fund-raising may become limited. Nevertheless in difficult times equity capital on which dividends do not have to be paid may look cheaper than a bank loan to the management of the company.

BANK FINANCE

Bank finance is debt issued by commercial banks, either singly or more often as a syndicate of banks. Banks normally require security over the project assets and the right to take the place of the SPV in the event of default. Bank debt must be paid back, in the default situation, before equity or subordinate (junior) debt and is therefore known as senior debt.

Bank debt can be drawn down as required during the course of the project and can normally include a standby facility to be called upon if required for project changes.

Bank finance will be priced with reference to the London Interbank Offered Rate (LIBOR) which is the interest rate at which banks lend to each other. One bank will normally act as an arranger who will establish the appetite of other lenders to form a syndicate. Lenders may each have differing amounts to lend and require different interest rates, e.g. one may offer £25 million at LIBOR + 350 whilst another may offer £20 million at LIBOR + 325. The numbers added to the LIBOR rate are in basis points where a basis point is one-hundredth of one per cent. Thus if LIBOR is 3.5 per cent then LIBOR + 325 is 3.5 + 3.25 = 6.75%. The arranger will total up all the loan offers and rates and identify the best deal and the rate at which to price the loan.

There are several types of syndications, 'underwritten', 'best efforts' and 'club'. A deal may be underwritten by the arranging bank. In this case it offers the full financial commitment and then syndicates it, absorbing itself any loan commitment that is not fully subscribed. A 'best efforts' syndication is where the arranger does not underwrite the whole funding requirement and the remainder is left to market forces. A 'club' is effectively a pre-existing syndicate looking for projects to lend to.

The LIBOR rate changes daily so LIBOR + X is a variable rate. The SPV will probably not wish to bear interest rate risk so at financial close it will enter into a swap whereby it swaps the variable interest rate for a fixed rate. The bank will of course charge for the swap.

BOND FINANCE

A bond is a formal contract to repay borrowed money with interest. There are numerous variations but the simplest form is where the issuer of the bond receives an amount of money, the principal amount, from the investor and promises to pay the investor interest payments (known as the coupon) at fixed intervals until the bond matures. At maturity the issuer pays the principal amount back to the investor.

Bonds are attractive to institutions such as pension funds and insurance companies who have long-term liabilities and want to match those with assets (i.e. bonds) that have a similar maturity.

Bonds can be freely traded in the market. An advantage of this to the SPV is that there will therefore be less restriction on the SPV and less monitoring of the project by the bond-holder than would usually be the case with a bank. On the other hand, if it is necessary to negotiate a relaxation of a restrictive covenant, for example, then since the bonds are freely traded amongst multiple investors it will be more difficult to contact and negotiate with the bond holders than it would be, through the arranger, with a bank syndicate.

Bond financing is less flexible than bank financing. In bond financing the total amount is drawn down at the beginning of the term and must be placed in an account from which the project costs will be paid as well as interest on the bond. Bond financing does not easily allow for a standby facility and therefore it is common to take up more finance than is initially required to provide this contingency. The raising of more finance than should be required is inefficient and a disadvantage of bond financing.

As mentioned earlier, bonds can be freely traded and the investors are not therefore able to monitor the project and step in, as a bank would, in the event of default. However, bond investors also require some security for their investment. This may be by means of parent company guarantees from the main contractors in the SPV, for example, or through wrapping the bond. Wrapping is when an insurance company with an investment grade rating AAA carries out due diligence on the project and guarantees payments against the bond. The AAA rating is thereby transferred to (or wrapped around) the bond. This makes the bond much more marketable and reduces the risk premium that investors would otherwise require.

Of course the insurer requires a premium for their risk. The insurers providing this service are normally specialists and therefore referred to as monoline insurers.

Traditionally bonds have been available with longer maturity periods than bank finance, and this can be an advantage to long duration PFI projects. However, as experience with PFI projects has grown, the gap between available bank finance terms and bond terms shrank to the point where there was no longer a significant difference.

The price difference between bank debt and bonds is subject to market conditions. On average it has favoured bonds but expert advice should be taken before deciding which route to adopt.

I imagine that most Project Sponsors and budding Project Sponsors will understand debt and interest on debt. Bonds are different and I hope that it will help sponsors if I explain a little of the theory of bond pricing.

Bonds, as we have said, can be traded and have a price. Bonds are securities where the issuer agrees to pay fixed payments on certain dates in the future and to repay the principal amount borrowed on maturity of the bond.

If we look at a simple example of a four-year bond for £100 principal with a 10 per cent coupon (interest rate on the bond) the cash flows which the investor would receive are as follows:

Year	1	2	3	4
Cash flows	£10	£10	£10	£110

If you recall the work we covered in Chapter 6 you will see how the face value of the coupon is calculated.

$$\frac{10}{1.1} + \frac{10}{1.1^2} + \frac{10}{1.1^3} + \frac{110}{1.1^4} = £100.00$$

If investors are looking for an interest rate of 8 per cent then they would discount the expected cash flows as shown below:

$$\frac{10}{1.08} + \frac{10}{1.08^2} + \frac{10}{1.08^3} + \frac{110}{1.08^4} = £106.62$$

Thus because the coupon is higher (10 per cent) than the current interest rate required (8 per cent) the investor would be prepared to pay more than the face value (£100) of the bond, i.e. they would be prepared to pay £106.62.

Of course if the interest rate had gone the other way, investors would be prepared to pay less. If the interest rate required had risen to 12 per cent then they would discount the expected cash flows as shown below:

$$\frac{10}{1.12} + \frac{10}{1.12^2} + \frac{10}{1.12^3} + \frac{110}{1.12^4} = £93.33$$

Thus bond prices move inversely with interest rate.

The longer a bond's maturity, the greater will be its change in price for a given change in interest rate:

$$\frac{10}{1.08} + \frac{10}{1.08^2} + \frac{10}{1.08^3} + \frac{10}{1.08^4} + \frac{10}{1.08^5} + \frac{110}{1.08^6} = £109.25$$

Or

$$\frac{10}{1.12} + \frac{10}{1.12^2} + \frac{10}{1.12^3} + \frac{10}{1.12^4} + \frac{10}{1.12^5} + \frac{110}{1.12^6} = £91.78$$

The lower the coupon rate, the greater the change in price for a given interest rate change:

$$\frac{5}{1.05} + \frac{5}{1.05^2} + \frac{5}{1.05^3} + \frac{105}{1.05^4} = £100.00$$

$$\frac{5}{1.03} + \frac{5}{1.03^2} + \frac{5}{1.03^3} + \frac{105}{1.03^4} = £107.43$$

$$\frac{5}{1.07} + \frac{5}{1.07^2} + \frac{5}{1.07^3} + \frac{105}{1.07^4} = £93.23$$

The other thing which by now you may be able to work out for yourself is that the sensitivity of a bond's price to interest rate changes increases with maturity but at a decreasing rate.

This is a brief introduction to the way that bond prices fluctuate with interest rates, coupon rates and maturity.

CREDIT CRUNCH

The credit crunch has had a severe impact on the willingness of banks to lend. Likewise the monoline insurers have been hard hit by guarantees given to sub-prime lending in the US housing market. Nevertheless markets are cyclical and normal service will, no doubt, be resumed eventually. Indeed there are many signs that this already seems to be happening.

Refinancing

Where a PFI project involves physical construction works such as a power station, road, hospital or school, much of the risk lies in the planning, design and construction phases. The funders and investors take account of this risk when pricing the returns that they require. Therefore, if construction is completed without all of the priced risk materializing, there is an opportunity to re-finance the project at a lower cost. This was a very controversial aspect of early PFI projects in the UK, where the private sector parties to PFI contracts did exactly this and significantly enhanced their profit margin. This issue was addressed, through voluntary amendments to the code of conduct, treasury guidelines and the model PFI contracts. The result is that, for PFI deals signed before 30 September 2002, the public sector can generally expect a 30 per cent share of the senior debt refinancing gain through the voluntarily agreed changes to the code of practice. For deals signed after that date the public sector share is 50 per cent. In Scotland this is extended to include refinancing of the junior debt, and there are also provisions to cap equity gains to the private sector.

Structure

The typical arrangement for a PFI project with respect to the cash flows is shown in Figure 9.2 and for the contractual agreements in Figure 9.3.

A current example of a UK PFI model is the Building Schools for the Future programme. This is the UK's largest single capital investment programme in the last 50 years. It aims to rebuild and renew all 3,500 of England's secondary schools by the year 2020. The programme was launched in 2003 and 146 schools had been completed by January 2010. The new schools are being delivered through PFI arrangements and the remodelling and refurbishment through conventional design and build contracts. Figure 9.4 illustrates the complexity of the arrangements.

Partnerships for Schools (PfS) is a non-departmental public body which is carrying out the programme management across the many local authorities involved and is funded jointly by the Department for Children, Schools and Families (DCSF) and Partnerships UK (PUK). Partnerships UK is classified as a private sector company and is a joint venture between HM Treasury, Scottish ministers and the private sector. DCSF and PUK also fund Building Schools for the Future Investments (BSFI) which is a limited liability partnership. Each local authority sets up a Local Education Partnership (LEP) to plan and manage the programme for its schools. The local authority has a 10 per cent equity stake in the LEP as does BSFI. They select a private sector partner, usually a consortium of contractors who will negotiate to provide services for the construction and maintenance of the infrastructure and information technology for the schools, whether this goes via the conventional of PFI route or not. The private sector partner contributes the remaining 80 per cent equity to the LEP.

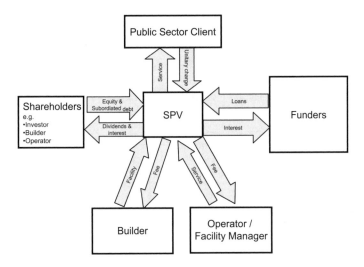

Figure 9.2   Typical PFI cash flow

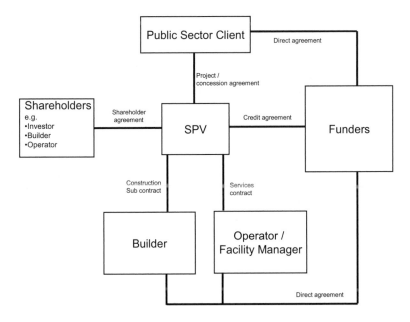

Figure 9.3   Typical PFI contract arrangements

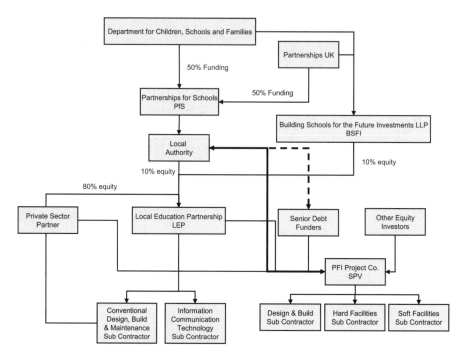

Figure 9.4   Building schools for the future organization. Hard facilities management is the maintenance of the school buildings and infrastructure whilst soft facilities management is cleaning and catering

PFI DEVELOPMENT PROCESS

There are variations in the development process, procurement options and differences between sectors. Consequently the following is intended to reflect the generic process for developing a project from identified need through to a PFI project delivering services. Table 9.1 identifies key stages, the main outcomes of each stage and an indication of the likely duration of each stage.

Table 9.1   The PFI development process

	Stage	Key stage outputs	Indicative stage duration
1	Strategy for change	Vision sets out what needs to be done Identification of advisers needed to scope and develop options Approval to proceed to next stage	2 months
2	Option appraisal	Procure advisers Develop output specification in consultation with stakeholders Identify options Scope options Preliminary costing and risk assessment of options Identification of preferred option Value for money assessment Approval to proceed to next stage	5–7 months
3	Outline business case	Develop preferred option Establish value for money, affordability and case for PFI procurement route Demonstrate rigorous appraisal process Demonstrate alignment with organization's policy and strategy Demonstrate buy-in of key stakeholders Obtain outline planning permission Prepare notices for inviting consortia to pre-qualify, e.g. An *Official Journal of the European Union* (OJEU) notice within the EU Approval to outline business case and proceed to next stage	8–12 months
4	Pre-qualification	Expressions of Interest invited, received and evaluated Shortlist 3–6 bidders	3 months
5	Negotiation	Outline agreement on key issues affecting price, risk allocation, payment mechanism and performance Designs typically 1:500 scale plans Select two bidders to proceed to next stage	6–20 months
6	Selection of preferred bidder	Detailed solutions typically 1:200 scale plans and 1:50 in key areas Full financial model Agreement on all contractual issues Preferred bidder selected	4–6 months
7	Financial close	Consortium due diligence Full business case All approvals in place All contracts and subcontracts in place	4–6 months
8	Design and construction	Completed design Detailed planning consents Constructed and commissioned facility	1–5 years
9	Operation	Delivered services	25–30 years

ADVISERS

The guidance in this chapter is necessarily very generic. The development of a PFI project is very complex, particularly in financial and legal terms. The Project Sponsor is very likely to need, as a minimum, the following advisers:

1. *Financial advisers* – usually from a merchant bank, investment bank or one of the top accountancy firms. They should have good relevant experience of PFI deals, preferably in the relevant sector. The financial adviser should assist with:
   - Business case preparation
   - Sounding out financial markets
   - Risk analysis
   - Structuring financial elements of bid documentation
   - Identifying payment structures to optimize risk/reward
   - Establishing financial bid evaluation criteria
   - Assisting with financial analysis of bids
   - Advice and support during negotiations.
2. *Legal advisers* – again they should have good relevant experience of PFI deals, preferably in the relevant sector. The legal adviser should assist with:
   - Advising on procurement approach and structuring the transaction
   - Advising on contractual issues
   - Advising on taxation, property, planning, environmental, competition, banking, employment and intellectual property law issues
   - Drafting contracts and bid documentation
   - Advice and support during negotiations
   - Drafting and settling final contracts.
3. *Technical advisers* – the Project Sponsor may need the support of architects, engineers, surveyors, project managers, actuaries and possibly more. Issues with which technical advisers may assist include:
   - Developing the output specification
   - Preliminary development of designs
   - Technical assumptions and estimates for the option appraisal and outline business case
   - Technical elements of the pre-qualification and tender documentation
   - Technical evaluation of pre-qualification and tender submissions
   - Valuation of assets to be transferred to the consortium
   - Actuarial advice where staff are transferred and there are pension issues
   - Advice and support during negotiations
   - Monitoring and advising on technical quality issues during consortium's design, construction and commissioning phases.

CHAPTER 10

PROJECT COMMISSIONING AND CLOSE OUT

The Project Sponsor should be thinking about project commissioning and close out from the very beginning. What is meant by project commissioning and close out will vary according to the type of project. Broadly speaking it is the transition between capital investment and revenue generation.

If we are talking about constructing a new airport, e.g. commissioning begins when all the construction and installation work is complete and systems are being powered up and tested. The systems like check-in, baggage handling systems, security, public address, arrival and departure information must all be proven to function as designed and that they are integrated correctly. Once this is done, or perhaps in parallel with it, the staff that will maintain and operate the new airport will need to be trained on the new systems. Stakeholders must be introduced to the new airport systems and procedures, probably with varying degrees of training and documentation. Stakeholders will include airlines, travel agents, emergency services, taxi drivers, bus operators, caterers, shops, car hire agencies, car park operators, security staff, cleaners and many more. Operations will need to be transferred from the old airport to the new one. Operating and maintenance manuals together with strategic spares will need to be handed over from contractors to the maintainers and operators. Every part of the airport will have to be inspected and any defects recorded. Plans will have to be agreed with contractors for the defects to be repaired during the defect liability period, usually while the airport is in operation. Accounts will have to be paid with some money retained until after all defects are rectified. Close out is finally achieved when all defects are cleared, final accounts have been settled and the airport is fully operational.

The project might be the staging of a pop concert. In that case although the duration of the project will be much shorter the overlap between capital investment and revenue generation will be larger. Ticket sales will commence as soon as contracts are placed with the bands and the venue. The stage building will take place shortly before the concert. Commissioning and close out will be complete when the bands, venue, roadies and so on are all paid.

In the case of an airport, the scale of design, procurement, construction and installation is so immense and the pressure to get it complete to budget and schedule so immediate that this can blind the project team to the issue of putting the completed airport to work. Terminal 5 at London Heathrow was recently completed. It is a fantastic work of architecture and engineering. It was completed on time and budget, with an excellent safety record. Unfortunately for a short period after opening it was an operational disaster. Baggage could not be handled properly and delayed baggage had to be sent to Milan for sorting. Flights were cancelled. Passengers were delayed for days. There may have been other issues but it appears that a major problem was that staff had not been told of the staff parking arrangements, they could not get to work on time, and chaos ensued.

You can imagine how compared to the design and construction of such a huge terminal, letting the baggage handling staff know where to park might have slipped the project manager's mind. But the impact on passengers and airlines and the fall out in the press totally wrecked what should have been a great celebration of an otherwise phenomenal achievement. The Project Sponsor must be the owner of the project/organization interface and planning or checking that the planning of all these details is done and carried through.

As soon as the project manager is appointed, the Project Sponsor should begin working with him or her on the plans for commissioning and close out. This may seem perverse but there are sound precedents. In sport the top players go through a visualization process whereby they visualize the desired outcome and then how it happened. So a champion golfer will stand on the fairway and imagine his golf ball rolling into the hole. Then he will see the flight of the ball as it heads for the green and finally he will see his swing which set the ball off on that trajectory. For projects the equivalent is to visualize the completed project in operation, next its transition from implementation into operation and then the implementation itself. As you think through the process for bringing your project into service, you may identify tasks that you will need suppliers to carry out or aspects of design that should be planned now so that they do not become a last-minute costly change to a supplier's scope of work.

STAKEHOLDERS

You should brainstorm a list of all the stakeholders who will be affected by the project and how they will be affected. What will their needs be leading up to the commissioning? What information, training or other assistance will they need to make the transition?

For staff, the project could be sensitive because it brings about greater efficiency and staff headcount reductions, involves relocation, or changes in working practices.

The project may in fact involve recruitment of new staff. In these instances the human resources department should be engaged early on because these are sensitive issues that demand careful handling through defined procedures.

Depending of course on the scale and type of project there can be a long list of stakeholders with complex commissioning and transition requirements. Some stakeholders will need only information. For example Dubai International Airport recently opened its new Terminal 3. This morning I arrived at Terminal 3 whereas my e-ticket said that I would arrive at Terminal 1, as indeed I had four weeks ago. My e-ticket says that my departure on Friday will be from Terminal 1, however an announcement by the flight crew advised that flights are gradually being transferred to Terminal 3 and to check with ground staff or on their website for flight number and date to see which terminal departing flights leave from. There are also notices in the local newspapers. So, as a passenger my information requirements have been quite easily met with simple, easy to obtain information. However, the logistics of moving airline operations and staff, immigration, baggage handling, security, catering, concessions, etc. will have been complex and well planned years in advance.

Many stakeholders will be internal to your organization, and with the earlier warning about involving the human resources department in sensitive staff-related issues in mind, other internal stakeholders should be approached as early as possible to identify what will need to be done to make the commissioning of the project and the transition as effective as possible. For external stakeholders, there are often internal stakeholders who are a communication channel to them. For example, internally you may have a maintenance manager dealing with several maintenance companies looking after various parts of the organization's operations. It is certainly worth channelling your stakeholder communications through these internal stakeholders for two reasons. First, on a major project you will have far too many stakeholders to deal with and therefore you will need all the help you can get. Secondly, the external stakeholders will probably appreciate project communications via a contact they already know and prefer a single point of contact within the organization. However, you will need to ensure that the right messages are getting through and that appropriate plans are in hand and that progress is satisfactory. Where there are no obvious internal surrogates for external stakeholders you will need to liaise with the external stakeholders. If you have a communications department they might be useful allies for this.

For each stakeholder I suggest the ICAPRO mnemonic.

- *Inform* – you need to tell the stakeholder as much as necessary and possible (there may be confidentiality issues) about the project and what you think it may mean for them.

- *Consult* – ask them for their thoughts on the project and what it means for them. How will they be affected? What will they need to ensure a smooth commissioning and transition to the new operational environment that the project brings?
- *Agree* – agree what needs to be done. There may be contractual issues of who pays, the organization or the stakeholder. It is worth researching, preparing and taking internal advice first on this.
- *Plan* – assemble what needs to be done, by whom and by when into an action plan that can be monitored.
- *Review* – there should be regular reviews of stakeholder plans to ensure that they are progressing satisfactorily and to take remedial action where they are not.
- *Other* – share your list of stakeholders with each stakeholder because they may be able to advise you of other stakeholders that you have missed.

Amongst the key issues critical to successful commissioning is the question of who will be operating and who will be maintaining the facilities provided by the project. Obvious choices are:

1. The organization itself.
2. The contractor(s) responsible for its implementation as part of a long-term contract.
3. A third party contractor.

OPERATION AND MAINTENANCE MANUALS

These questions should be addressed early in the project. Operation and maintenance manuals (O&M manuals) will need to be provided both to the organization and to those responsible for the operation and maintenance. There is a common problem with O&M manuals. They are often a folder or box filled with all the manuals and drawings for each component part of the project systems with at best a contents list. There is seldom a holistic approach to this with a manual that explains how to operate and maintain the whole system as opposed to its component sub-systems.

Whereas car manufacturers usually provide a plastic wallet with an operator's manual for the car and often one other manual for the entertainment system, an organization taking ownership of a new building may only receive a box of drawings and manuals for the fire alarm system, the air conditioning system (or more likely separate manuals for each part of it, e.g. one for the air handling units, one for the chillers, one for each pump), the lifts, the burglar alarm, the telephone switchboard and so on. The building industry is not the only culprit. Despite the parallels that could be drawn with cars, if you buy a yacht you will be disappointed if you expect a manual of similar quality. Although you will have parted with an enormous amount of money you will get a plastic wallet containing the manufacturers' manuals for the toilet, the engine, the radio, the GPS, the radar, the depth gauge and many other components. There is seldom any guidance on the actual yacht into which all these parts have been installed or how the yacht should be operated as a complete system.

It may not be possible to change cultures overnight but I recommend asking early, relevant questions about O&M manuals and demanding to see examples of previous offerings and to give feedback on what you expect to see in yours.

TRAINING

Another closely related issue to address is training of operators and maintainers. You may wish to incorporate a training requirement into the implementation contractor's contract or, if not, develop a suitable training arrangement. Another issue to build into the contractor's contract and schedule are visits during manufacture, construction and commissioning for operating and maintenance staff because they seldom get the opportunity to see what they will subsequently operate or maintain put together and it can be very useful.

Operator training can be a very complex issue. For example, I have worked on railway projects where the signalling system is upgraded. Because the changeover from the old system to the new system necessarily takes place whilst the railway is not operational, perhaps over a Christmas or Easter bank holiday, it is not possible to provide training for the train drivers on the new system. Therefore it is necessary to provide training using simulations. This used to be by making a video film of the route from the driver's cab of a train and then superimposing the new signals on the film footage. This video is then shown to all the drivers who will drive over the route by trainers who will provide training in all the issues necessary for the drivers to do their work safely. Even obtaining the in-cab video of the route required months of planning because there are safety concerns about having a video camera and cameraman in the cab with the possible distraction of the driver. Consequently a special non-passenger-carrying train had to be run with a specially trained driver and for this to be done during daylight required considerable forward planning. Fortunately, computer simulation techniques have simplified this process considerably.

Prototypes, mock-ups, trials and pilot projects are valuable aids to commissioning and to project development in general. The Modern Facilities at Stations project was set up to provide railway stations across the UK with suitable access for mobility impaired passengers, waiting room facilities, public conveniences and passenger information where these were lacking. The Strategic Rail Authority was sponsor for the project which was being delivered by Network Rail. However, the operators and maintainers for the facilities would be the train operating companies for the stations concerned, of which there are many. The construction of a prototype on the roof of Euston station in London allowed many of the design and commissioning issues to be resolved with train operating companies before construction started in earnest. Four pilot projects were built in advance of the main programme. One was severely damaged by vandalism and another was locked out of use by the operator to avoid maintenance. Thus important lessons were learnt from the commissioning of these pilot projects, which helped to make the main tranche of projects highly successful. They were modified to be more resistant to vandalism and contracts were amended to ensure that operators would maintain them. Prototypes and mock-ups are very useful for training purposes and for trials of uncertain construction or commissioning methods.

DECOMMISSIONING EXISTING FACILITIES

Another aspect of commissioning for the Project Sponsor to consider is whether the bringing into operation of new facilities by the project must be accompanied by de-commissioning of existing facilities. If it is, then judgement is necessary over exactly how much overlap should be allowed. If anything goes wrong with the new facilities you might be grateful that the old facilities are still available. However, you cannot afford to keep the old facilities too long because that would reduce the cost efficiencies that the new project brings and undermine the business case. You may have headcount reductions to make or land and equipment that cannot be sold until the old facilities are closed down. Am I being too pessimistic about the new facilities not functioning perfectly from day one? How can we decide how long to retain the existing facilities? Let me introduce you to Dr Weibull. Waloddi Weibull was a Swedish engineer who amongst many other things did important research into fatigue analysis. The Weibull probability function is named after him and it is much used in the science of availability, reliability and maintainability (ARM). The relevance of Dr Weibull and ARM to this issue is the bathtub curve shown in Figure 10.1.

Systems (and the human being is no exception) tend to suffer a high failure rate early in their life. Then they bed-down and perform reliably for (hopefully) an extended period of time until they start to wear out. I suggest that you discuss with your project manager the recording of failures during the commissioning period and commencement of operations and plot failure rates so that you can estimate the point at which you will have sufficient confidence to de-commission the redundant facilities.

The Project Sponsor should make sure that the wider commissioning plans discussed above are incorporated in the project manager's project plan so that they are monitored and managed.

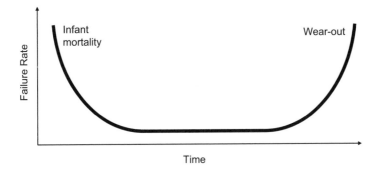

Figure 10.1   The Weibull bathtub curve

In summary of what we've covered so far, the Project Sponsor should be asking these questions:

1. Have we identified all the stakeholders that are involved in putting the new project into operation?
2. Have we got all the staff necessary to operate and maintain the facilities?
3. Will the staff get to the workplace on time, reliably?
4. Will the staff have all the equipment, manuals and training they need to do the job?
5. Have we done everything possible to ensure that all other stakeholders have all the information they need to ensure that the project is successfully put into operation?
6. Do all stakeholders have sufficient plans in place to ensure a successful commissioning of the project?
7. Do we have adequate checks in place to ensure that these commissioning plans are working?
8. Are necessary plans in place and being progressed satisfactorily for the de-commissioning of redundant facilities?

PROJECT CLOSE OUT

If all of these issues are robustly identified, planned and carried through then there is every prospect of a well-executed project moving successfully into the operational phase. Given all the effort that you and the project team put in, it would be a terrible shame if it did not. Take the Heathrow Terminal 5 project for example. I visited the site during construction. It was probably the best managed construction site that I have seen. The project was delivered on time and budget and with an enviable safety record. My wife and I travelled through the new terminal around three months after it opened and found it a joy to travel through and a magnificent building to behold. However, as I write the BBC are reporting[1] on the House of Commons Transport Committee's investigation as follows:

> *What should have been an occasion of national pride was in fact an occasion of national embarrassment ... most of the problems were down to insufficient communication between British Airways (BA) and BAA, the report found. It also criticised poor staff training and system testing by the airline company.*

The process of closing out a project often involves some contention in the agreement of the final accounts for the consultants, contractors and suppliers involved. If you selected a good project manager and they did their job well then this should not be too onerous. The main cause of messy final account settlement is change to the project scope which has not been properly priced at the time the change is instructed. This may be because the project manager and the contractor wished to avoid protracted debate and get on with the project, leaving the arguments over money until later. That can appear to be a successful tactic (for either side), but if an issue cannot be resolved at the time, it becomes increasingly difficult to solve later. The best project management practice is to evaluate the cost, time and performance impact of any requested change and then confirm whether or not the sponsor still requires the change. If this is done, then closing out the project will be much easier. Do not be too discouraged if changes to the project appear impossible due to their high cost. Around 1990 my boss at Bovis undertook a short research project into why building projects that we undertook in the United States were delivered around 30 per cent faster and cheaper than equivalent projects in the UK. In both countries clients wanted to make changes. In the UK we would endeavour to accommodate the client's changes which would result in an often unforeseen chain of changes which caused delay and extra cost. In the USA the client would be politely told that we would finish the project as planned first and then go back and make the change afterwards. This might seem counterintuitive but it did result in 30 per cent efficiency savings. It also meant that the management team in the USA was considerably smaller because it did not have to deal with change and that itself contributed to the efficiency saving.

Finally there are three more things.

1. You should make sure that there is a lessons learned workshop so that the lessons of your project can be available to the next project. Note, however, that you should ensure that this is the last in a series. If lessons can be learned why leave it until the end?

---

1   http://news.bbc.co.uk/1/hi/england/london/7704846.stm.

2. You should celebrate with an end of project party. Note, however, that you should ensure that this is the last in a series. Celebrating success is an important part of motivating teams. There should be many key milestones that can be celebrated.
3. You should ensure widest possible publicity for your project's success on behalf of your organization, your team and yourself.

PART 3

UNDERSTANDING PROJECT MANAGEMENT

CHAPTER 11

THE PROJECT TEAM

In Chapter 8 we looked at selection of the project manager and the sponsor's leadership of the top half of the project hourglass, the client organization. These are the essential leadership tasks that the sponsor is responsible for. In this chapter we will focus on the neck of the hourglass and discuss the relationship between Project Sponsor and project manager and the qualities and behaviours that the Project Sponsor should be looking for in the project manager.

In Chapter 8 we examined how important it is to make the project manager the first person hired on the project, because the remaining selections should be seen to be his or her choice. That way the team owes a debt of loyalty to the project manager rather than feeling that the project manager is an interloper, coming between them and you, the sponsor. In the same way, since you have picked the project manager they owe you loyalty. At the very beginning you should establish a climate of honesty with them. You should be clear about their role, which is to lead the lower part of the hourglass in delivering the project. You should explain your role which is to 'lead' the existing organization in procuring, receiving and assimilating the project results and being responsible for the business case.

You should be clear that if the business case turns sour you will, with regret, have to cancel the project. You should give what guidance you can to the project manager with respect to any relative priority within the project triangle of cost, time and performance. For example, time is often of the essence. A new shopping centre opened in January rather than in time for Christmas shopping may be a much bigger disaster than a 10 per cent cost overrun.

You should agree what limits of financial authority the project manager has and what needs to be referred back to you. You will not wish to be bothered every time the project manager needs to procure a new box of paper clips but you will perhaps want to know before new project team appointments are made. You should also agree the circumstances under which you want to be involved when the project manager has dialogue with the upper part of the hourglass. You may know, for example, that some members of your organization need more careful treatment than others. You will not want to keep the organization totally off limits to the project manager, but there may be particularly sensitive people and/or subjects which you will need to control.

I don't think that I can emphasize enough the importance of choosing the right people for the project team. In his book *Good to Great*[1] Jim Collins explains the extensive and exhaustive research that he and his team conducted into the factors that differentiate great companies from good companies. Collins found that the first distinguishing factor common to great companies was a self-effacing leader obsessed with achieving results for the company. The second factor was that all the great companies focused first on getting the right people 'on the bus' (and the wrong people off the bus) and only then identifying what they were going to do. On projects we do not usually have the option of deciding what we are going to do, but we do have the power of decision over how we will go about it. Collecting the right people around you is the single most important step you can take to ensure the project's success. The golfer Gary Player was once asked what made the difference between a good golfer and a bad one. His answer was that he had never seen a good player with a bad grip (how you hold the club) or a bad player with a good grip. I would say that I have never known a successful project with a bad project team or an unsuccessful project with a good project team.

QUICK WINS OR EARLY SUCCESSES

One of the outstandingly successful projects which I have been involved in was the replacement of the signalling system on the London Tilbury and Southend railway in the mid-1990s. The project was suffering from more than a year's delay and huge cost escalation when the project manager was changed. The incoming Senior Project manager, Tony Ingle-Finch, took stock and then set about augmenting and replacing the project management team with the right people.

The next thing that he did was create early success. Railway projects of this nature involve a series of major commissioning periods when the old system is changed over to the new system. For obvious reasons these changeovers need to happen when trains are not running and therefore tend to be at weekends or, for the larger commissionings, over bank holiday periods such as Christmas or Easter. After careful deliberation Tony postponed the first major commissioning period. He decided that the project wasn't ready and that it would more than likely be a failure. He considered that the effect of a failure on team morale would be worse that the additional eight-month delay until the next opportunity. That was a hugely courageous and job-threatening decision to make. It was not a decision born of inspiration. Tony had already said that the biggest motivation for anyone is success. He then worked the team hard to ensure that everything was planned

---

1   Collins, J. 2001. *Good to Great*. Random House Business Books, London

in minute detail for the postponed first commissioning. It was a success and the team celebrated that success. Everyone felt that they were now part of a winning team and Tony cultivated that. In each part of the project people felt an *esprit de corps*. They found ways to do their job better than it had been done before. Each subsequent commissioning period became more successful than the last. Tony became an ambassador for the LTS project and the project team appreciated that.

Another important factor in assembling the project team is to get the right mix of people. The perfect project team contains a mix of skills and behaviour styles. A rugby team with 15 scrum halves won't work and neither will a project team in which every member thinks and behaves the same way. Teams take time to establish how they can best work together and given that projects often bring together team members who have never worked with each other before it is very useful to invest in some focused team building.

When you ask a project manager candidate what the most important factor in project success is going to be, and they reply that it is the project planning software, keep looking. If their reply is that controlling scope change is the most important factor, give them another chance. It is pretty important, but the right team will make sure that it happens.

When you ask them how they are going to motivate the team and they reply with bonus payments, keep looking.

LEADERSHIP

At the beginning of this chapter we noted the importance of letting the project manager select their team. The sponsor should be involved in the selection of the senior members of the project management team and should advise the project manager, in private, of any preferences or concerns that they have. It is, however, very important that the project team believe that the project manager is responsible for their appointment. This does not mean that you should divorce yourself from the project team. You are the Project Sponsor and the embodiment of the client. Whilst you should not do anything to undermine the project manager you certainly should visit the project office and site to show your interest.

The nature of projects is that they bring together, for a relatively short time, a diverse group of people who probably have not worked together before. Consequently the team dynamics and the leadership of the team is particularly important to project success. In this chapter we will examine leadership in a project environment and how teams work together. First of all I would like to look at the difference between leadership and management.

Warren Bennis[2] identified twelve differences between leaders and managers which are summarized in Table 11.1.

Clearly there is a role for both managers and leaders. I have not yet come across anyone with the title 'Project Leader'. The titles project manager or project director are the norm. Both project directors and project managers can fall into the categories of leader and manager. Leadership is a state of mind and behaviour. One would hope that, thanks to greater experience and seniority, project directors will have greater leadership skills than project managers but this is not necessarily so. The title project director suggests a senior manager who has a number of project managers under their wing guiding them in the right direction when they stray from the right path. Of course a programme manager will also be directing a number of project managers, so what is the difference between a project director and a programme manager? A programme is where a number of distinct projects fit together to make a whole. Consequently a programme manager will be managing or directing project managers towards the ultimate goal of the programme. However, a project director may be directing several project managers whose projects have absolutely no relationship with each other.

Table 11.1   Leadership styles

Managers	Leaders
Administer	Innovate
Ask how and when	Ask what and why
Focus on systems	Focus on people
Do things right	Do the right things
Maintain	Develop
Rely on control	Inspire trust
Have a short term perspective	Have a longer-term perspective
Accept the status quo	Challenge the status quo
Have an eye on the bottom line	Have an eye on the horizon
Imitate	Originate
Emulate the classic good soldier	Are their own person
Copy	Show originality

2   Bennis, W. 1989. *On Becoming a Leader.* Addison Wesley, New York.

THE IMPORTANCE OF LEADERSHIP

Teams can be managed by a manager and will work reasonably successfully – for a while. Imagine yourself working in a team in which the manager is doing all the things above on the left, but none of the things on the right. How long will it survive? How long will you stay?

How far would Greek culture have spread without Alexander the Great? Would Britain have defeated Napoleon without Nelson and Wellington?

Throughout human history, tribes have always required leaders. Some are good, some are bad. There are often leadership contests and coups. Leaders die and are mourned but are always replaced. The king is dead, long live the king!

DIFFERENT TYPES OF LEADERSHIP

Hersey, Blanchard and Johnson[3] characterized leadership style in terms of the amount of direction and the amount of support that leaders provide to their followers.

Leadership is characterized as:

- Directive
- Coaching
- Supporting
- Delegating.

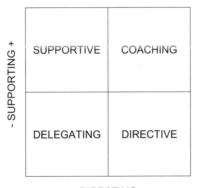

Figure 11.1   Leadership styles

---

3   Hersey, P., Blanchard, K.H. and Johnson, D.E. 1988. *Management of Organizational Behaviour*, 9th edn.Prentice Hall, Englewood Cliffs, NJ.

Leaders need to be flexible with their management styles because the effectiveness of each of these styles depends on the competence and commitment of those following the leader. Inexperienced and uncommitted staff will need more direction whereas highly experienced and committed staff can be delegated to (but not ignored) with confidence.

It is worth remembering that great leaders can be very different and have very different yet successful styles.

Some people say that not everybody has the inherent skills to be a leader. I think that by the time you have finished reading this chapter you might question that. What is certainly true is that some people prefer to lead and some prefer to follow at any particular point in their personal development. It is a question of comfort zones with respect to responsibility, confidence and trust.

John Adair[4] has modelled leadership using overlapping circles, as shown in Figure 11.2.

Adair's point is that leaders must address the needs of the task, the team and the individual to succeed in leading a project. It is only through the power of the team that major tasks will be achieved and the team need to clearly understand what the task is. Equally the team will fall apart if the needs of each individual are not addressed and their role in the team well recognized and valued.

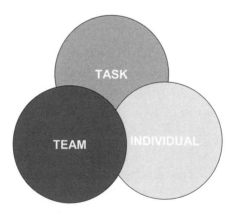

Figure 11.2   Task – team – individual

---

4   Adair, J. 1988. *Effective Leadership*. Pan, London.

This model might seem simplistic but there is much to recommend keeping things simple. The human brain can cope well with three things but begins to struggle with four. Perhaps we learn this as children, or perhaps it is recognized that this is the case and influences the way we are taught. A, B, C, ... 1, 2, 3, three blind mice, the three musketeers, airway, breathing, circulation; faith, hope and charity, three kings and so on. Politicians will often try to make three points in their speeches, even when there is only one, for example Tony Blair's 'education, education, education'.

To exploit the 'power of three' myself, I offer the model shown in Figure 11.3 to represent what projects are all about.

The vision is paramount. Without a clear sense of purpose, stated objectives and understanding of the tasks to be achieved a project will achieve nothing.

The players must be inspired to achieve the project objectives and be clear about their roles and responsibilities. They must become a team and work together productively with a culture that encourages success.

The project must be appraised to check that it will add value to the organization. Thereafter it must be planned carefully so that the team know the tasks to be done, what quality is required, when the tasks must be done and the budget available to perform those tasks. The performance of the project must be measured to ensure that it is on track towards a successful outcome and if not corrective action taken.

In so far as leadership can be considered a process, Figure 11.4 seeks to illustrate it.

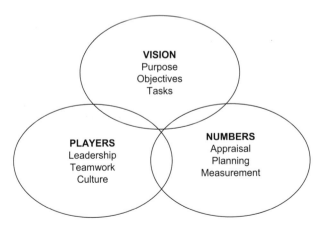

Figure 11.3   Vision – players – numbers

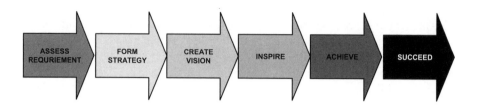

Figure 11.4   The leadership process

The paragraphs that follow explain each step's part in the leadership process.

Assessing the Requirement

Managers ask how and when, leaders ask what and why. Managers do things right, leaders do the right things.

Good leadership includes having a long hard look at what your team is required to deliver: is it the right thing? Is there something else that better meets the need? A value management approach could yield important insight as well as helping the team to gel together.

Forming a Strategy

If you have worked out what needs to be done then forming a strategy is about deciding on the best way to deliver it. That will include aspects of:

- Risk assessment – what could make us fail and how to prevent it
- Team selection
- Roles and responsibilities
- Identification of deliverables, level of detail and so on
- Tools to be used and compatibility of systems
- Communication channels to be used, frequency of meetings and so on
- Plan – who does what when?
- How can this project develop our team, our people and our reputation?

Creating a Vision

See Chapter 7 and the SERVE model.

Inspiring

The DTI's Inspired Leadership study[5] found the following six essential elements of 'inspirational leadership'.

Inspirational leaders:

1. Genuinely care about their people
2. Involve everybody
3. Show lots of appreciation
4. Ensure work is fun
5. Show real trust
6. Listen a lot.

These are not difficult things to do, are they, but how many of our leaders exhibit these traits? The memorable ones I bet! Because simple as they are, they are really, really rare and valuable traits.

If you can inspire your team through communicating a shared vision of the objective, then your team will deliver the equivalent of landing a man on the moon for you.

ACHIEVING

Good news, you can start to relax now. It isn't you but your team that will deliver success. The leader can relax. You've done all the hard work. You've identified the right things to do, the strategy, turned it into a communicable vision and inspired your team to deliver it. Of course you still have to keep it fun, ensure that everyone is involved, make sure that everybody is happy and keep cheering them on. By this stage you should also be a great ambassador for them, singing their praises from the hilltops and ensuring that they get the recognition they deserve.

Arrrrgh, I almost forgot. You don't double up as the manager do you? In that case you've got to do all that boring administrating, doing things right, watching the bottom line etc.

Perhaps you should have trained someone in your team to do that!

---

5   http://www.berr.gov.uk/files/file10989.pdf.

Succeeding

> *Succeed: verb 1 achieve an aim or purpose. 2 attain fame, wealth, or social*
> *status. 3 take over an office, title, etc., from (someone). 4 become the new*
> *rightful holder of an office, title, etc. 5 come after and take the place of.*
> *ORIGIN Latin succedere 'come close after'*. Oxford English Dictionary

What a wonderful word succeed is! The difference between achieving and succeeding is that success looks to what comes afterwards. Kennedy sadly never saw Armstrong and Aldrin step onto the moon, but he had set in place the vision that would ensure that they did.

The mark of a leader is their focus on the people. A leader will develop the team and nurture the next generation of leaders.

It is your team who will achieve for you, therefore there are two tools included below that will help you to understand your team and the process of building a team.

Arguably the two most important insights into how teams work have come from Belbin[6] and Tuckman.[7]

TEAM COMPOSITION AND ROLES

Belbin found through his research that an effective team has members that cover eight key roles in the management of the team. These roles may be separate from the role that that person has in carrying out the work of the team.

On Belbin's website you will find his definition of the roles that he identified and questionnaires to identify what your own Belbin team role style is (http://www.belbin.com).

The important thing is to recognize the important contribution that each role makes to an effective team. When I first learnt of Belbin's team roles I immediately recognized each of these roles in action within the civil engineering department of Foster Wheeler where I worked. You will also see the roles played out on successful company boards and even in films: the classic war film *The Great Escape* is a

---

6   Belbin, R.M. 1981. *Management Teams: Why they Succeed or Fail.* Butterworth Heinemann, London.
7   Tuckman, B. 1965. Developmental sequence in small groups. *Psychological Bulletin*, 63, 384–399.

good example. I would like to translate Belbin's team roles into the vernacular and illustrate them with some examples.

Executive	Provides the drive and motivation to get things done. The Chief Executive Officer of a company perhaps. Executives can ride roughshod over people in their desire to get things done. Richard Attenborough's character in *The Great Escape* was a typical Executive.
Chair	The chair ensures that due process is observed and that all team members have their say. The requirement to separate the CEO and Chairman roles on company boards as required by good corporate governance is obvious when looked at from the team perspective. James Donald's character was the senior British officer and played this role.
Ideas person	Steve McQueen was always coming up with new escape ideas. Inventors and creative people often struggle to get their ideas implemented without the support of a team of marketing, finance and production people. However, it should also be remembered that nothing happens without the flow of creative ideas.
Worker	Workers take ideas and start assembling systems to implement them. James Coburn played the manufacturer who made many of the tunnelling tools and bellows for pumping air underground. Likewise, Charles Bronson was the tunnel king doing much of the work on the tunnels.
Detailer	Attention to detail is not everyone's speciality. However, the permits and travel documents forged by Donald Pleasence obviously required great attention to detail.
Procurer	Procuring raw materials, equipment and specialists is an important role in any project. James Garner played the scrounger who had a particular skill for bribing German guards and finding other ways to obtain items necessary for the escape.
Critic	The critic is often not a popular role but it is vital to have someone who can identify the flaws in an idea. Gordon Jackson played the intelligence officer and was rigorous at looking for and identifying where things could go wrong.
Human resources	With all the activity taking place on a project, and with each team member focusing on their role, it is inevitable that people will clash. It is therefore useful to have someone on the team attuned to the 'atmosphere' and team member's feelings.

TEAM BUILDING

Tuckman proposed the forming, storming, norming, performing model of the phases in the development of a team. He argues convincingly that these phases are all necessary and inevitable for the team to develop and deliver results.

I have never watched it myself but a colleague (who shall remain nameless to protect his dignity) has watched *Big Brother* on the TV and says that this process of forming, storming, norming and performing is clearly demonstrated amongst the contestants in the Big Brother House.

Since projects have to deliver results in a relatively short period of time it is desirable that teams reach the performing stage as quickly as possible. However, it is equally important that they perform really well which means that they must get the most out of the forming, storming and norming stages. It is not helpful to skip a stage. Teams can in fact jump back from performing to storming if a team member is changed, particularly the leader.

So what use are these tools? How often do you get to choose your team? Not often perhaps, but you can do the following:

Assess which Belbin team roles you have in your team and which are missing. You might then be able to recruit the missing ingredient into the team or encourage someone for whom the missing role is a secondary one of theirs, to turn the volume on it up a bit.

You can use a team building event to speed up the forming, storming, norming, performing process. Please note that, for this to work, the team do actually need to be engaged on a task involving teamwork. Drinking large volumes of alcohol won't work on its own. An outdoor adventurous activity is a favourite with many,

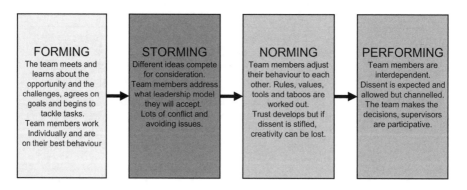

Figure 11.5   Tuckman's forming, storming, norming, performing

but for the less adventurous making a model of a nuclear power station out of cereal packets and egg boxes can work. A trainer/facilitator is essential to coach the team through each phase and debriefs afterwards.

In conclusion, teamwork is the vehicle that will deliver the project. The ingredients of good teamwork are good leadership, with a clear vision of the objective and the strategy for getting there and rounded team composition, with the necessary diversity of ideas and behaviours.

CHAPTER 12

PROJECT PLANNING

BACKGROUND TO PROJECT MANAGEMENT

At the beginning I would like to try and avert any difficulty with terminology. The key deliverable of project planning is, unsurprisingly, a plan which documents what needs to be done, when and by whom. This is, as shown in Figure 12.1, often expressed in the form of a Gantt chart. You will find this document sometimes also referred to as a bar chart, a plan, a programme or a schedule. In the UK you will often hear this sort of plan referred to as a project programme, whereas in the USA it is a schedule. Use of the word programme causes additional confusion both because Americans spell it program and because it means a portfolio of projects. I will endeavour to use the word schedule rather that programme and if I want to refer to a portfolio of projects I will use the American spelling.

The science of modern project management really began in the early 1900s with what we know as the Gantt chart, after Henry Gantt who made it popular in the Western world, although the engineer, economist and management researcher Karol Adamiecki had introduced a similar chart slightly earlier in Poland. A Gantt chart (see Figure 12.1) represents tasks or activities as horizontal bars against a background of time. The length of the bar is how long the task is expected to take and where it is positioned to the left or right is when in time it is expected to take place.

The next step in the development of project management science came in the 1950s when the Program Evaluation and Review Technique (PERT) was developed to help the US Navy control the Polaris nuclear missile programme. At roughly the same time the Du Pont Corporation developed the critical path method. Both of these methods graphically modelled the logical sequence of tasks in a project or programme. A network diagram is produced and the longest path (in time terms) from start to finish is the critical path and represents the expected duration of the project.

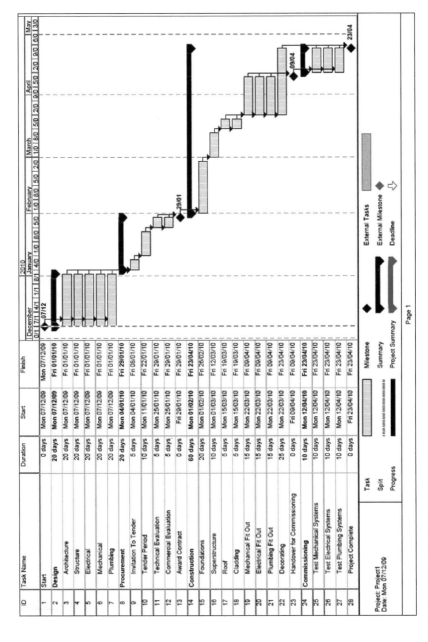

Figure 12.1   A Gantt chart

PROJECT LOGIC NETWORK

Project planning is virtually always done now using computer software. However, in order to understand what the computer is doing and the terminology it is useful to know how planning was done on paper. I will use preparing Christmas dinner as a simple example.

The network is prepared using node symbols such as shown in Figure 12.2.

Using these symbols a network is drawn which represents the logic connecting the activities. For the Christmas dinner example the network is shown in Figure 12.3.

For this example I have chosen to use minutes as the units for activity durations.

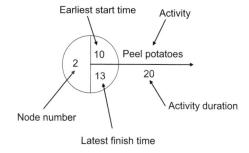

Figure 12.2   A network node

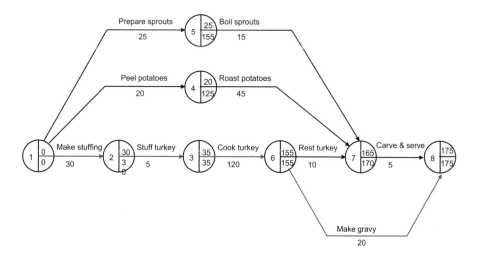

Figure 12.3   A critical path analysis network

CRITICAL PATH ANALYSIS

There are four possible pathways through this network. The path through nodes 1 – 2 – 3 – 6 – 7 – 8 I shall call the turkey path. The path 1 – 4 – 7 – 8 I shall call the roast potato path. The path 1 – 5 – 7 – 8 I shall call the Brussels sprout path, and finally the path through nodes 1 – 2 – 3 – 6 – 8 I shall call the gravy path. For each pathway we make a forward pass through it adding activity duration to the earliest start of the previous node in order to find the earliest start of the subsequent node. We look for the longest path through the network and this is known as the critical path. In this example the path 1 – 2 – 3 – 6 – 8, the gravy path is the critical path. The final node (node 8) will have a latest finish time equal to its earliest start time as determined by the critical path. For each path we then do a backwards path where we subtract the activity duration from the each node's latest finish time in order to determine the latest finish time of the preceding node. For each node the difference between the latest finish time and the earliest start time is the float that we have on the activity preceding that node. Thus I have 5 minutes spare for resting the turkey because from when the turkey comes out of the oven and I take the juices for the gravy it will take 5 minutes longer to make the gravy than I need for resting and carving the bird. I also have 105 minutes float available for peeling the potatoes. Either my wife can start peeling them at the same time as I start making the stuffing and keep them in cold salted water until the potatoes need to go in the oven or she can leave me to start peeling them 20 minutes before they need to go in the oven. There are 130 minutes float available for preparing the Brussels sprouts for similar reasons. Note that these large floats do not apply to cooking the potatoes or sprouts because they need to be completed just prior to serving for best results.

COMPUTER PLANNING PACKAGES

With the advent of computers more powerful planning and analysis become possible on more complex project networks. The Christmas dinner project has been modelled in one of the many powerful project management software packages available. The network appears as shown in Figure 12.4.

The network layout is useful for tracing the logical relationships between activities and when project networks were drawn out by hand on A0 sheets of drawing film it was the vehicle for calculating float and determining the critical path. Personally, I feel that the human eye and hand can lay out a network more efficiently than the computer can, as I think the examples show. These days if I do feel the need to print off a network diagram I regret it because a relatively simple network uses far more sheets of paper than a hand drafted network would, precisely because the planning software is not as economical at laying out the diagram as the human eye is. The

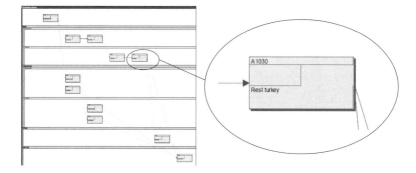

Figure 12.4   A software-drawn network

Gantt chart is a more compact way of showing the schedule and the relationship logic. The Gantt chart for the Christmas dinner project is shown in Figure 12.5.

Planning software does allow us to do sophisticated things, such as creating a range of calendars and assigning calendars to particular activities or resources. For example, although most activities and resources will work to a standard five-day calendar with holidays as non-work periods there may be some activities that can only take place at weekends or on bank holidays.

From the mid-1970s, due to developments in computing, it became realistic to consider the effect of resource requirements (manpower, money, materials) for tasks and to defer, in the plan, tasks which would otherwise compete for resources with more critical tasks. This is (hopefully) a simple explanation of resource levelling.

With the development of powerful personal computers, project management software has become easily available to even the smallest of projects. Given that virtually all project management software packages are designed to analyse resource usage (planned and actual) as well task linkages and durations, then the Gantt chart and budget, arguably the project manager's two most referred-to documents, are available in one package.

COST REPORTS AND FORECASTING

For the Christmas dinner project I have entered resources i.e. Chef; Assistant Chef; turkey; potatoes; brussel sprouts and gas. I have entered costs per unit for the materials (turkey, potatoes etc.) and costs per hour for the chefs and the gas. I have

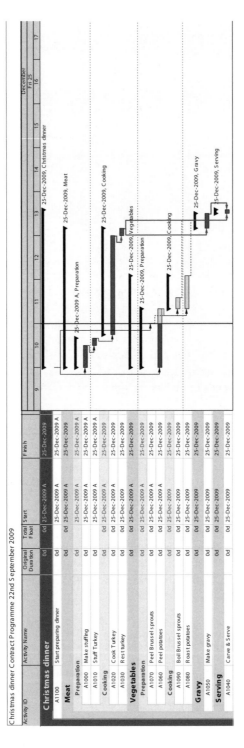

Figure 12.5 The plan for Christmas dinner

then assigned resources to the activities. I now find that my project budget for Christmas dinner is £126.98 as shown in a cost report (Figure 12.6).

CC-01 Cost Control - Summary by Activity

WBS Activity ID	Activity Name		Budgeted	Pct Cmp	Actual	Actual This Period	Estimate to Complete	Forecast
Innovative Construct								
NEWPROJ-1								
A1100	Start preparing dinner	ES: 25-Dec-2009 EF: Dec-2009 LS: 5-Dec-2009 LF: 5-Dec-2009 TF:						
	RD: 0d	£0.00		100%	£0.00	£0.00	£0.00	£0.00
NEWPROJ-1.2								
NEWPROJ-1.2.1								
A1000	Make stuffing	ES: 25-Dec-2009 EF: Dec-2009 LS: 5-Dec-2009 LF: 5-Dec-2009 TF:						
	RD: 0d	£26.03		100%	£26.03	£25.03	£4.17	£30.20
A1010	Stuff Turkey	ES: 25-Dec-2009 EF: Dec-2009 LS: 5-Dec-2009 LF: 5-Dec-2009 TF:						
	RD: 0d	£4.17		100%	£4.17	£4.17	£4.17	£8.34
Subtotal			£30.20		£30.20	£29.20	£8.34	£38.55
NEWPROJ-1.2.2								
A1020	Cook Turkey	ES: 25-Dec-2009 EF: Dec-2009 LS: 5-Dec-2009 LF: 5-Dec-2009 TF: 0d						
	RD: 0d	£22.53		62.5%	£34.42	£34.42	£5.01	£39.42
A1030	Rest turkey	ES: 25-Dec-2009 EF: Dec-2009 LS: 5-Dec-2009 LF: 5-Dec-2009 TF: 0d						
	RD: 0d	£0.83		0%	£0.00	£0.00	£0.83	£0.83
Subtotal			£23.36		£34.42	£34.42	£5.84	£40.26
Subtotal			£53.56		£64.62	£63.62	£14.18	£78.80
NEWPROJ-1.1								
NEWPROJ-1.1.1								
A1060	Peel potatoes	ES: 25-Dec-2009 EF: Dec-2009 LS: 5-Dec-2009 LF: 5-Dec-2009 TF: 0d						
	RD: 0d	£13.35		0%	£5.01	£0.00	£8.34	£13.35
A1070	Peel Brussel sprouts	ES: 25-Dec-2009 EF: Dec-2009 LS: 5-Dec-2009 LF: 5-Dec-2009 TF: 0d						
	RD: 0d	£17.94		50%	£15.85	£8.34	£0.00	£15.85
Subtotal			£31.29		£20.86	£8.34	£8.34	£29.20
NEWPROJ-1.1.2								
A1080	Roast potatoes	ES: 25-Dec-2009 EF: Dec-2009 LS: 5-Dec-2009 LF: 5-Dec-2009 TF: 0d						
	RD: 0d	£12.10		0%	£0.00	£0.00	£12.10	£12.10
A1090	Boil Brussel sprouts	ES: 25-Dec-2009 EF: Dec-2009 LS: 5-Dec-2009 LF: 5-Dec-2009 TF: 0d						
	RD: 0d	£5.42		0%	£0.00	£0.00	£5.42	£5.42
Subtotal			£17.52		£0.00	£0.00	£17.52	£17.52
Subtotal			£48.81		£20.86	£8.34	£25.86	£46.72
NEWPROJ-1.3								
A1050	Make gravy	ES: 25-Dec-2009 EF: Dec-2009 LS: 5-Dec-2009 LF: 5-Dec-2009 TF: 0d						
	RD: 0d	£18.35		0%	£0.00	£0.00	£18.35	£18.35
Subtotal			£18.35		£0.00	£0.00	£18.35	£18.35
NEWPROJ-1.4								
A1040	Carve & Serve	ES: 25-Dec-2009 EF: Dec-2009 LS: 5-Dec-2009 LF: 5-Dec-2009 TF: 0d						
	RD: 0d	£6.26		0%	£0.00	£0.00	£6.26	£6.26
Subtotal			£6.26		£0.00	£0.00	£6.26	£6.26
Subtotal			£126.98		£85.48	£71.96	£64.66	£150.13
Subtotal			£126.98		£85.48	£71.96	£64.66	£150.13
Total			£126.98		£85.48	£71.96	£64.66	£150.13

Figure 12.6   A cost report

If we have allocated resources to the activities in the schedule and if we have assigned appropriate costs to the use of the resources then we have a very powerful method for measuring progress available to us called earned value analysis (EVA).

EARNED VALUE ANALYSIS

After we have completed our plan with all activities scheduled and resources assigned and the cost of using those resources estimated the plan 'knows' at any time in the schedule what value of work we should have achieved. This is known as *budget cost of work scheduled* (BCWS). We may have achieved more or less progress than we had planned to, and the value of the work that we have achieved is the *budget cost of work performed* (BCWP). We may have used more or less resources and they may have cost more or less to use than we had planned. Therefore there is an *actual cost of work performed* (ACWP). At the point in time when we measure our performance, the difference between the BCWS (the value of work which we had planned to do) and the BCWP (the value of work which we have actually done) is a measure of our performance in terms of time. The difference between BCWP (the value of work we have actually done) and ACWP (the actual cost of the work we have actually done) is a measure of our performance in cost terms.

There are various ways in which these can be interpreted. The indicators I find useful are schedule variance index (SVI) and cost performance index (CPI).

$$SVI = \frac{(BCWP - BCWS)}{BCWS}$$

If the SVI is positive then we are ahead of schedule, if it is negative then we are behind schedule.

$$CPI = \frac{BCWP}{ACWP}$$

If the CPI is more than 1.0 or 100 per cent then that indicates that we are under budget. A CPI less than 1.0 or 100 per cent indicates that we are over budget.

As we cook our Christmas dinner we update the schedule with details of progress together with how much time the chefs have actually spent and how much the ingredients actually cost.

The earned value plot (Figure 12.7) shows that we have gradually fallen behind programme until time now (12 noon). Also we have actually been spending more to achieve what we have achieved than budgeted. The BCWP, i.e. what we budgeted to have spent to achieve the progress that we have made, and the ACWP i.e. what we have actually spent to achieve the progress that we have made, are forecast ahead as dotted FBCWP and FACWP lines based upon current trends. Christmas dinner looks like it will be about 45 minutes late and £20 over budget. If we are unhappy with that we have to examine our options.

Projects are traditionally a balance of cost time and performance (or quality) as represented by the triangle in Figure 12.8.

We could bring in additional chefs to assist perhaps, although where we will find them on Christmas day I don't know. Perhaps we could turn the oven temperature up to cook the potatoes and turkey faster. These options would cost more in labour and energy costs respectively. We could try microwaving the turkey and potatoes for a while to accelerate the cooking. That will probably be detrimental to quality. If it's breaking the budget that is our main worry then we could fire the chef and leave the assistant chef to finish off. That would save money but almost certainly be detrimental to both quality and time.

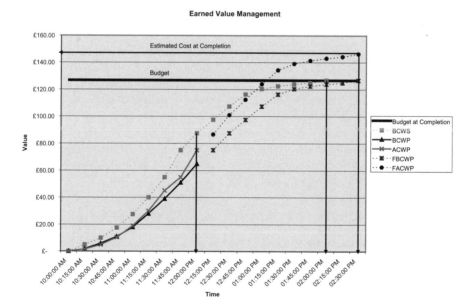

Figure 12.7   Earned value analysis

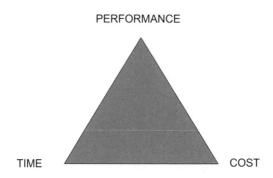

Figure 12.8   The project triangle

The Project Sponsor will be faced with these sort of trade-offs and will need to have a clear understanding of which is the most important factor. History suggests that quality problems usually persist long after budget or schedule overruns are forgotten. However, there are some projects like staging the Olympic Games, or opening a shopping mall for Christmas, where completion on time is fundamental.

OTHER METHODS OF MEASURING PROGRESS

There are other ways of measuring progress such as the achievement of milestones or weeks ahead of or behind critical path, but only earned value analysis gives us the whole picture. For example, if you try to monitor progress on your project by achievement of milestones you may be feeling confident that six out of eight milestones have been passed successfully and only two-thirds of your budget has been exhausted. However, the final two milestones may require half of the total effort, in which case your sense of confidence is unfounded. If you focus on how far ahead or behind plan you are relative to the critical path then you will miss lack of progress on activities which are not on the critical path. You may even find resources diverted from non-critical to critical activities. This is a logical course of action pursued by those who do not want the expense of bringing in additional resources from outside the project. The problem is that this may show some schedule recovery on the critical path initially but as the project end date approaches all activities will start to become critical and the project resources will be overwhelmed by the incomplete activities that have been starved of resources.

The reason why progress monitoring by milestone and/or by critical path is popular is that neither of these methods requires an assessment of the resources or even the cost of activities in the project schedule, and that is a time-consuming exercise. In truth all three methods of measuring progress should be employed.

As I have said, virtually every project planning software package on the market supports these processes. That's because this is the correct way to plan and monitor projects. However, I have to inform Project Sponsors that very often the planning software is used more like a drawing package for producing Gantt charts without accounting for resource requirements and quite often without even identifying the logical relationships between activities. This makes for poor planning, resource constraints that go unnoticed, over-optimistic schedules and suboptimal monitoring of progress.

I encourage Project Sponsors to discuss with prospective project managers their approach to project planning and see what they have to say about resources. You should also ask them to confirm how they will check that logical relationships between activities are correctly identified and incorporated within the plan.

It is very important to carry out a risk assessment and analysis on the schedule because it highlights the problem of parallel activities. This will be discussed in Chapter 15. There is almost always inherent, asymmetric risk in project schedules which passes unnoticed without a risk analysis and is a key reason why so many projects finish late.

Plans should be saved as a baseline, that is in the sense of a starting point used for comparisons. Although undesirable, it is often the case that plans change during the course of the project. Project managers, contractors and consultants will work to the latest plan. However, it is good practice to report progress against the baseline plan as well as the latest plan, not least because the baseline will usually be the plan against which the board has given authority to proceed.

CHAPTER 13

PROGRESS REPORTING

Project Sponsors are interested in progress reporting because they want to know how the project is going and to be reassured that it will be delivered on time, within budget, perform as required and that those working on it will be safe. Whenever this assurance is not forthcoming the sponsor needs to ask 'what is the plan to recover from the deficiency?'

The Project Sponsor should hold regular progress meetings with the project manager. The project manager will also hold regular progress meetings with the project team. It is perfectly reasonable for the Project Sponsor to attend the project manager's progress meetings occaisionally, as long as the Project Sponsor and project manager present a reasonably united front to the project team. The project manager's authority over the project team can be undermined by the sponsor, with the Project Sponsor becoming effectively the project manager as well. This happens if the project team see that all decisions are actually made by the sponsor. On the other hand the sponsor is the embodiment of the client and if the project manager and sponsor work effectively together this can send a powerful message to the project team.

It is really a matter for the Project Sponsor and project manager to work out between them how they are going to run project progress meetings. It is also a question of the time that the sponsor has available for attendance at project progress meetings and how frequent the meetings are. What I think works well is for the Project Sponsor and project manager to meet privately once a week for the project manager to update the sponsor on progress, any changes and key issues that are being tackled. In private the sponsor can air any concerns that they have and have an open exchange of views with the project manager. The attendance of the Project Sponsor at progress meetings should be made a special event with, perhaps, presentation of emerging design or tour of the site. These special events should not be isolated occasions but it is helpful if the sponsor's attendance is something a bit special and the sponsor is not seen by the team as a project manager of higher rank.

For the sponsor and project manager to have a useful dialogue it is important that the sponsor receive a written progress report and have time to read it before meeting with the project manager. The project manager's progress report will in fact summarize progress reports from project team members as well as including their own assessment. Consequently, the timing of progress reports and meetings will need to be carefully choreographed by the project manager to allow for processing of written reports in time for meetings.

The format of progress reports can be many and varied. However, the key items that Project Sponsors should look for are as follows:

HEALTH AND SAFETY

Nobody wants the joy of a successful project to be marred by the death or serious injury of a worker in delivering it. Consequently it is right and proper to have health and safety at the top of the agenda. If there have been any accidents or near misses since the last progress meeting these should be reported together with results of investigation into the cause and the steps that have been taken to prevent any further incidence. Projects often boast of the number of man-hours since a time losing injury. Whilst it is laudable to be proud of an excellent record for safety this must not become a report of how lucky the project has been not to have had an accident YET. It is far better to report proactively on the steps being taken to establish a safe working environment and safe methods of working. For example, I would rather see reports on safety inspections and the elimination of potential hazards, risk assessments and the risk management plan, safety training records and certification than how lucky we have been so far.

Sadly at present the phrase 'health and safety' has become a frequently used excuse for inaction – 'Can't do that, health and safety!' The press frequently publish news stories in which health and safety rules have seemingly prevented worthwhile activities. Hardly ever is this as a result of actual guidance or intervention by the health and safety regulators. Indeed, in the UK the Health and Safety Executive (HSE) have a page on their website dispelling myths of such activities supposedly prevented by the HSE.

I would like to redress the balance and affirm that not only is attention to health and safety important from the point of view of preventing accidents but that it positively helps get the job done too. It is said that a tidy ship is an efficient ship and an efficient ship is a happy ship. Certainly on a construction site tidiness promotes efficiency as well as safety. If it requires health and safety regulation to tidy up sites and instil efficient working practices, then so be it. You wouldn't want to entrust your life to surgeons in an operating theatre where the surgical instruments were strewn randomly across a trolley. Even in a well-ordered environment in which information can be found easily promotes efficiency, safety and quality.

QUALITY AND PERFORMANCE

It is said that the taste of poor quality will linger long after cost and delay issues are forgotten. I wouldn't want to suggest that cost and time are less important, because the business case depends on what the project costs, how soon it starts delivering results and how good those results are. However, there can be a tendency for project progress reports to focus on cost and schedule performance to the exclusion of quality and performance issues.

The Project Sponsor should seek to have quality control inspection and test results reported in the progress reports. Any trend towards deteriorating quality should be pounced on no less vigorously than schedule delay or cost overrun.

The project manager should identify in the progress report the action plan for correcting quality problems and reversing any adverse trends.

SCHEDULE

As discussed in Chapter 12, it is very easy to get a misleading view of project progress if project planning is inadequate, in particular if the plan is not resource loaded. Where the plan is not resource loaded (that is where the quantum of resource required for an activity is identified in the schedule) then the only way of reporting schedule process will be in terms of days or weeks ahead or behind schedule. Thus, a project manager or contractor may report, for instance, that they are one week behind schedule but will catch up this time. What they mean is that on the project's critical path they are one week behind where they had planned to be. This is an important measure of progress, but it masks what is or is not happening on non-critical activities. There is a natural tendency for resources to be diverted from non-critical onto critical activities. The problem with doing this is that non-critical activities fall farther behind and eventually all activities become critical with no time left to address them.

The sponsor should require both a report of progress against critical path *and* an earned value report with a graphical display of progress against plan in terms of the total volume of work achieved at the reporting date versus the total volume of work that should have been achieved.

We discussed earned value analysis (EVA) in Chapter 12. In Figure 13.1 the BCWP (budget cost of work performed) curve shows the actual progress achieved

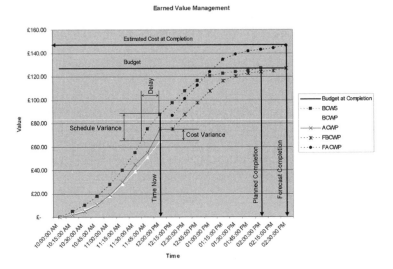

Figure 13.1   Project reporting using EVA

whilst the BCWS (budget cost of work scheduled) curve shows the progress which should have been achieved. Clearly we are behind schedule and action needs to be taken to address this.

The progress report should include a plan for getting back on schedule and, if it does not, the sponsor should demand to know why not.

COST

The performance of the project in cost terms is also portrayed in the earned value graph above. The ACWP is above the BCWP so we are heading for an overspend. This method of monitoring cost performance is excellent if the cost is actually known. This will be the case where all costs are completely reimbursable by the client and all cost data is transparent. However, this will rarely be the case. More commonly there will be one or more contracts for a fixed price and a process for agreeing contract variations or changes which result in additional cost. Consequently there will probably be a mixture of agreed additional costs, changes being negotiated and early warning of change requests yet to come.

All of this information should be clearly summarized in the progress report together with the reasons for the changes.

The Project Sponsor must reach an understanding with the project manager that a fair but robust approach should be taken with respect to agreeing contract changes. Contractors must be paid for changes to which they are legally entitled but not where they have submitted a low tender price and are seeking to recover losses through exploiting the change control process. The best way to avoid this is to minimize changes to the contractor's scope of work. If this is unavoidable then try to agree the cost of changes before instructing the change to be made and ensure that the agreed cost of change is based upon the tendered rates. However, whilst the project manager must negotiate robustly, reporting of the anticipated final cost should, whilst striving to be as accurate as possible, be a prudent assessment and not the project manager's optimistically hoped for outcome.

RISK

The progress report should include an update on the risk register and progress with mitigating outstanding risks. This should also be coordinated with the cost report. Where risks have been realized as changes these should be identified. Where the possibility of risk has passed then this should be noted and the risk removed from the risk register. The project manager should identify where contingency sums can be released or where the contingency is at risk of being insufficient.

CONTINUAL IMPROVEMENT

It is all too easy to bask in the glory of a project which is performing ahead of expectations or panic when the project is behind expectations. Time should be set aside for learning lessons from what has gone better than expected as well as what has gone worse than expected. Whatever lessons can be learnt should be incorporated into future plans and promulgated through the other projects in the organization.

CHAPTER 14

VALUE ENGINEERING

Value engineering alternatively known as value management or value analysis is a structured technique for achieving greater performance from the project at less cost – more bang for your buck, in other words.

The method was conceived by Lawrence D. Miles during the Second World War at General Electric, an American defence contractor that was struggling with shortages of materials. Miles focused on the function that a component is required to perform and sought to understand if there might be another way of fulfilling the function that was cheaper, faster or of better performance.

This concept is defined by the equation Value = Function/Resources. Function is the performance that the customer wants the project to deliver and resources are money, materials, time, labour etc. Consequently we look for ways of increasing the ratio of function to resources in a way that pleases the customer. Miles developed the technique of describing function with a verb and a noun. For example the basic function of a column might be *support beam*. There are often secondary functions. Columns in buildings are often decorated and designed to impress the owners of, or visitors to the building.

Figure 14.1 illustrates the principle that value engineering is most effective at the beginning of a project and of no benefit when the project is completed.

The process of value engineering through the means of a workshop is as follows:

1. Preparation:
   - Determine the scope and objectives of the workshop.
   - Organize the team and venue for the workshop including an experienced value engineering practitioner.
   - Gather information, e.g. vision statement, design information, cost information, areas of concern.
2. Workshop:
   - Review information. Understand the current project status and key constraints.

　　　　– Function analysis. Build a picture of the system under consideration starting from the highest order function. A FAST diagram (described later in this chapter) is an effective way to do this. The focus is what the project must do rather than what has already been done or conceived.

3. Creativity. Generate ideas about other ways in which the functions can be performed. Brainstorming can be a useful method to generate ideas (see Chapter 15) as can TRIZ (described later in this chapter). The way to have a good idea is to have many ideas and to discard the bad ones.

4. Evaluation. Identify which ideas look most promising and shortlist those ideas that warrant further development.

5. Development. Work up the shortlisted ideas with sketches, costs, benefits and risks.

　　　　– Present the ideas to the Project Sponsor for a decision on which idea to progress.

6. Implementation.

7. Document the value engineering workshop results.

8. Develop and action the plan for implementing the approved idea.

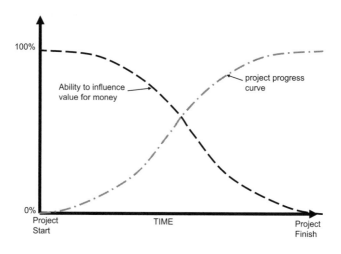

Figure 14.1   The effectiveness of value engineering

FAST TECHNIQUE

FAST – function analysis system technique – was devised by Charles W. Bytheway. It uses the verb–noun description of function in a box on a diagram (Figure 14.2).

You start at the left hand side of the paper with the highest order function and then work to the right describing the supporting functions and secondary functions.

You should build the diagram in the left to right HOW direction and test the project in the right to left WHY direction. Figure 14.3 shows the function to record information being broken down through supporting functions, the resulting product of which is likely to be a pencil. There is an apocryphal story told of the research effort that NASA put into designing a pen that would work in zero gravity: the Russians just used a pencil.

When we have developed our value engineering ideas or proposals we need a system for recording them and managing their development until they are either incorporated in the design or discarded. Figure 14.4 shows a typical value engineering proposal form. Notice in the bottom left-hand corner of the form an area where the impacts of the proposal in monetary terms can be estimated. It is important to assess operational costs and revenues as well as capital costs. Note also the outcome area in the bottom right-hand corner where the proposal will be marked as accepted, rejected or recommended for further development.

Figure 14.2   The FAST process

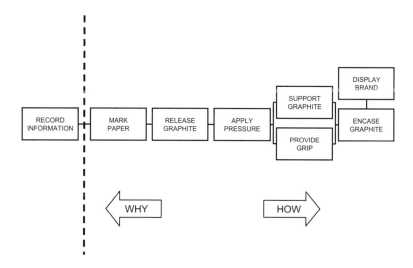

Figure 14.3   An example of FAST

VALUE ENGINEERING PROPOSAL   Proposal No   1

Proposal Title
Backfill disused dry dock.

Description of Current Solution
Redundant dry dock is to be used as a water feature adjacent to the new office building.

Description of Proposed VE Solution
Backfill dry dock and install shallow tray, say 250mm deep to form shallow water feature.

Advantages of the Proposal	
Overcomes problem of waterproofing basement car park. Safety benefits. Easier to maintain.	Consider safety, capital cost, operating & maintenance costs, quality, programme, revenue opportunity, risk & opportunity
Disadvantages of the Proposal	
Slightly less visually convincing as a water feature. Modification to design drawings required and short (approx. 1 week delay to tender).	

Implementation Plan
Change design and notify short-listed tenderers of 1 week delay to tender issue.

SUMMARY OF IMPACTS		OUTCOME	
Capital Cost Saving	£200,000	A= ADOPT	✓
PV of Operating Cost Saving	–		
PV of Maintenance Cost Saving	£15,000	R = REJECT	
PV of Revenue Enhancement	-£1,000		
Cost of Implementation	£5,000	D = DEVELOP	
Total of Proposed Saving	**£209,000**	FURTHER	

Figure 14.4   A value engineering proposal

A large project may have many hundreds of value engineering proposals to keep track of. If this is the case then a value engineering proposal register is helpful. Figure 14.5 shows a typical format for such a register.

VE Proposal No.	Date Entered	Proposal Title	Whole Life Cost Saving	Status	Proposal Owner
		VALUE ENGINEERING PROPOSAL REGISTER			
1	09/12/09	Backfill disused dry dock	£ 209,000	A	DW
2	09/12/09	Franchise kiosk in staff canteen	£ 150,000	D	JB
3	09/12/09	Steel frame instead of concrete frame	-£ 135,000	R	CD
4	09/12/09	Reduce number of lifts	£ 75,000	D	BH
5	12/02/10	Reduce car parking allocation	£ 10,000	D	DW
6	12/02/10	Degrade floor & wall finishes in offices	£ 110,000	A	BH
7					
8					
9					
10					
11					
12					

Figure 14.5   A value engineering register

TRIZ

TRIZ is the Russian acronym for the *theory of inventive problem solving* which was devised by G.S. Altshuller and colleagues. For further reading on this subject visit the website http://www.triz-journal.com, where many examples and resources for creativity can be found.

TRIZ works on the principle that someone somewhere has solved a similar problem in the past. You therefore generalize your specific problem, research how the general problem has been solved in the past and then see how the general solutions can be applied to your specific problem

Of particular interest on the website noted above is the 'Forty Inventive Principles' document where the 40 most common generic solutions to problems have been listed together with examples of their application.

CHAPTER 15

RISK MANAGEMENT

Projects are inherently risky because they are a departure from the organization's normal operations and rely (usually) on a team brought together especially for the project. Consequently project risk management assumes a very important profile.

WHAT IS MEANT BY RISK?

Uncertainty is inherent in risk. Risk events may or may not happen – they are not certain. For the purpose of analysis and planning we can assess the probability of a risk event happening and also assess the impact that the risk event will have if it does occur. For example archaeological artefacts may or may not exist under our site. We can assess the probability that artefacts exist on the site by reference to historical maps, consulting local historians and perhaps by non-intrusive surveys if access is available to do so. If they are present then the project will incur some delay and extra cost. That delay and extra cost is in itself uncertain and depends on the importance and extent of the finds.

Thus uncertainty is at the heart of risk, so much so that risk is often taken to be the probability of the risk event rather than the risk event itself. The *Oxford English Dictionary* defines risk as 'the possibility that something unpleasant will happen'.

Engineering risk is defined as the probability of the risk event multiplied by the consequence of the event if the risk event occurs.

$R = P$ (of the Event) $\times C$

Therefore risk is the expected consequence of the risk event.

The Health and Safety Executive define risk as the chance that a hazard might cause someone harm combined with an indication of how serious that harm might be.

In summary, risk is the probability of an uncertain event occurring multiplied by the consequence of that event if it were to occur. However, there is much sloppiness in terminology and you will find that sometimes the word risk will be used where the risk event (or hazard) is meant, sometimes it will be used in place of the probability of the risk event occurring and sometimes it will be used as defined above for the expected consequence of the risk event.

Whilst the OED defined risk in terms of something unpleasant, in projects opportunities may also be uncertain. The techniques for identifying, analysing and managing risks and opportunities are the same really, so from here on in please remember that risks may also be opportunities and that cost, time or quality impacts could be beneficial as well as detrimental etc. Indeed it is very important that the Project Sponsor pushes hard for the identification of opportunities. There will be a tendency for the project manager, designers and contractors to emphasize risk because this will have the effect of increasing their contingency allowance. The identification of opportunity helps provide a balance.

Often the difference between a risk and an opportunity depends upon what has been assumed in the budget and/or schedule. For example we might have a situation in a refurbishment project where we may or may not be able to reuse some existing equipment. If we cannot reuse the existing equipment, then new equipment will be required which will cost more and take longer. If we have made the assumption in the budget and schedule that the equipment will be reused, then there is clearly a risk that it will be found to be damaged and not reusable with consequent cost and schedule impacts. If however we had assumed in the budget and schedule that the equipment would need to be replaced, then there is the opportunity that the equipment will be found to be OK and there are cost and schedule 'upsides'.

AN OVERVIEW OF THE RISK MANAGEMENT PROCESS

At its simplest level the risk management process involves three key stages:

1. Identifying the risks – assessing what might happen.
2. Analysing the risks – assessing the expected impact of the risks on the project, prioritizing the risks for treatment and weighing the expected impact against the cost of treating the risk.
3. Risk treatment – doing something about the risk.

The process diagram (Figure 15.1) shows a circular process, because risk management should be iterative and new risks are always lurking around the corner.

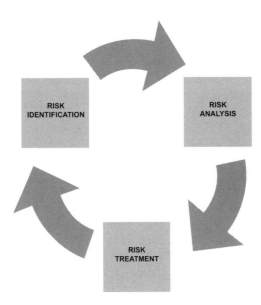

Figure 15.1   The risk management process

Some models of the risk management process include additional stages such as risk treatment planning, decision making, risk reporting, risk treatment monitoring, residual risk reporting etc. I think that they over complicate the process and I feel sure that you can see how these additional 'sub-stages' would fit into the simple process that I have drawn.

RISK MANAGEMENT TOOLS OVERVIEW

Tools for Risk Identification

A crystal ball would be handy, but they take a lot of training, embarrassing costumes and natural talent to use reliably. Consequently I recommend:

- Reviews of project documentation
- Benchmarking against previous, similar projects
- Checklists of typical risks
- Interviews with key project team members and stakeholders
- Brainstorming workshops.

Tools for Risk Analysis

Risk analysis has two main purposes:

- To prioritize the risks identified so that the most critically important risks receive urgent and effective attention.
- To forecast the impact of the risks upon the project cost and timescale such that the scale of risk treatment required can be assessed.

At its simplest level, the first purpose can be achieved by a risk matrix (Figure 15.2). Risks that have been identified are assigned a probability of occurring in a high, medium, low-type format and also an impact if they do occur. They can then be plotted on a matrix such as that shown here and clearly those risks expected to have a high probability of occurring and also a high impact if they do occur are the top priority. However, a risk matrix doesn't do anything to help with the second purpose of forecasting the effect of risk on the project's cost and timescale. To achieve that, a Monte Carlo simulation is now the tool of choice.

Monte Carlo simulation packages exist as add-ins to spreadsheet and project planning software. They work by modelling probability distributions such that the uncertainty surrounding inputs such as package costs or activity durations can be replaced by an appropriate probability distribution and the effect on the output can be shown. Identifying the probabilities and potential impacts is usually a matter of judgement based on the collective experience of the project team. The inputs that we provide to the Monte Carlo simulation are generally speaking probability distributions in place of the key discrete numbers. Using the Monte Carlo software we can do this for activity durations, costs, resource availability, resource cost etc. For example, we can replace a duration of five days with a triangular probability distribution in which the most likely duration is five days, the minimum duration is three days and the maximum duration is ten days. Or we can say that project approval has a 70 per cent chance of being submitted at this month's board meeting

	Very Low	Low	Medium	High	Very High
Very High	009		008, 025	006, 031, 036, 044	019, 022, 027, 033, D7, E2
High		032	004, 005, 016, 020	011, 012, 013, 015, 017, 024, 026, 028, 037, 040, 042, 053, C9, C10, E6	001, 021, A1, E9
Medium			010, 034	003, 041, E10	049
Low		048	007	046, 047	054
Very Low					

Figure 15.2   A risk matrix

but if not then it will definitely be ready for the following month. Probabilistic branching can also be created in which various alternative scenarios can occur and each can be given its own probability of occurrence. This might be useful for the earlier example of archaeological remains being found in which excavation will be planned differently depending on whether remains are found or not.

This is important because discrete numbers or averages don't always convey the full picture.

The Monte Carlo simulation runs thousands of iterations in which a random number generator works to replicate the probability distribution identified for each duration or cost risk. For each iteration there will be a result in terms of the project end date and total cost. These are stored and the next iteration is run. Thus thousands of results for project end date and cost are built up and these are displayed as histograms and the chances of achieving any particular end date or budget cost can be seen. Also the influence of any one risk on the final outcome can be determined more accurately than with the risk matrix.

TOOLS FOR RISK TREATMENT

Having identified risks and prioritized them, the next step is to identify risk treatments. These can be identified using similar techniques to identifying risks, i.e. by brainstorming amongst the project team, looking at what other projects have done and asking experts. The main thing then is to ensure that the appropriate risk treatment actions are followed through. A risk register in which risks, probabilities, impacts, consequences, owners and actions are logged is useful for tracking this.

THE BENEFITS OF PROJECT RISK MANAGEMENT

In the project management environment, as in so many walks of life, we can get so carried away with what we are trying to achieve, what we have to do, and the urgency of it all that we simply don't take time out to think about what might go wrong.

Edward de Bono, in his book *Six Thinking Hats*,[1] describes how you should look at problems with six different mindsets, symbolized by different coloured hats. One of these is the black hat. As de Bono *says* 'Black Hat thinking is one of the real benefits of this technique, as many successful people get so used to thinking positively that often they cannot see problems in advance. This leaves them under-prepared for difficulties.'

---

1   de Bono, E. 1985. *Six Thinking Hats*. Harmondsworth, Penguin.

Another key benefit of project risk management is that it exposes the problem of parallel activities. In most projects, overlapping of activities occurs. This is entirely appropriate since it speeds the project up, but it is at the cost of increased risk.

The simple project shown in Figure 15.3 would clearly have a three-week overall duration, any project planning software would confirm that. However, if we consider the three parallel activities in the middle and make the assumption that each of them can either finish early (E) or late (L) then the possible scenarios for the three parallel activities are: EEE, EEL, ELE, ELL, LEE, LEL, LLE, LLL. One of these scenarios (EEE) is a happy outcome and seven are unhappy because they include at lease one late outcome which delays the subsequent activity. Thus although planning these three activities in parallel was a good idea because it turned what would have been a five-week schedule into three, it has stacked the odds seven to one against achieving that schedule. Monte Carlo simulation would allow us to model the risk, perhaps by saying that the duration of each activity can be represented by a triangular probability distribution with a most likely duration of five working days plus or minus two. This symmetrical modelling of risk many experienced project managers, who haven't thought through the example above, would expect to show a most likely overall duration as per the plan.

The simple project Gannt chart that was shown in Figure 12.1 has been modelled using Monte Carlo simulation in which each activity has been given a triangular probability distribution in which the most likely duration is as planned: the minimum duration is 90 per cent of the planned duration and the maximum duration is 110 per cent of the planned duration. The resulting distribution of end date is as shown below in Figure 15.4.

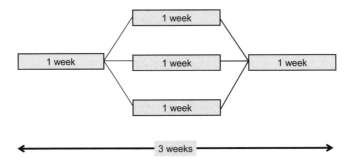

Figure 15.3   The problem of parallel activities

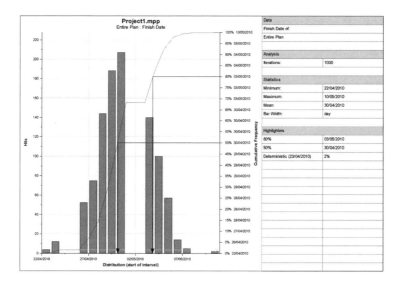

Figure 15.4 A Monte Carlo simulation

The result is that the probability of achieving the planned end date of 23 April 2010 is only 2 per cent. This is a fundamental reason why so many projects finish late, yet surprisingly few project professionals understand it. A sensitivity test on the schedule using Monte Carlo with, say, plus or minus 10 per cent applied to all activity durations will help identify this problem and allow a more robust schedule to be created. Project sponsors must push for this to be done as early as possible before the schedule becomes cast in stone. In order to achieve an acceptable schedule with a realistic chance of completion on time it will probably be necessary to shorten a number of activity durations. This must be done early on so that those responsible for delivery prepare themselves for the earlier delivery. If someone is given three weeks to deliver an activity they will usually take three weeks, even if they could have done it in two.

THE PROCESS OF RISK MANAGEMENT

Risk Identification

Ideally, each of the following methods should be used for risk identification. It is probably also useful to revisit some of them. For example, after the workshop it might be beneficial to carry out more interviews or benchmarking to obtain more information on a risk issue loosely identified at the workshop. If, however, time is strictly limited then a workshop probably provides the greatest value of any one method. When using any of the methods below bear in mind what information you need to obtain and capture in the risk register.

A first stage in risk identification is to review project documentation. For example:

- *Contracts* Check commitments made to clients. Are these fully covered back to back in subcontracts? What compensation events are there in subcontracts? What interfaces are there between contractors/designers? Are there any items of scope that fall down the gaps between contracts?
- *Cost plans* Are there and assumptions or exclusions stated or inferred? Are there any omissions?
- *Schedule* Is the schedule logic linked? Does the critical path seem sensible? Is the schedule resourced?

Any exclusion, assumption, caveat, gap or omission is a risk.

It makes sense to review previous, similar projects where possible and review what risks they faced to see what might be relevant for your project. Likewise, examine lessons learnt and contract variations incurred on similar projects.

Interviews are useful for exploring issues in depth and getting team members to open up in a way that they might not in front of their peers or superiors. The interviewers will create a climate of trust and may need to guarantee anonymity for any attribution of contentious risk statement.

A risk identification workshop has several advantages over the other methods:

- The lateral thinking encouraged by brainstorming is most likely to identify risks that the other methods will not.
- A workshop is useful for securing the buy-in of the project team to the risk-management process.
- It is a useful vehicle for getting the wider project team and stakeholders together and can be exploited as a team-building event.

The risks identified from the above methods should be captured and recorded in a risk register or risk log. A risk register can be a document, spreadsheet, database or proprietary software tool. Typically it will aim to capture the following information.

Risk ID	A sequential number given to each risk for ease of identification.
Risk title	In as few words as possible summarize the risk such that people who have read the risk register once will know exactly what you mean by reference to the risk title.
Risk description	Elaborate on the risk so that first-time risk-register readers will understand the risk.
Risk Consequence	Describe what will happen if the risk occurs. Since quality/ performance impacts are difficult to quantify this is where a qualitative description of quality/performance impact is best captured.
Probability	Define the probability of the risk occurring. This might be a % or a high, medium, low-type rating, preferably against pre-agreed criteria defining what in % terms is meant by high, medium or low.
Activity affected	Identify which activity or activities in the project schedule are affected by the risk. Be clear whether the impacts identified are applicable to each activity identified or are the effect on the project as a whole. This will affect the analysis.
Cost impact	Define the cost impact if the risk does occur. This might be in monetary units or a high, medium, low-type rating, preferably against pre-agreed criteria defining what in money terms is meant by high, medium or low.
Schedule impact	Define the schedule impact if the risk does occur. This might be in time units or a high, medium, low-type rating, preferably against pre-agreed criteria defining what in time terms is meant by high, medium or low.
Risk owner	Who is responsible for ensuring that risk treatment actions are completed? The risk owner should be the party who is best able to manage the risk.
Risk treatment action	Describe the actions agreed necessary to treat the risk.
Risk treatment cost	Estimate the cost of treating the risk.
Action by	Record a date when the risk must be treated by.
Risk status	Used to record the status of a risk, e.g. Open, Closed, Occurred.

A further level of sophistication is to consider the risk probabilities and impacts both before treatment (or mitigation) and afterwards. Having identified the risk and a treatment (or mitigation) for the risk, it would be too pessimistic, perhaps, to ignore this in the risk analysis. A common approach is to assess the contingency allowance necessary, both in time and money, on the basis of post-mitigation assessment. In other words we make a contingency allowance for the residual risks assuming that the risk treatments or mitigations that we have identified are as successful as we expect them to be. There is inevitably an element of risk in this approach. However, since we have encouraged the team to engage in black hat thinking, I think a degree of optimism associated with the risk treatment plan is a reasonable balance. I recommend that the project manager maintains a risk priority order based on the pre-treatment ranking until the treatment is seen to be effective. Figure 15.5 shows an example of a risk register spreadsheet with pre-mitigation and post-mitigation risk scoring. The risk score is the product of probability and cost impact where, for each, the most severe probability and impact are assigned a 5 and the least severe are assigned a 1. Therefore risk scores range from a maximum of 25 down to 1.

RISK ANALYSIS

Risk analysis has two main purposes:

1. To prioritize the risks identified so that the most critically important risks receive urgent and effective attention.
2. To forecast the impact of the risks upon the project cost and timescale such that the scale of risk treatment required can be assessed.

As described earlier in the overview of tools, prioritization of risks can be achieved through a simple risk matrix. However, the impact assessment is likely to be a mix of cost, time and performance impacts. It is unlikely to take account of the project's critical path accurately.

By carrying out a Monte Carlo simulation analysis using the data captured in the risk register above we can measure which risks are having the most effect on end date and also on cost. This can be displayed in a Tornado diagram, as shown in Figure 15.6. This enables the greatest possible efficiency in allocating resources to mitigating risks.

Monte Carlo simulation is the best tool for forecasting effects of risk on cost and timescale. Using this, outputs such as histograms of project cost versus probability, project end date versus probability and probabilistic cash flow can be obtained.

Risk ID	Risk Description	PRE - MITIGATION			Risk Response	Risk Mitigation Owner	RESIDUAL RISK POST MITIGATION		
		Probability of Occurrence	Cost Impact if Occurs	Overall Risk Score			Probability of Occurrence	Cost Impact if Occurs	Overall Risk Score
3	Surveys may find unknowns esp. condition of existing road.	Very Likely	H	20	Get surveys underway ASAP	CH	Likely	M	12
13	Agreement to street furniture may be delayed	Very Likely	L	10	Apply pressure on members & make consequences of delay known based on longest lead times	SJA	Very Likely	VL	5
36	Stats may need to be diverted	Unlikely	VH	10	Liaise with utilities & explore design changes to avoid diversion	CH	Unlikely	H	8
2	Objections to traffic orders permanent e.g. removal of loading facility	Likely	L	8	None	CH	Likely	L	8
16	Effect of construction on existing businesses. Borough may require sections of road to be kept open which would be extremely difficult to achieve safely.	Likely	L	8	Commence discussions with Borough and local businesses	SJA	Fairly Likely	L	6
23	H&S risks and consequent claims from trip injuries insurance excess.	Likely	L	8	Appropriate site management and careful selection of site management	TMF	Fairly Likely	L	6
14	Events in Wellingborough can affect construction programme	Fairly Likely	L	6	Discussion with Borough to discover timing of events & routes etc.	SJA	Fairly Likely	VL	3
11	This scheme sets materials to be used for the major town centre scheme. There may therefore be pressure on which supplier to use. Opportunity to negotiate bulk discount and need for security of supply for whole townwide schemes	Fairly Likely	L	6	Establish total material volumes for whole core area. Negotiate with suppliers to establish bulk discounts and security of supply.	SJA / SA	Fairly Likely	VL	6
18	Damage to existing stats	Fairly Likely	L	6	Radar surveys prior to excavation. Appropriate site management and careful selection of site management	CH / TG	Unlikely	L	4
32	Acceleration costs if project is delayed and acceleration imposed.	Fairly Likely	L	6	Robust project management	TG / SJA	Fairly Likely	L	6

Figure 15.5   A risk register

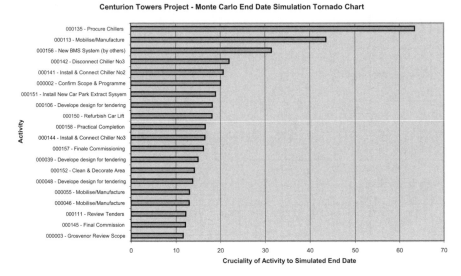

Figure 15.6   A tornado chart

RISK TREATMENT

Having prioritized risks for mitigation a number of techniques can be used for identifying mitigation actions. These include:

- Workshops with the project team, harnessing their combined intellect and experience.
- Benchmarking against other projects. What has been successful elsewhere in similar situations?
- Consulting experts.

Generically speaking risks can be:

- *Avoided*: change plan or method of working such that the risk is avoided
- *Transferred*: risks can be transferred to other parties through insurance or contracts
- *Reduced*: you can take mitigation actions to reduce the probability of the risk occurring or its impact if it does
- *Accepted*: you may decide that the risk should be accepted because the costs of avoiding, transferring or mitigating it outweigh the expected cost of the risk

MANAGING, TRACKING AND REPORTING RISK MITIGATION ACTIONS

The risk register is the tool for this. The risk register, as previously described at the end of the previous risk identification section, records a description of the risk and its consequences together with the risk treatment actions, risk owner and status. There are three secret keys to success:

1. The risk treatment/mitigation actions are no different to any other project activities designed to ensure the project's success. Incorporate them in the project plan
2. Review and report risk treatment at the project progress meetings and through the same channels as all other project reporting. If risk management is seen as something separate to the project it will fail
3. Do something! Action does need to be taken, don't just talk about it! Here's a question for you:

> There are five men sitting on a fence. One man decides to get off the fence, how many are left sitting on the fence?

Answer: five. There is a huge difference between deciding to do something and actually doing it!

Risks should be owned by the party best able to manage the risk.

TOOLS

Experts

I hope that this chapter has done much to demystify the subject of project risk management. However. there are several aspects for which calling in some expertise is efficient and adds value:

- As a fresh pair of eyes, ears and brain. Sometimes you can be so close to the project that you can't see the risks or their solutions even with the black hat on.
- To facilitate the risk brainstorming workshop. Facilitating a brainstorming meeting is different to chairing a meeting.
- For the risk analysis.

Workshop Facilitation Techniques

- Objectives – be clear about what you want to get out of the workshop. This might just be a completely freely brainstormed list of risks which your project may face that you can use to worry about and keep yourself awake at nights. However, to do the job properly you will need to get the following in order to inform the risk analysis stage:
  - A description of the risk.
  - Identification of the project activity or activities that it will impact.
  - An estimate of its probability of occurrence.
  - An estimate of its schedule impact if it does occur.
  - An estimate of its cost impact if it does occur.

Once the risk analysis has been done risks will be prioritized. Then a follow-up workshop can aim to generate:

- Risk mitigation actions for the top priority risks.
- Revised estimate of probability of occurrence if the mitigation action is progressed.
- Revised estimate of schedule impact if the mitigation action is progressed.
- Revised estimate of cost impact if the mitigation action is progressed.

Participants – this will vary depending on the project circumstances, suggested participants include:

- The facilitator – highly recommended. It's very different from chairing a meeting and it's very hard to both facilitate and contribute.
- Project sponsor.
- Project manager.
- Cost estimator – will know what risks were anticipated at pricing stage and what allowances are built into the budget.
- Planner – likewise will know what risks were anticipated at planning stage and what risk allowances may have been built into the plan.
- Design engineers – they're the guys thinking about the problems and how to solve them.
- Contractors – they have the construction perspective.
- Other stakeholders – consider those whose approval is required, particularly if they have approved similar projects in the past and will know what failings those projects had.
- A note-taker is helpful.
- Above all – a mix of skills, experience and viewpoints. You don't want a group all thinking the same thing.

Agenda – there are three aspects here:

- The agenda that tells the participants where to be and at what time; that reassures them that there is a structure to the workshop and that they will get an introduction as to what it is all about. They will need to know that they get coffee breaks and probably lunch. They will also need to know what time it finishes.
- The division of the workshop into two parts. The first part will be a structured brainstorming of the risk issues. The structure is to ensure that all aspects of the project are considered so that risk can be allocated to the project activity it relates to. However, it should still be a brainstorming with brains stimulated to roam across all potential risks. The second part of the workshop will be to quantify the probability, cost, time and performance impacts of the risks, either numerically or against pre-agreed high, medium, low scales. The quantification requires a less brainstorm more consensus view approach.
- The 'agenda' that stimulates brainstorm thinking about risk. Given that for a risk analysis of the schedule we will need to associate risks with the schedule activities they will affect, it makes sense to use the schedule for this. Since the schedule should include all the activities to be undertaken it also represents an agenda that will ensure that every aspect of the project is considered for risk. However, two things to remember:
  i) The size of the schedule. If you're dealing with a schedule of several hundred or even thousands of activities then you will have to work with headings from the work breakdown structure. The risk analyst will then need to use their judgement, in conjunction with the planner, to identify allocation of risk to specific activities.
  ii) Don't forget to ask the assembled brainpower if there is anything required of the project that has not been captured in the schedule.

If it is such early days in the project that there is not yet a schedule or budget (and I do encourage early risk management thinking) then STEEPLE is a useful mnemonic for stimulating risk thinking: social, technological, environmental, economic, political, legal, ethical.

Venue – this needs to be a room capable of comfortably accommodating the required attendees. It should be reasonably quiet and also isolated from interruptions. There should be space for the facilitator to move around and for flipcharts. It may be useful to have projection facilities for an introduction and project briefing. If there are a large number of participants then a PA system may help. Ability to stick flipchart pages around the room is useful.

Equipment/materials – whatever the facilitator needs but likely to include: copies of the agendas (both, see above) for all participants; flipcharts (several) and flipchart stands (two); Post-it™ notes (several packs, assorted colours); flipchart pens (assorted colours); projector and screen (possibly).

Ground rules – the traditional ground rules of brainstorming as set out in the 1940s by Alex Osborne[2] (if you're interested) are:

1. The goal of a 'brainstorming' session would be to come up with as many ideas as possible.
2. There would be absolutely no criticism of any thoughts or ideas.
3. No idea should be considered too outlandish and such ideas would be encouraged.
4. Members of a brainstorming team should build upon one another's ideas.

These rules hold good today and apply to the first part of the workshop, i.e. the risk identification rather than the quantification part. They will also very much apply to a follow-up mitigation identification workshop.

RISK CHECKLISTS

Checklists are a useful way of benchmarking against previous experience. For example, it can be very effective to review a schedule of the contract changes that were required on similar previous projects.

A sample risk checklist for a development project is shown in Figures 15.7a and 15.7b.

---

2   Osborne, A. 1942. *How to 'Think Up'*. McGraw Hill, New York.

Opportunity Identification	Site Identification	Team Assembly	Feasibility Study	Project Appraisal	Site Acquisition
Demand - the market cycle. If residential is the requirement now, will it still be so when the opportunity comes to market?	Prospects of obtaining planning permission	Competency?	Planning context	Identification of sunk costs	Site valuation - paying too much will severely constrain development potential
Emotions!	Owner's willingness to enter into options / conditional contracts / development agreements/ Clawback/ Overage etc.	Roles defined?	Design options	Rental value	Negotiation timescales
Competing developments	Land assembly	Objectives defined?	EIA	Market Dynamics Demand / Supply	
Development lag - Early cycle / Late cycle	Adjoining owners	Scope defined?	Design requirements for planning application	Land value	
	Over-sailing licences	Outputs defined?	Project planning	Costs	
	Party wall notice periods	Payments defined?		Finance costs	
	Rights of light infringements	Working relationships?		Capital allowances	
	Access, rights of way, ransom strips	System compatibility?			
				Phasing	
	Archaeology	Bitter flavour of poor quality lingers long after the sweet taste of low price		Accuracy - QRA	
	Contaminated ground	Contracts based on divorce not marriage			
	Geology, soft ground, water table	Project Manager			
	Flood risk	Architect			
	Asbestos	QS			
	Ecology & habitat	Structural Engineer			
	Restrictive covenants	Services Engineer			
	Vacant possession	Planning Consultant			
	Underground services, pipelines	Environmental Consultant			
	Overhead cables	Traffic Consultant			
	Highway constraints	Surveyors			
	Vendor retained operational activities	Marketing			
	Capacity of existing substations, water supplies, gas, sewage treatment etc.	Legal			
		Spin Doctor			
		CDM Co-ordinator			

Figure 15.7a Typical risks in the project life cycle

Marketing	Planning Approvals	Funding	Design	Procurement	Construction	Letting / Disposal	International
Local opinion	Consultation	Procurement route?	Procurement route?	Form of contract?	Insurances	Market conditions	Language created problems of understanding
Local community needs	Connectivity, urban design, massing, variety, townscape	Pre-let or Speculative?	Scope change	Market capacity & volatility	Insolvency	Pre-lets not completing on lease	Cultural differences in approach to projects
Fit out - Cat A / Cat B?	Archaeology	Guarantees? Security?	Technological innovation	Efficient risk allocation	Delayed completion		Differences in procedures and standards
Lease agreements	Agreements (planning obligations)	Rates	Configuration control		Increased costs		Exchange rate risk (FOREX)
CAD Graphics	Planning conditions	Economic cycle changes to interest rates	Changes in standards		Damage to works		Legal differences of law and jurisdiction
	Highway agreements	FOREX?			Latent defects		Time Zone differences
	Time for negotiation of agreements				Underground services		Translation requirements e.g. translate all specifications and drawings into another language
					Weather		Political Risk
					Fire		Security Risk
					Flood		
					Unexpected ground conditions		
					Security		
					Vandalism		
					Claims culture		
					Long lead items		
					Tight tolerance requirements		
					Fragile long lead items		
					Design changes		
					Temporary works		
					Health & Safety Risks		
					Approvals required		
					Other construction in vicinity		
					Logistics of material supplies		

Figure 15.7b Typical risks in the project life cycle

CHAPTER 16

QUALITY MANAGEMENT

As Project Sponsor you are very interested in getting the highest possible quality from the project within the cost and time boundaries. Project managers are, in my experience, also very committed to achieving high quality. Most take great pride in a job well done. The same is true of most consultants and contractors that I have met during my career. However, as previously discussed, projects are a balance between quality, time and cost. In the short term the most immediately obvious performance measures for the project manager and the project team are first time, then cost (since the final account will often be settled months after the project is completed) and lastly quality. Of course if quality problems become apparent during the project then they will be dealt with, but quite often quality problems lie dormant for years.

The project manager and team may be long gone by the time quality issues come to light, whereas you, as Project Sponsor, will still be there to face the wrath of unhappy people in your organization. Consequently I urge you to take quality management seriously.

Quality management encompasses three interdependent disciplines:

1. Quality control
2. Quality assurance
3. Quality improvement.

Quality control is the process whereby we strive to ensure that the quality of the project's outputs meet the specified requirements. We need a Quality Plan to describe the checks, inspections, tests and so on that we will undertake and the system for instructing corrective action where defects are found.

Quality assurance is the process by which we can provide confidence that quality has been satisfactorily controlled.

To give an example of quality control, where concrete is being used for structural purposes the engineer will specify a minimum strength requirement for the concrete.

The mix of concrete will be designed with an appropriate ratio of cement to water that should ensure this strength (it is the cement to water ratio that determines the strength of concrete, the proportions of sand and aggregate affect workability). As the concrete is poured, samples of the concrete will be taken in cubes which are subsequently crushed in a laboratory to prove that the concrete batch was of the required strength. If the concrete strength is not proven to be up to standard then further tests may be undertaken, such as drilling cores out from the structure and testing these. If the strength is still not adequate the affected part of the structure may have to be demolished and rebuilt.

Records of the tests will be kept and these test records form part of our quality assurance. If the records were not kept then we would have controlled quality but no way of assuring, say, insurers, building control officers or subsequent owners as to the quality of the structure.

Processes for achieving good quality management are set out in national and international standards, notably ISO 9000. This standard is generic to any enterprise and sets out the requirements of a quality management system. In essence it requires that:

- There should be procedures which cover all key processes of the enterprise.
- The processes should be monitored to ensure that they are effective.
- Adequate records should be kept.
- Outputs should be checked for defects.
- Corrective action should be taken where necessary.
- The processes and the quality system itself should be regularly reviewed for effectiveness.
- Continual improvement should be facilitated.

There are a number of bodies accredited to certify that an organization's quality management system meets the appropriate standard. These can be found at the International Accreditation Forum (http://www.iaf.nu/).

Quality management has actually been around as long as there have been craftsmen, craft guilds and apprenticeships. The act of learning, improving and teaching crafts through guilds, or professions through professional institutions is an example of continual improvement in action.

DEMING TO SIX SIGMA

Obviously training plays a very important role in quality improvement on projects and within organizations. Other initiatives for achieving continual quality improvement have been pioneered by, amongst many others, William Edwards Deming who was credited with increasing US armament production during the Second World War. Subsequently he transferred the philosophy of continual improvement to Japan. Genichi Taguchi did much to further the use of statistical methods for quality measurement and improvement. In recent years Six Sigma has been a popular philosophy for quality improvement. Six Sigma was originated in Motorola in the mid-1980s. The Greek letter sigma or σ is used in mathematics to denote the standard deviation of a Gaussian probability distribution. Many things do conform to Gaussian (or normal) distributions, concrete strength from a particular mix and the height of adult human beings included.

In Figure 16.1 three Gaussian distributions are shown with standard deviation (sigma, σ) values of 2, 1 and 0.5. You can see that the smaller the standard deviation the narrower the range of outcomes. If we express the tolerance, or range of acceptable quality, as a multiple of σ then for a particular quality tolerance the smaller σ is, the fewer outcomes will fall outside of the tolerance.

If the acceptable tolerance is σ either side of the mean then 69 per cent of our output will fail this quality standard. If it is 2 σ then 31 per cent of our output will be substandard. If the tolerance is 6 σ either side of the mean, then only around 0.0003 per cent will fail the standard. Consequently Six Sigma seeks to drive down the σ (standard deviation) or variability of output until the tolerance specified is equivalent to six standard deviations, either side of the mean.

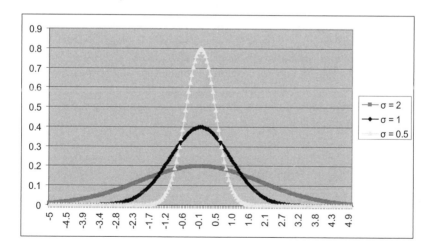

Figure 16.1   Sigma – standard deviation and quality

The process of Six Sigma is:

- Define improvement goals consistent with customer requirements and the organizational strategy.
- Measure key parameters of the current process and collect appropriate data.
- Analyse this data and look for cause and effect relationships.
- Improve the process informed by the new understanding of the cause and effect relationships.
- Control the process to ensure that any deviations from required quality are rectified.

Consequently Six Sigma is founded in measurement and the belief that what you can measure you can improve. Another notable feature of Six Sigma is the ranking of practitioners. Six Sigma Master Black Belts are Six Sigma champions who train practitioners within the organization. Black Belts devote all of their time to Six Sigma and Green Belts practice Six Sigma alongside their day job.

Six Sigma is the currently popular process for managing quality. There have been previous processes known as kaizen, quality circles, and total quality management (TQM) (*kaizen* is the Japanese word for improvement). The application of quality management which William Deming transferred to Japan after the Second World War was enthusiastically embraced by Japanese car companies such as Toyota, where kaizen was practised at many levels from CEO down. At any particular workstation on the production lines small teams would be lead by their supervisor to find ways of improving quality. These small teams are known as quality circles. The application of kaizen across an entire company is known as total quality management. I do not necessarily advocate any one philosophy of quality improvement over others. I do advocate that Project Sponsors probe the people that they employ to try and establish whether they have invested in obtaining quality certification for marketing purposes or they have a genuine pride in their work and seek to keep learning and improving.

CONFIGURATION MANAGEMENT

A topic related to quality management is configuration management. There seem to be an almost unlimited number of definitions of configuration management.

The US Department of Defense *Military Standard 973, Configuration Management* says that:

Configuration management is a discipline that applies technical and administrative direction and surveillance over the life cycle of items to:

- Identify and document the functional and physical characteristics of configuration items.
- Control changes to configuration items and their related documentation.
- Record and report information needed to manage configuration items effectively, including the status of proposed changes and implementation status of approved changes.
- Audit configuration items to verify conformance to specifications, drawings, interface control documents, and other contractual requirements.

According to British Standard BS 6488, *Configuration management of computer-based systems*, configuration management is the discipline of identifying all components and their relationships in a continually evolving system (taking into account relevant system interfaces) for the purpose of maintaining integrity, traceability and control over change throughout the life cycle.

The dictionary definition of configuration is 'an arrangement of parts or elements in a particular form or figure'.

Projects often take a system and change components of that system in order to form a new, better system. Configuration management is the process of ensuring that the system retains its coherency and consistency during the change process.

If the project involves a complex piece of software that is being upgraded it is possible that two or more programmers may be working on the same program. In that case it is perfectly possible for one of them to destroy another's work by making changes in code in their part of the program that is referred to by code in other parts of the program. To use a more visual analogy, if a team of designers are working on designing a building, the architect may decide to move a column slightly. This will affect the structural engineer's drawings, the mechanical and electrical engineers drawings and every other discipline. If each discipline doesn't keep up the builder may find that the foundation he has built is no longer underneath the column, and that a ventilation duct he is trying to install clashes with the column.

Each programmer or designer's work contributes to the overall system and configuration management seeks to ensure that all of their contributions are coordinated. Each programmer or designer should be addressing these questions:

- What is my current design configuration?
- What is its status?
- How do I control changes to my configuration?
- What changes have been made to my design?
- How do I inform everyone else of my changes?
- Does anyone else's change to their design affect my design?

In those halcyon days when computers were fed by punched cards and drawings were done by hand with pen or pencil, the way that configuration was managed was as follows. Each discipline involved in a design would circulate prints of its drawings to every other discipline for comment and/or information. Whenever changes were made to a drawing the revision number or letter in the drawing title block would be incremented by one. There would be a table above the title block where each revision letter would have the date of the revision and a description of the revision recorded. The part of the drawing which had been revised would have a cloud drawn around it with the revision letter or number adjacent to draw attention to the feature that had been changed. Each time a drawing was revised a print was sent to all the other disciplines. By following this procedure each design discipline involved in the project could assess the impact of other disciplines' changes on its own design and make appropriate adjustments.

Nowadays technology supports this process considerably. Because most drawings are produced using Computer-aided design (CAD) packages, revisions are recorded automatically. Information is shared between disciplines either because disciplines are allocated separate layers on the same drawing, or by uploading drawings to project collaboration websites where all other disciplines can have access to each others' designs.

It is important that the project manager establishes, before design commences, how configuration is to be managed. Ideally this would be agreed whilst all designers are being appointed. Everyone can be clear regarding the design software to be used, design conventions, collaboration tools and procedures for circulating information. However, if some designers are appointed before others this procedure must be established with the first designers and then imposed on all subsequent designers. If subsequent designers cannot comply, perhaps because they have different software, then a solution will have to be agreed with all parties such that configuration can still be controlled. This may mean appointing an intermediary who can convert the output of one designer into that which is readable by the others, for example.

The project manager should also ensure that the project's quality plan contains provision for audits of the configuration management process.

In summary, as technology evolves and systems become increasingly complex, the management of quality (or the performance of the final product) is becoming more and more the science of integrating systems (system integration) and ensuring their compatability as it is about the strength of concrete or the quality of a weld.

CHAPTER 17

COMMERCIAL MANAGEMENT

The commercial management of a project is an enormously important part of the project. On small projects the project manager will probably manage the commercial aspects himself. However, on large projects the project manager will probably have a planner, commercial manager, risk manager and other specialists to support them. Some of the work areas which may fall within the remit of the project commercial manager are:

- Estimating – producing cost estimates for project work or of changes to the work scope.
- Grant application – if the project is eligible for government grant funding.
- Procurement – managing the process of procuring suppliers, consultants and contractors.
- Insurance – making sure that the project and all suppliers carry appropriate insurance cover.
- Budgeting – transforming estimates and/or contract sums into a budget and ensuring that each member of the project team knows what they have got to deliver for how much money.
- Contingency management – establishing a contingency between budget and the funding available such that money is available to pay for unexpected expenditure. Monitoring and managing the expenditure of contingency.
- Cost control – keeping accounts for the project and tracking what has been spent against what should have been spent.
- Change control – ensuring that the cost effect of changes to the project are identified and agreed. Although change control is part of commercial management it is also closely bound up with controlling the project scope. Consequently I am giving it a chapter to itself (Chapter 18) and just flagging it up here as an important commercial management function.
- Payments – agreeing valuations of work done by suppliers, contractors and consultants, receiving their invoices and ensuring that they are paid.

ESTIMATING

See Chapter 7 for my general guidance on estimating. Now that a project team is on board access to experts and industry standard estimating manuals should be more readily available. Issues that may require special attention are regional variations; accounting for inflation effects; local constraints such as restrictions on working hours; traffic; ground conditions and so on.

The nature of estimating is such that there will be a degree of uncertainty inherent. It is therefore important to make these uncertainties explicit and managed via project risk management (see Chapter 15). Most estimates will be converted into contract sums either fixed or target as the project is procured.

GRANT APPLICATION

For projects which provide a social good and meet government objectives in one form or another there are often grants available. The types of projects which meet these criteria might be projects increasing environmental sustainability, improving public transport, enhancing the landscape or providing employment or education and training.

Sometimes grants from several different bodies can be obtained, the cost of which is filling in a form and providing progress reports on the project and how the money has been spent. However, it can also be a bureaucratic, costly and time-consuming process. It is therefore important to make an assessment of whether or not applying for a grant is worth the effort.

If your project does provide benefits to society it is certainly worth making enquiries of government to see if grants are available and what the process for obtaining them is.

PROCUREMENT

Much of the advice in Chapter 8 relating to procurement of the project manager is also relevant to procuring the other consultants, suppliers and contractors.

A procurement strategy should be thought through. Key issues to resolve are:

- Level of aggregation of the work
- Transfer of risk.

What is meant by level of aggregation of the work? Well, at the level of maximum aggregation you could let the project as a turnkey project inviting tenders for a contractor to do the whole thing, simply handing the keys over to you at the end. Most of the interfaces will be within the turnkey contract and are for the contractor to manage itself and its subcontractors. However, each tendering contractor will need to assemble their team of subcontractors in competition with the other tendering contractors. It is quite unlikely that one tenderer will succeed in assembling all the best value subcontractors within their consortium.

At the level of minimum aggregation you could seek tenders for each specialism involved in the project of which there might be many thousands. In this way you can pick 'horses for courses' and obtain the best people for the job with the maximum price competition. The downside is that there will be many interfaces to manage and an open cheque for claims if these interfaces are not well managed.

The project team should carefully consider the needs of the project and the state of the market to find the right balance between these extremes.

The other question is how much risk to transfer to contractors. At one extreme you could try to transfer the maximum amount of risk to contractors, seeking fixed lump sum prices for each package of work. Provided that you do not change your requirements after the contract is let, and provided there are no interface problems between contractors, which they may try to blame on the client, this route will give you maximum cost certainty. However, this route also gives you minimum flexibility. If you change anything you may pay dearly. You will also pay a premium for the risk that you are asking contractors to bear. Of course, competitive tendering should minimize the price that you pay for this risk premium. A contractor with a fixed price contract will have an excellent incentive to complete on time and at minimum cost. But remember the cost–time–quality triangle and pay particular attention to specifying the quality of output that is required and rigorously check that you are getting it.

Alternatively you could employ contractors on cost plus contracts. This will give you maximum flexibility to make changes but minimum cost certainty. In theory, since the contractors take very little risk, they will not price in risk and you will get a cheaper job. However, there will be little incentive for them to complete on time and at minimum cost. There should, however, be no compromise on quality.

The accepted wisdom with respect to risk transfer is that risk should be borne by the party best able to manage the risk. Therefore the greater the contractor's remit the more they have risk within their control and the more they should bear. A procurement route that makes particular sense to me for building projects is a variation of 'design and build' which is 'detailed design and build'. Design and build provides very good cost certainty for the client because the contractor really has hardly anywhere to turn if there are design or construction problems. However, the drawback is that the client has very little control over the design and may not ultimately get what they really wanted. I have been involved with several building projects for the UK Ministry of Defence where detailed design and build has been successfully used. How it works is that the client directly contracts with a project manager and team of designers to develop the concept and schematic design of the facility they want. When the client is happy that the designed solution meets their needs in the best possible way, tenders are invited for the detailed design and construction. It is in the detailed design that problems affecting construction generally occur, for example where ducts clash with beams. This procurement route therefore has the advantage of giving the client very good control over both the design and cost certainty.

CONTRACTS

There are a wide variety of contract documents that can be used to formalize and control the project. The GW Works suite of contracts has been developed by the UK government over many years and can be obtained from Her Majesty's Stationery Office. Further information on their suitability can be found on the Office of Government Commerce website at http://www.ogc.gov.uk/documents/ InformationNote2699.pdf

Alternatives include the New Engineering Contract suite of contracts which can be found at http://www.neccontract.com, FIDIC which can be bought from http://www1.fidic.org/resources/contracts/ or IChemE which can be found in their bookshop at http://www.icheme.org/learning/.

Once a procurement strategy is decided upon the next step will depend on any applicable procurement regulations. For example contracts entered into by public sector organizations in the European Union, above a fairly low threshold value, must comply with the European Procurement Regulations (http://www.ojec.com/ Directives.aspx). These set requirements for advertising the opportunity.

The project commercial manager will work with the project planner and project manager to develop an Out To Tender (OTT) schedule. This will be a table which for each tender package specifies all the key dates from information available to compile the tender information to date of contract award.

A shortlist of tenderers should be drawn up informed by responses to the advertisement if you are in the public sector, or by other research methods if not. See Chapter 8 where the description of tendering for the project manager can be applied more widely to the tenders for each package.

INSURANCE

The insurance required for a project depends on the type of project. For construction projects there are three main types of insurance:

1. Professional indemnity – this covers the professionals (e.g. designers, project manager etc.) from risks such as negligence or breach of duty of care, unintentional infringement of copyright or loss of documents or data.
2. Product liability – this covers the insured against damages awarded as a result of damage to property or personal injury caused by the insured's product.
3. Contractor all risks/third party – this is an insurance policy specially designed for contractors and subcontractors working at a contract site. The cover can include public and employers liability, contract works, own plant, hired-in plant and employees' tools.

There is a good case for projects, particularly major projects, to consider providing these insurances to cover all parties involved on the project rather than each party insuring themselves alone. Heathrow Terminal 5 is an example of where project insurance has been used. Project insurance helps to avoid wasteful blame and counter blame if something goes wrong. It also helps to avoid any gaps in cover and allows cover against the broadest possible range of risks. In the case of Terminal 5 BAA, already a very experienced construction client, took out project insurance for the whole project rather than requiring each contractor to insure themselves.

If after due consideration you believe that project insurance is not for you, you will at least have to ensure that each party holds the appropriate insurances sufficient to cover the risks, which will of course vary from project to project.

For guidance, UK government departments usually require professional indemnity cover of at least £5 million from each consultant and contractor.

In the UK all employers are required to have employers' liability insurance which will enable the employer to meet the cost of compensation for employees' injuries or illness. Public liability insurance covers claims made against the insured by members of the public or other businesses, but not claims by employees. While public liability insurance is generally voluntary, employers' liability insurance is compulsory.

You should ensure that your consultants and contractors are insured for these risks where their engagement on the project could result in such liabilities. Include a requirement for proof of insurance cover in the tender.

BUDGETING

In its simplest form a project budget is a list of all the expected expenditure on the project so that the final cost can be anticipated. A budget also allows a check of what has been spent compared to what should have been spent and the anticipated final cost (AFC) to be kept up to date. Corrective action can be considered if costs are getting out of hand.

For reasons set out in Chapter 12 on project planning, I strongly believe that time, resources and cost are inextricably linked in a project and should be managed holistically. All of the major project planning applications that I know of such as Microsoft Project, Primavera P6 and Asta Powerproject are designed to plan and track time, resources and cost. After university I began my career with a major American process contractor and for this I am eternally grateful. I have since worked in many roles and in many industries internationally, and in my view the holistic approach to managing project time, resources and cost that I learned then, from the Americans, is the right one.

Sadly this is far from a universally held opinion. It is commonplace for project planning software packages, such as those noted above, to be used, at a fraction of their real power, simply for time-scheduling project activities, and for cost planning to be done and cost expenditure monitored on a spreadsheet. If time and cost are separated in this way EVA is not possible (see Chapter 12) and progress monitoring is severely hampered. Likewise if resources are not loaded into the scheduling there is no real control of resource levelling and it is more likely that resources will be under- or over-allocated. Also project cash flow projections are less easily arrived at and less likely to be accurate.

I believe the problem is a historical one. In the UK construction industry the task of managing cost falls to the quantity surveyor. This profession evolved in the nineteenth century from the earlier trade of measurer. The measurer quantified all the materials and labour required for a building project and recorded these in a structured schedule (or Bill of Quantities). This allowed builders to submit tender prices which could be compared like for like. Thus the way of structuring these Bills of Quantities has developed over a long period of time and is defined by a standard method of measurement. In the USA the task falls to Cost Engineers, a discipline which began in the 1950s. Consequently, in the USA project planning and cost engineering grew up side by side, whereas in the UK project planning is the new kid on the block.

It is unlikely that quantity surveyors will be persuaded to abandon their beloved spreadsheet budgets. Nevertheless the project manager should bring the quantity surveyor and project planner together at the beginning of the project with the objective of developing a work breakdown structure that allows information to be readily transferable between the project schedule and the project budget and allows the project schedule to be easily cost loaded.

CONTINGENCY

The budget should include sufficient contingency, that is, an allowance for unexpected costs. In Chapter 6 we discussed optimism bias and the contingency that should be incorporated in the business case. Budget contingency should be less than this because there should be some headroom between the budget including contingency and the point at which the project becomes unviable. You should undertake a quantitative risk analysis to assess how much contingency to allow (see Chapter 15 on risk management). An assessment of the risks which can affect the budget should be made together with the probability of the risk occurring and the minimum, most likely and maximum cost impact if the risk does occur. The use of Monte Carlo simulation software to model the risk will generate a graph which indicates the confidence that you can have in a particular level of contingency being sufficient to cover the possible risks. Figure 17.1 indicates that, based upon the assessment of risks a contingency of somewhere between £0 and £600,000 will be required. It shows that we can have 50 per cent confidence in a contingency of £270,000 being sufficient. That means that in the 5,000 iterations that were used in the simulation 2,500 of those iterations required less than £270,000 and the same number required more. The chart also shows that we can have 80 per cent confidence in a contingency of £340,000. That means for 4,000 of the 5,000 iterations in the simulation, £340,000 was sufficient.

We refer to the 50 per cent confidence figure as P50 and the 80 per cent confidence figure as P80 and so on. There are no hard and fast rules about which confidence level you should adopt for your contingency. The very cautious may want to adopt P100 as the contingency. The problem with this is that it may tie up capital that could be usefully deployed, perhaps on another of the organization's projects.

In the example shown in Figure 17.1 this would be setting a contingency of £600,000 when on average £270,000 should be enough. The key phrase here is 'on average'. If your organization only has one project then you probably will not be content with a contingency that is equally likely to be inadequate as it is to be adequate – you will want more comfort than that. However, if your organization has a large portfolio of projects then you will be happier that 'on average' each project holds enough contingency. The projects which overspend their contingency will be balanced by the projects which underspend. In my experience where there is not a large portfolio of projects to balance risk out contingency pitched at the P80 level is a sensible compromise.

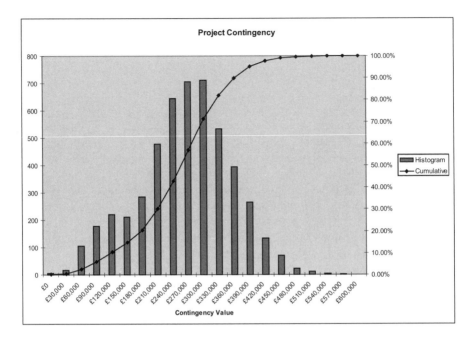

Figure 17.1   Project contingency

If you do not have Monte Carlo simulation software then you can total up the probability of each risk multiplied by the average impact of each risk.

$$C = \sum p \times {(\mathrm{Im}\,ax + \mathrm{Im}\,l + \mathrm{Im}\,in)}\big/_{3}$$

Where C = contingency

p = probability of risk

Imax = Maximum cost impact of risk occurs

Iml = Most likely cost impact if risk occurs

Imin = Minimum cost impact if risk occurs

This will give you an approximation of the P50 level risk contingency and adding a further 25 per cent to the P50 should put you in the ball park of P80.

CONTINGENCY MANAGEMENT

The objective of good contingency management is to:

- Ensure that sufficient contingency is retained for the remaining risks *and*
- Release surplus contingency as risks are passed without impact.

These objectives can be best achieved by regular review of the risk register and accounting for what has been spent.

Imagine, for example, that £100,000 had been identified as the contingency requirement against a risk of unforeseen ground conditions on site. The foundations have now been built without encountering any ground problems. Therefore, on the face of it, £100,000 can be released back into the organization's budget. However, the project should check before doing this that there have not been any unidentified risks that have incurred additional expenditure. There should also be consideration given to any new risks emerging. If there has been unexpected expenditure or if there are new risks emerging then a view must be taken on how much contingency should be released.

$$CFR = Cu - UExp - Rnew$$

Where CFR = contingency for release

Cu = Unused contingency where risk has passed

$UExp$ = Unidentified Expenditure

$Rnew$ = Risk allowance for new risks that have emerged

COST CONTROL

Cost control involves monitoring week by week, month by month, how much money has been expended against what had been budgeted. A review of the section on EVA in Chapter 12 will make it clear that this should be combined with the actual achievement of progress. Obviously if you are in month 12 of a 20-month schedule and you have spent 15 per cent less than you had budgeted to spend by month 12 then you might be pleased with that. If however you have achieved only 40 per cent of physical progress and you had planned to have achieved 70 per cent then you might not be so pleased.

There is also a dependency on the contractual arrangements. Where you have members of the project team who are being employed on a time-reimbursable basis, the above situation does indeed point to overspending that element of the budget. If however you are paying for the amount of work delivered, the schedule situation is serious but you should not pay for undelivered work. Therefore the cost control situation is less serious.

In order to control costs we must first estimate the project expenditure, then assess the risks and opportunities and set appropriate contingency allowances. We must rigorously control change (which we will discuss in Chapter 18, Change control) and we must monitor, reporting period by reporting period, how we are doing against budget. Where we see cost expenditure going off track we will need to explore ways to get it back on track.

There are many ways of presenting periodical cost reports. Figure 17.2 is fairly typical, if simple, example of a monthly cost report for a building project.

The first column on the left is a list of the packages of work which make up the project with the budget for each of these shown in column two. Skip column three for a moment, we will come back to that. Column four shows cost actually incurred to date. Column five shows cost committed which is the amount from now on that we are committed to spend on the package. Column six shows cost exposure and represents an assessment of additional cost exposure on the package which is not yet committed. Now we will go back to column three which is the estimated final cost and is arrived at by adding together Cost to date + Cost committed + Cost exposure. Finally, column seven is variance which is Estimated final cost – budget.

Let's see what this tells us. The earthworks package is complete. We have overspent the budget by £2,476, perhaps because there were some unexpected ground conditions. However, we have settled the final account with the earthworks contractor and there is no further exposure.

November 2009 Project Cost Report						
Package	Budget	Estimated Final Cost	Cost To Date	Cost Committed	Cost Exposure	Variance
Earthworks	£30,000	£32,476	£32,476	£0	£0	£2,476
Foundations	£45,000	£44,100	£42,500	£0	£1,600	-£900
Superstructure	£60,000	£62,000	£58,500	£1,500	£2,000	£2,000
Roofing	£10,500	£10,500	£10,500	£0	£0	£0
Cladding	£21,700	£19,750	£19,750	£0	£0	-£1,950
Mechanical & Electrical	£18,650	£21,599	£6,754	£12,345	£2,500	£2,949
Plumbing	£9,760	£9,595	£3,345	£5,000	£1,250	-£165
Decoration	£6,450	£5,500	£0	£5,500	£0	-£950
External Works	£12,350	£11,200	£9,575	£1,125	£500	-£1,150
TOTAL	**£214,410**	**£216,720**	**£183,400**	**£25,470**	**£7,850**	**£2,310**

£   208,870

Figure 17.2   Cost reporting

The foundations package is also complete. We have actually spent £42,500 and there is no further committed cost. However, there is a minor dispute with the foundations contractor and we estimate that this might cost an additional £1,600. Therefore although we hope to be £2,500 under budget on the foundations package we are prudently allowing for the £1,600 exposure and are showing a variance of –£900.

The superstructure package is almost complete. There is some minor finishing work to do on it, partly as a result of a design error but partly as a result of poor quality control. We have actually spent £58,500 but accept that £1,500 is a committed additional expenditure for correcting the design error by our engineer. The contractor does not accept that the quality control error is entirely his fault and therefore we are reporting a further potential exposure of £2,200.

The roofing package is complete and came in on budget. There is no further commitment and no further exposure. The cladding package is complete and came in £1,950 under budget.

The mechanical and electrical package and the plumbing package are both in progress. For both of these there is some exposure which tips the mechanical and electrical package over budget by £2,949 but the plumbing package is still £165 under budget even with the predicted exposure.

Decoration hasn't started yet. We have committed to a contract sum of £5,500 which is £945 under the budget which we had set. We don't believe that any of the minor issues which other contractors have had can spill over to affect decoration.

The external works package is almost complete. We have spent £9,575, have committed expenditure remaining of £1,125 and possible exposure to a further £500. Nevertheless the external works package is £1,150 under budget.

Overall we are committed to expenditure of £208,970 against a budget of £214,410: £7,850 hangs in the balance as provision against items disputed or which we believe may yet be disputed. We have left it too late for further value engineering. If our estimate of exposure is correct we will be £2,310 over budget. What are our options?

1. As Project Sponsor you should know whether you can absorb this additional expenditure and still have a good business case.
2. We can look for items of scope remaining that we can cut out. Perhaps we can look at the number of electrical sockets specified and cut these back because we believe we had over-provided for these. We need to check that we have over-provided and then negotiate this with the mechanical and electrical contractor.

3. Since the decoration package hasn't yet started we could see if there are options for cheaper paint perhaps. This may have implications for long-term maintenance.
4. We should look carefully at our cost exposure column and attempt to negotiate this down. For contractors there is an incentive to do a deal and settle now rather than a long time-consuming argument over something slightly more, even if they feel it is justified.

There are various ways of reporting cost on projects and the above is a simplified, typical example. We could split the budget column into estimate and contingency. The above report does not differentiate between the originally tendered work which remains to be done and contract changes which we have agreed.

PAYMENTS

Paying the consultants, suppliers and contractors engaged on the project is a core commercial management function. Each contract will specify the amount to be paid and when it is to be paid together with how contract changes are to be accounted for.

The types of payments typically include:

- Time-reimbursable contracts where staff submit timesheets to a responsible manager for sign off and standard time and overtime is paid against agreed rates.
- Re-measurable contracts where a Bill Of Quantities estimated the amount of work to be done and the contractor provided a rate per unit of work. It is necessary to reach agreement with the contractor as to the actual amount of work done each period and make payment accordingly.
- Lump sum contracts where there is a fixed amount to be paid with periodic instalments. These can be subject to adjustments according to the physical progress achieved.
- Day works where a contractor has been asked to do works that were not previously incorporated into their scope of works and they charge for labour, materials and equipment used on an hourly or daily basis.
- Payments for work performed off-site, for example items of equipment that may be manufactured in a factory. Payment might be on delivery or, more likely, by stage payments. If stage payments, it will be necessary to verify that the stage has been achieved and ensure that the work is suitable labelled as property of the project client in case the manufacturer becomes insolvent.

For all of the project suppliers it is necessary to ensure that payments are made properly so as to support progress but not to overpay and put the project at risk.

CHAPTER 18

CHANGE CONTROL

It is ironic that whilst projects are designed to bring about change and that is a good thing, changes to a project are to be avoided like the plague if you wish to retain any hope of completion on time and budget.

In the early 1990s my managing director at Bovis Construction undertook a short research tour of our company in the USA, the object of which was to discover why they were able to construct buildings around 30 per cent cheaper than we were able to in the UK – and this was despite higher salaries in the USA. The two big reasons that he uncovered were:

1. Once construction was underway changes were put on hold until the project was finished as originally intended. Then prices would be negotiated to change the project as required. Of course, sometimes once the project was complete, the client would be content with it and no longer require the change. Nevertheless it was still considerably cheaper to finish and then change than to change halfway through.
2. There was a much smaller and tighter project management team on our American sites.

Actually the second reason is really part of the first, because much of the management required on UK sites is there to manage change.

In Chapter 9 on project finance we saw that a major benefit of PFI/PPP project arrangements is that they require huge investment of time at the beginning, getting the scope right and ensuring that risks are allocated and that contractual arrangements significantly inhibit change. The result of this is that 89 per cent of these projects were finished on time or early and all were finished within budget. This contrasts with only 30 per cent finished on time or early and 73 per cent which were over budget under traditional contract arrangements.

The message is clear – project change leads to delay and extra cost. However, what constitutes a change depends on your point of view.

The Project Sponsor will probably recognize the following as changes:

- The sponsor has found some aspect of the project as currently defined that should be changed to improve the business case. This may be because it was overlooked earlier or because the operating environment has changed and the project needs to as well.
- A department of the organization has decided that it needs a change of some sort.
- An external stakeholder requires a change that could not have been reasonably anticipated.

The project team will perceive a change where:

- They have presented a design solution that meets the requirement. The steps towards that solution have been discussed with the sponsor yet when finally presented the sponsor doesn't like it and wants something else.

An individual member of the design team may perceive a change when:

- Another member of the design team makes a change which is necessary for their design to comply with the requirement but it causes other design team members re-work. There is a grey area between 'design development', which is a normal part of design and for which all design team members should be prepared for some changes, and errors by other designers which cost money.

A contractor may recognize change where:

- The design changes in some way.
- Designers have made errors which need to be corrected.
- An aspect of the design which had not been clearly specified has been implemented by them in what they believe to be an adequate way but the designers do not.
- Their work is interfered with or inhibited by a third party.
- An aspect of the project beyond their control is not as they had assumed it would be, for example ground conditions.

Each contract entered into should be as clear as it can be concerning what constitutes a compensation event, i.e. under what circumstances a contractor, consultant or supplier is entitled to additional time and/or money to complete their obligations.

The process for controlling change is also usually defined within the contract and differs slightly from contract type to contract type. Without fail there will be forms to fill in. Self-carbonating pads are still used but increasingly change control is built into project management software and project collaboration websites. These forms may include:

- *Request for information (RFI)* – these are normally raised by contractors. They may simply be requests for information with no contractual consequence. However, very often they are signalling a change that will cause delay and additional cost. For example a contractor's RFI which states 'high voltage cable found at grid reference XYZ, not shown on existing drawings. What action do you require?' is seeking an instruction which will probably result in a change.
- *Architects instruction (AI)* – these will be used by architects to instruct changes or to clarify design.
- *Engineer's instruction (EI)* – these are similar to architect's instructions but exist where the engineer has power to make changes under the contract.
- *Project manager's instruction (PMI)* – these are similar to architect's and engineer's instructions but exist where the project manager has power to make changes under the contract.
- *Site instruction (SI)* – these are common where a management contractor or construction manager is managing other contractors on behalf of the client.
- *Change request (CR)* – this may be raised by the contractor or a member of the project team. It differs from the others listed above in that it is explicitly stating a request for a change which will have cost and/or schedule implications.
- *Change order (CO)* – this will be raised by the project manager with the client's authority (and should be signed by the Project Sponsor). It instructs a change. It should define what the change is and the additional cost and/or time granted to execute the change.

There are quite a few problems with change control processes on projects. I will list the problems first and then suggest steps that can be taken to ensure the best possible change control system.

- There can be a disconnect between the change control process used and the contract. Often a project manager or contractor will have standard forms and processes which they adopt without checking what the chosen form of contract requires.
- There will be changes requested by various parties on the project, e.g. designers, contractors, suppliers etc. and change orders to issue to these parties. There will probably be different types of contract under which each party is engaged and the adopted change control process may not suit all of them, or indeed any of them.

- The pressure of project work on site often means that contractors require an immediate instruction detailing how they should tackle a problem. Representatives of the project team usually do try to identify a suitable course of action to overcome the problem but are reluctant to agree, on the spot, the cost implications. They may leave that to the accountants or quantity surveyors to sort out later. Contractors will build up a large file of instructions and many months later will claim that they were instructed to do this, instructed to do that and the cost of all of it is £X million.
- It may become difficult to distinguish changes caused by designer error from other changes. In clear cases of designer error a claim against the designer's professional indemnity insurance may be appropriate.

My tips for ensuring the best possible change control system are:

1. Try to adopt forms of contract that are from the same stable e.g. GC Works, NEC etc. for all parties on the project.
2. Review the requirements of each contract for requesting and instructing change or agreeing compensation events.
3. Agree a change control process and appropriate forms that will comply with these contract processes for all contracts. If a computer-based system is used then generic forms within the computer system will need adaptation to suit.
4. Ensure that each form has:
   - A unique number.
   - The identity of the person who raised it.
   - To whom the form is sent for action, and who is copied for information.
   - A description of the requirement for instruction or change as appropriate.
   - A description of the cause for the instruction or change.
   - The date by which a reply is required (which should conform to contract requirements.
5. Where a paper-based system such as a self-carbonating site instruction pad is required because of the remoteness of the site from the nearest networked computer terminal, then a process should be identified for logging such hard copy instructions into the system.
6. There should be a clear process for establishing the cost and time implications of a change as quickly as possible.
7. There should be a regular meeting at which the project manager reviews all changes with the Project Sponsor, explaining the implications of each change and suggesting a course of action.

CHAPTER 19

STAKEHOLDER MANAGEMENT

WHAT (WHO) ARE STAKEHOLDERS?

Stakeholder **noun 1** an independent party with whom money or counters wagered are deposited. **2** a person with an interest or concern in something. *Oxford English Dictionary*

The first definition is the historical one – we are going to focus now on the second.

Stakeholders are those people and organizations who have an interest in our project, particularly those who could influence the project for good or ill.

BENEFITS OF STAKEHOLDER MANAGEMENT

Stakeholder management helps us to understand who can influence the success of our project and which ones to focus our attention on. It provides techniques for gaining support for the project and it improves our chances of success.

THE STAKEHOLDER MANAGEMENT PROCESS

1. Identify who the stakeholders are.
2. Analyse stakeholder influence.
3. Prioritize stakeholders.
4. Research the stakeholder issues.
5. Develop a strategy for influencing the stakeholders.
6. Implement the stakeholder management plan.

Identify who the Stakeholders are

This is probably best accomplished by brainstorming with your team. See Chapter 15 for advice on brainstorming. The number of stakeholders will probably turn out to be very much higher than you imagine.

Stakeholder Analysis

You now need to assess each stakeholder against three criteria:

1. How much interest do they have in the project?
2. How much power do they have?
3. Are they for the project, neutral or against?

It should be reasonably obvious from Figure 19.1 that we need to focus maximum attention on those with the most interest and most power.

Research Stakeholder Issues

Having prioritized stakeholders we should next set about identifying what their issues are. If they are in favour of the project; why? If they are against the project; why? What are their priorities? What are their interests?

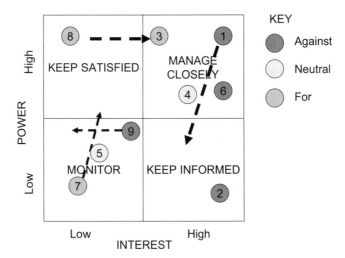

Figure 19.1   Stakeholder power and interest matrix

How one goes about the research depends upon the nature of the project and the organization's role in it. At one end of the scale we may simply be interested in discovering how to make our design more useful to a stakeholder. At the other end of the scale we may be trying to minimize objection to a planning application or even a parliamentary act such as a Transport and Works Act.

Informal	Formal
• Speak to stakeholder	• Consultation
• Speak to mutual acquaintances	• Market
• 'Google' the stakeholder	research

The guidance below allows you to carry out consultation effectively.

1. Don't ask questions without good reason. Check what you know already and make sure that you can use the results of your question.
2. Plan ahead. Make sure that you can provide clear guidance to consultees about timetables, costs, and their likely areas of interest.
3. Wicket rolling – prepare the ground with key stakeholders. Ensure that key stakeholders are informed prior to wider consultation and that they will be on your side.
4. Manage expectations. Be clear about the objectives of consultation, what people can really influence, what the constraints are and what options are available.
5. Identify your target audience.
6. Pick your method of consultation carefully. Do you want qualitative or quantitative information. What messages are you trying to get across? What method will best suit the target audience?
   - Meeting
   - Questionnaire
   - Road show
   - Exhibition
   - Presentation
   - Public meeting.
7. Make sure that your presentation material is easy to understand and complies with the Data Protection Act. Use plain English, avoid jargon.
8. Act on what you find.
9. Tell people what you learned, provide feedback on the results and what you are doing about it.
10. Evaluate how it went and disseminate lessons learned.

Develop a strategy for influencing the stakeholders

A simple strategy for influencing stakeholders is set out below, follow the REBECA mnemonic:

Redesign	Can we redesign the project economically to remove the stakeholder's objections or further strengthen stakeholder benefits?
Benefits	Have we fully identified the benefits that the project and its design has for stakeholders?
Communicate	How can we best communicate the project's benefits to stakeholders? Keep communicating. As Churchill said, 'Jaw jaw is better than war war' Face-to-face, newsletters, websites, presentations, right language, right message
Allies	What allies can we mobilize who will help persuade the objectors or at least counterbalance them? How can you raise the interest of powerful but disinterested allies? How can you help interested allies achieve greater power? How can you turn interested and powerful neutrals into allies?

Implement the Stakeholder Management Plan

A register such as that shown in Figure 19.2 is recommended for keeping track of stakeholder management actions.

Stakeholder	Key Interests	Issues	Current Status	Interest	Power	Message	Action	Who	When
Planning Authority	Conservation, Design context	Massing, listed building	Neutral	High	High	Locally sourced materials design intent	Arrange meeting	DC	04/04/2008
Neighbours	Traffic, noise	Construction traffic	Against	High	Med	Jobs generated, BREEM rating, travel plan & investment in bussing	Presentation & consultation, newsletter	PT	15/06/2008
English Heritage	Listing, conservation	Portico	Against	High	Med	Conservation of Portico	Arrange meeting	JW	03/07/2008
Client Head Office	Reputation, profit	Environmental issues, costs	For	Med	High	Jobs generated, BREEM rating, travel plan & investment in bussing	Demonstrate newsletter & website	PT	15/06/2008
Local MP	Votes	Fear of traffic generated, noise	Neutral	Med	Med	Jobs generated, BREEM rating, travel plan & investment in bussing	Arrange meeting	JM	12/05/2008
Chamber of Commerce	Business growth	Jobs, growth	For	Med	Med	Jobs generated, growth predictions, construction labour purchasing power	Presentation & consultation, newsletter	PT	15/06/2008
Local Press	Circulation, local issues	Whatever interests the public	Neutral	Low	Med	Jobs generated, BREEM rating, travel plan & investment in bussing	Press release	DC	02/01/2008
Local School	Traffic, noise	Children crossing the road, noise during class time	Against	Med	Low	Travel plan, jobs, bussing	Presentation to Govenors, site visit	PT	05/03/2008
Highways Dept.	Traffic	Construction traffic & visitors	Neutral	Low	Med	Travel plan, bussing	Letter	DC	10/04/2008
CABE	Design quality	Portico, Wiltshire vernacular	Neutral	Low	Med	Locally sourced materials design intent, restoration & re-use of portico	Letter & sketches	JM	04/04/2008
Ramblers Association	Right to roam	Access to parkland at rear	Against	Med	Low		Monitor	DC	On-going
Local Shopkeepers	Sales, parking	Loss of sales, loss of parking	Against	Low	Med	Jobs generated, growth predictions, construction labour purchasing power	Presentation & consultation, newsletter	PT	15/06/2008
Local Farmer	Access	Access for combine harvester	Neutral	Med	Low		Monitor	DC	On-going

Figure 19.2 A stakeholder management plan

INDEX

Figures are indicated by **bold** page
numbers, tables by *italic* numbers.

If you have found this book useful you may be interested in other titles from Gower

Managing Project Uncertainty
David Cleden
Paperback: 978-0-566-08840-7
e-book: 978-0-7546-8174-8

Essential Prince 2
Simon Harris
Paperback: 978-0-566-08768-4

Project Management
Dennis Lock
Hardback: 978-0-566-08769-1
Paperback: 978-0-566-08772-1
e-book: 978-0-7546-8634-7

**Accelerating Business and IT Change:
Transforming Project Delivery**
Alan Fowler and Dennis Lock
Hardback: 978-0-566-08604-5

**Making the Business Case:
Proposals that Succeed for Projects that Work**
Ian Gambles
Paperback: 978-0-566-08745-5
e-book: 978-0-7546-9427-4

GOWER

59 Checklists for Project and Programme Managers
Rudy Kor and Gert Wijnen
Paperback: 978-0-566-08775-2
e-book: 978-0-7546-8191-5

**A Handbook of Corporate Governance
and Social Responsibility**
Edited by
Güler Aras and David Crowther
Hardback: 978-0-566-08817-9
e-book: 978-0-7546-9217-1

Strategic Project Risk Appraisal and Management
Elaine Harris
Paperback: 978-0-566-08848-3
e-book: 978-0-7546-9211-9

Project Governance
Ralf Müller
Paperback: 978-0-566-08866-7
e-book: 978-0-566-09156-8

Project Reviews, Assurance and Governance
Graham Oakes
Hardback: 978-0-566-08807-0
e-book: 978-0-7546-8146-5

Visit **www.gowerpublishing.com** and

- search the entire catalogue of Gower books in print
- order titles online at 10% discount
- take advantage of special offers
- sign up for our monthly e-mail update service
- download free sample chapters from all recent titles
- download or order our catalogue